Forward
Into Hell

Forward Into Hell

Vince Bramley

JOHN BLAKE

Published by John Blake Publishing Ltd,
3, Bramber Court, 2 Bramber Road,
London W14 9PB, England

www.blake.co.uk

First published in paperback in 2006

ISBN 1 84454 217 3

British Library Cataloguing-in-Publication Data:

A catalogue record for this book is available from the British Library.

Design by www.envydesign.co.uk

Printed in Great Britain by Bookmarque Ltd, Croydon

1 3 5 7 9 10 8 6 4 2

Papers used by John Blake Publishing are natural, recyclable
products made from wood grown in sustainable forests.
The manufacturing processes conform to the environmental
regulations of the country of origin.

Every attempt has been made to contact the relevant copyright-holders,
but some were unobtainable. We would be grateful if the appropriate
people could contact us.

This book is dedicated to the soldiers of 3 Para, whose comradeship and determination throughout the campaign make the author proud to have served with them. So that those members of 3 Para who never returned are not forgotten, their names and ages at death in action are listed below.

Private Richard Absolon, Military Medal 19

Private Gerald Bull 18

Private Jason Burt 17

Private John Crow 21

Private Mark Dodsworth 24

Private Anthony Greenwood 22

Private Neil Grose 18

Private Peter Hedicker 22

Lance-Corporal Peter Higgs 23

FORWARD INTO HELL

Corporal Stephen Hope 27

Private Timothy Jenkins 19

Private Craig Jones 20

Private Stewart Laing 20

Lance-Corporal Christopher Lovett 24

Corporal Keith McCarthy 27

Sergeant Ian McKay, Victoria Cross 29

Corporal Stewart McLaughlin 27

Lance-Corporal James Murdoch 25

Lance-Corporal David Scott 24

Private Ian Scrivens 17

Corporal Alex Shaw 25

Private Phillip West 19

PREFACE

My grandfather fought in the Second World War, although the family know little of what he went through, for he remained silent about his war. Perhaps he was right to forget and carry on. But I have always been saddened when history dies with a soldier.

One veteran did share his memories with me and I was always intrigued by his reminiscences of the 1914–18 war. Mr Smith told me when I was seventeen that I would make a soldier and later, after his death, I became one. His stories have remained with me and inspired me to write an account of my own war as a soldier of junior rank. I have described what I saw and felt, not what an officer or tactician experiences, nor for that matter what any other ordinary soldier goes through, for every soldier sees war differently and has his own tale to tell.

ACKNOWLEDGEMENTS

On the military side, many serving and former members of 3 Para have lent their valued support, notably Johnny Cook, Dominic Gray and Grant Grinham. Also a tower of strength was Johnny Weeks, who is and will always be a professional soldier's soldier.

Bravery is not confined to the field of action. In this connection, I cannot thank enough Rita and Bill Hedicker, who allowed me to relate the tragic death of their son and my friend, Pete. This is bravery and strength of a special order.

I should like to thank my family: Fred, Pam and Brian, who have unfailingly supported me through thick and thin; and my brother Russell, who gave me invaluable encouragement from the start.

Finally, my thanks to Wally Camfield, formerly of 3 Para, who inspired me to join that elite regiment, and also to my wife Karon who at times lives with my battles when everyone else is asleep.

GLOSSARY

ACC Army Catering Corps
a.s.a.p. as soon as possible
AT Anti-Tank

basher improvised sleeping shelter, often using a poncho
bergen backpack containing mess kit, food rations,
    sleeping bag, spare clothing, etc.
blowpipe hand-held, wire-guided, ground-to-air missile
blue-on-blue accidental clash between forces fighting on
    the same side

Cabbagehead Marine
Chinook powerful twin-rotor helicopter used by both the
    British and the Argentineans
chopper helicopter
CO Commanding Officer
compo standard-issue dried food rations for use in the
    field: GS (General Service) – canned; Arctic – dried

Craphat soldier not of one's own regiment (not applied to the SAS)

CSM Company Sergeant-Major

DF defensive fire

Endex end of exercise

Exocet variable-range guided missile particularly used in sea warfare

FAP first aid post

FIBUA fighting in built-up areas

FN Belgian-made automatic rifle

FOO forward observation officer

FPA final protection area: target on which a machine-gun is locked, or registered

GPMG general-purpose machine-gun

H hour the time at which an action or battle is to commence

HE high explosive

IWS individual weapon sight: infra-red for night use

JNCO junior non-commissioned officer

MG machine-gun

Milan short-range, wire-guided, anti-tank missile; also used against bunkers

Mirage French fighter-bomber used by the Argentineans

MOD Ministry of Defence

MT Motor Transport

NCO non-commissioned officer
ND negligent discharge (of a weapon)
NOD night observation device

OC Officer Commanding
OGs durable cotton-denim battle dress; often preferred,
    particularly in cold conditions, to standard-issue
    'lightweights'
OP observation post

PC Platoon Commander
Pucará twin-piston-engined ground-attack aircraft used
    by the Argentineans

QM quartermaster

RAC Royal Armoured Corps
RAMC Royal Army Medical Corps
R & R rest and recuperation
RMP Regimental Military Police
RSM Regimental Sergeant-Major
rubber dick hoax, wind-up

SAS Special Air Service
SBS Special Boat Squadron
Scimitar light tank equipped with a seventy-six-millimetre
    gun and particularly suited to cross-country use
Scorpion light tank equipped with a thirty-millimetre
    automatic cannon and particularly suited to cross-
country use

Seacat medium-range sea-to-air missile
Sea King anti-submarine helicopter for naval use with a
    capacity of up to twenty persons
SF sustained fire
SLR self-loading rifle
SMG sub-machine-gun
stag duty guard duty
stand down cease guard duty
stand to begin guard duty

tab Parachute and other regiments' term for a brisk
    march or run
Tom private soldier

CONTENTS

1
'ON THE BUS, OFF THE BUS'

March 1982. Our battalion was on twenty-four-hour standby 'Spearhead', ready for emergency action. Early that morning, I was seated with other members of Support Company in the Intelligence lecture room at our barracks in Tidworth. The Intelligence officer stood in front of the squad.

'Well, lads, the picture is as normal every time we get lumbered with Spearhead. The only possibility at the moment is that the situation in Northern Ireland may require our assistance. The Gulf situation is really well out of our hands.'

After a half-hour brief, we were packing away our notebooks when he suddenly said, 'Oh, yeah, this little island near the South Pole has been getting some bad vibes from the Argentines, but it's really very little. As far as the latest report is concerned, we can, and must, concentrate on the Ireland problem.'

'What's the island called?' shouted a lad from the back.

'Ireland,' came the reply, everyone turning to face the lad who had asked the question.

'No, sir, I meant the one down south.'

The Intelligence officer looked more closely at the map on the wall and turned around, still smiling at his little joke.

'It's called the Falkland Islands.'

Skip and myself had just arrived in Aldershot for a three-week course with 9 Squadron. We were on Pioneer Procedures, which would include one week on explosives – the main reason the thirty members of our battalion had grabbed the opportunity to come, the other being that we all wanted to go on the town in Aldershot and get away from battalion bullshit for a while. Once we had finished the course, we would straight away go on Easter leave.

At the end of the first week, riding back to camp in a four-tonne lorry, Dennis O'Kane said to me, 'The news of the day is that some island down south has had some Argies raise a flag on it and the island is British, stupid fuckers. Anyway, are you staying in town, or heading home?'

'Home, I reckon,' I said.

The second week of that course saw me go down with the worst bout of flu I have ever had. To this day, I have never been as ill as I was that week. Dennis, who was in charge of the party, told me, 'Go home tonight and forget the homework.'

My body was shaking and sweating with fever. I sat at my in-laws' house and Holly, my mother-in-law, gave me hot whisky to help me sleep.

Next day, feeling very weak, I tried to get to my class but

this bug was unreal. For three days, it had me flat out. By the time I felt a bit better, we had finished week two of the course and were to have the afternoon off, so it must have been a Friday. We arrived back at camp and I packed my weekend kit into my grip and made my way to my in-laws', where I watched TV with Holly.

My wife, Karon, rang from the officers' mess to tell me that Dennis had been trying to contact me to return to camp as soon as possible. She said it was something to do with an invasion of some sort.

'Yeah, yeah, Karon, winding me up like that is the oldest one in the book.'

'Well, this is what Dennis says, anyway,' she answered.
'Karon, you know what the lads are like. I'll see you down here later, OK?'

An hour after I put the phone down, it rang again.

'Vince, is that you?' It was Dennis.

'Yeah.'

'Well, for fuck's sake, get back up here or make your way back to Tidworth, mate. Haven't you heard the news?'

'No.'

'That fucking little island down south has been overrun with a full-scale invasion by Argentina.'

'Dennis, is that a wind-up?'

'No, gen. up.'

'OK, I'll see you at camp.'

Dennis was doing his best to round everyone up, but the lads who hadn't heard about the invasion laughed and said it was 'a cracker of a rubber dick'.

I turned the channels of the TV over and over, still thinking that it might all be a joke. Ten minutes later, a grim-faced newscaster confirmed Dennis's story. Looking at Holly, I simply said, 'It looks like I'll be doing an "on the bus, off the bus" until something is decided.'

I met Karon outside the Queen's pub, then made a fast return to camp. When I arrived back at camp, it was calm, with only a few bodies running about. Walking into the storeroom, I found most of the platoon sitting around chatting. Tommo grinned and said, 'Took your time.'

'We will probably sit here all night until someone up top decides to tell us what's happening,' shouted TP from the back.

'Well, can anyone tell me the score so far?' I asked.

'Argentina one, England nil,' said Johnny Cook, laughing as usual. His sense of humour had always been an asset to the platoon.

As predicted, we did sit around for some four hours. Then GD, our platoon sergeant, came in with Lieutenant Oliver and told us, 'Go home. Be back at 0900 hours tomorrow, OK?'

Walking home with Tommo, I said, 'Looks like a "hurry up and wait" job again, doesn't it?'

'Yeah. As usual, it'll fuck up our leave too.'

When I got home, Karon was standing there with hands on hips, looking sternly at me. 'Well,' she said, 'I suppose you'll be going off again, and I have to tell you this, Vince: in the six months we've been married, you have been away four of them.'

'Karon, it's not just a little fucking exercise this time, OK?' I said. 'We may go, we may not. I'll find out tomorrow.'

Saturday, 3 April. At 0800 hours, we arrived at the platoon storeroom to be told a briefing would be held for the whole battalion at lunchtime. Until then, we were to pack our kit and clean our weapons. So all morning we packed and unpacked kit. Young Rob Jeffries walked in just before dinner, late for the call-back. Every member of the battalion had been called back from all walks of life and throughout Britain, some even from abroad. 'Wob', as we called him, placed his grip on the floor and asked, 'What's all this crap about the Argies invading Scotland?'

We all looked at him and laughed and threw items of kit as he retreated from the storeroom.

At dinnertime, we paraded in the square and formed up, waiting for the CO. The RSM arrived just ahead of him and called the battalion to attention.

'Gents, just to let you know the full implications and developments. We will be going to Southampton on Wednesday or Thursday to embark on a ship yet to be named. We will then sail south. There will be a lot of running about and a lot of changes between now and then, so please be patient. You will have tomorrow (Sunday) off and then, by Monday the fifth, you and I will have a better idea of the coming events. Good day.'

We walked back to the stores, chatted for some minutes, then dispersed into our separate little worlds, saying goodbye in the face of what seemed unreal, almost a joke, to us all. I went back to Aldershot and stayed there with my parents. I could see the fuller implications of what was coming, but my family seemed more concerned about the weather. Certainly, Karon was more worried that it was another tour away than about any danger I might be in. Me? I really thought that the end might be upon me, but I waited to see if we would go the full way, or if it was just a bluff by the government.

Steve Wake and his girlfriend Julie came back to

Tidworth with us to have the last few days together. Although they were good company, I still don't know if this was a wise idea, or whether Karon and I should have spent the time alone together.

Monday, 5 April. After a few hours' dry drill, we cleaned and packed away our SF machine-guns. We now had a better idea of the weather and terrain we would be working in, so our kit had to be unpacked and packed yet again. We also had the pleasant information that the battalion was to travel on the SS *Canberra*, at least as far as Ascension Island. As far as the MOD were concerned, this was a small island mid-way to the combat zone. It would be the staging area for the invading task force. I went home with Steve and we watched the news, seeing the Navy leave Portsmouth in a blaze of farewells.

The next day we rearranged our kit yet again, this time moving it from the army suitcase to the sausage-bag. We then witnessed the unbelievable manoeuvres involved in unloading six hundred body bags from the column of four-tonne army lorries that had been arriving since it all started. TP and myself walked over to watch the quartermaster's party unloading. Our sneak peep into the QM's stores was enough for us to realise that the government meant business. The platoon gathered around us as we ran through the list of kit that had arrived, which included Arctic clothing, Clansmen radios and socks. In fact, everything the battalion had asked for we now had in our grasp, all within hours. As Johnny said, 'Makes you wonder how long that fucking stuff has been on some twat's shelf.'

That afternoon, we all piled up to Perrum Down ranges and zeroed our weapons. As I lay down to zero my SLR, looking at the figure-twelve target, I scarcely imagined that less than a month later I would be aiming at a live target of Argentinean soldiers.

On Wednesday, we got the green light to go the next day. The day was slow and uneventful because we were stood down early. The whole battalion had received all the latest intelligence and were packed and ready for the last time.

That last night at home, sad as it may sound, I wanted to go, as Karon hadn't stopped complaining. The tension was to blame for most of it, though the frustration of not knowing what would happen made it all seem unreal still.

After dinner on Thursday, 8 April, we climbed on to the fleet of coaches for the two-and-a-half-hour journey to Southampton. The last goodbyes were short and sad and the lads just sat for the first few minutes of the journey, deep in their own thoughts.

The arrival at the docks was a sight, even though we were the main reason for the massive activity. Standing in a huge hangar, we listened to the regimental band playing over the shouting and screaming of the hundred people all wanting to be in charge. Sitting on his kit, Johnny said, 'This is just to get us on the bloody boat. Christ knows what it'll be like if we reach the Argies.'

'Yeah,' I said, 'I can see it now: "Bramley, Cook, go kill that Argie, please, he's spoiling my view."'

We were still grinning as we received the order to follow a long line of troops and members of 3 Para on to the gangway. As I picked up my kit, I caught sight of Jez Hemming, a bandsman from our battalion and also a very good friend. We stood looking square into each other's eyes. We never had time to say goodbye properly. The activity around me broke our stare and the quick 'I'll see you around, you wanker' from me was said as I climbed the plank on to the ship.

The SS *Canberra*, or the 'Great White Whale' as she became nicknamed, was no doubt having the most attention paid to her since her maiden voyage. The dockers did us proud; working flat out like a chain-gang, loading the ship. The whole dockyard was like a beehive with loading, shouting and movement of troops.

Amid weapons, kit and bodies pushing and shoving, our platoon, moaning and swearing, found the small corridor with the cabins allotted to us. Mark Rawlings ('Rawley') and I were in the same cabin. We had shared before in many corners of the world and we were both happy with this arrangement. For the first few hours, we sat around unpacking the basic items we would need and watched the activity outside, through the porthole.

That first night, we sat in the bar and watched the news, all wondering very much the same as we did on day one: 'Who do you believe?'

Friday, 9 April. All morning, the SNCOs were coming down on the lads like it was going out of fashion: 'Do this, do that.' Around dinnertime, I managed to slip away to ring home. My conversation with Karon was brief. I mainly wanted to know: 'Are you coming down to see the ship off?'

'No, I can't, really. I'll get lost in the car.'

As I put the phone down, I felt rather angry. I rang my parents. The same thing happened. 'Vince, you'll be home shortly, plus we have visitors here.'

They meant Peg and Stan, family friends for years. Feeling somewhat niggled after Karon's answer, I said, 'Yeah, you're right. I'm just overreacting as usual.'

I walked to the front of the ship to watch the crowds of

families gathering. My good friends Paul Reid and Johnny were there and we took some photos or 'catch me naturals' as we called them. After tea, we hung around awaiting the order to line the decks for the big send-off.

There were now some two and a half thousand troops on board, elite units put together to form 3 Commando Brigade: 3 Para and attachments and 45 and 42 Royal Marine Commandos. Mixing with the Marines was not our idea of pleasure. We had hated each other for years, and the atmosphere of rivalry was very apparent. The cold stares we gave each other at first caused some concern among the high brass, but we came together in a united front as we watched the families and listened to the bands playing below. We were all now quiet and self-absorbed.

I could not help thinking that my family were really planning to come. However, as we lined the decks, the reality was upon us all, whether we had family below or not. The ship slid quietly away from the dock, to cheering and frantic calls from girlfriends, wives and mothers below. Marines and Paras alike forgot the war and even the silly hate between us, and waved and shouted back. The TV crews on the decks with us tried to capture this personal moment, but they did more harm than good, because we all just wanted to be left to our own thoughts.

The lights of Southampton, with its night-time activity, flickered from the coast. I watched from the deck and an almost eerie silence took over as we moved away from the dock. The only noise now was the rushing of water as the great liner cut a path through the Channel. Gone was the sound of cheering families and friends. Almost gone, too, was the sight of England. Would I see her again? Would we really go in, or was all this just a game for the politicians?

I didn't feel, nor have I ever felt to this day, that our actions were wrong – nor did any member of that task force I spoke to then, or since. The unknown was our only pain.

As the coastline disappeared, my trance was broken by singing from below. Walking from the deck, I noticed that it was filled with Marines and Paras, all leaning over the side, gazing into the darkness. One Marine turned at the same time as me and said, 'Looks like something from a film, don't it, mate?'

'Yeah. Perhaps we'll be cannon fodder – not that I'm worried about it as yet,' I replied.

'I was on Naval Party 8910 last year. Same of the lads who were down there when the fuckers invaded say they blew the fuck out of Moody Brook, our old barracks.'

'We were told that they didn't touch it,' I said.

'Ah, you'll see. Over the next few weeks, we'll hear bullshit after bullshit.'

When we went for a drink, we found that the powers that be had separated the Paras from the Marines, so that each now had their own bar. The Marines all sat in theirs around a TV set flickering with the last news bulletin. Standing on chairs to see the screen, the Marine and I watched the docks and the SS *Canberra* sailing from England with all pomp and circumstance. The picture flickered once more and then was gone forever.

I rejoined my own battalion, who were happily downing as much beer as they could. Then, having sunk a few myself, I made my way back to my cabin, to find Rawley already asleep. Once I was in bed, the new surroundings didn't bother me, nor did Rawley's snoring. The first day of the campaign slipped away as our ship drew nearer to the war zone.

2

EVERYBODY LOVES A SOLDIER

Saturday, 10 April. I awoke and quickly dressed. Rawley gaped through the porthole at a mass of sea, with us in the middle of nowhere. The ship's movement was barely noticeable as we clambered to the galley for breakfast.

Soon after breakfast, the platoon gathered in Tommo and Johnny's cabin for the first of many hundreds of briefings. GD was OK in camp, but out of it he was a bloody pain. Not one member of the platoon liked his attitude. He was our SNCO and we all had to know it every day. I don't mean that I hated or even disliked him, but he just didn't give us the freedom that the other platoons were allowed at times.

The routine on ship was to be something the Paras had never encountered before. Suddenly we had to know the meaning of every word the Navy uses. For example, 'heads' meant the toilet, 'port' was left, 'starboard' right, 'galley' the cookhouse. A list of these equivalents was pinned on the Support Company noticeboard, which was on D Deck. It was soon covered in graffiti correcting it to our standard. For example, the heads were to remain 'The shithouse, OK?' The amended list disappeared from the board within hours.

Often a naval officer would come around on inspection, or rounds as they called it, and ask a Para, 'Ah, good. Can you tell me what "the bow" means, please?'

The answer was always, 'The arse, sir.'

This never failed to turn the officer's face a glowing red.

We all had a daily training programme to complete, and it was in many cases very much needed. We revised all military subjects that would be required for the terrain we would be living in. The intelligence and information being gathered by the superiors of the brigade were constantly brought round to us during the teaching.

The first subject we had to cover in depth was fitness. Secretly, we were not keen on this. We all felt that we were fit enough already. We were wrong, as usual. The whole company pounded the deck, and by the time the first week was over we would be doing twenty-four circuits in one session – about ten kilometres in all. We built up to 'tabbing' around the deck with full kit, often doing more than fifteen kilometres. This was funny when the sea was rough, because as we ran around in company formation the whole column would suddenly sway to one side with the ship. Sometimes, in rough weather, the PT instructors would stand debating whether or not a fitness run should take place. If it did, we ended up running in a snake motion. However, it was calm most of the time and before long we had got up a good pace.

As the early days of April slid by, we crossed the Bay of

Biscay. The news was that the politicians were at a stalemate. On board we would often say, 'Fuck the bloody twats sat there arguing. Let's get it over and done with.'

The general attitude of the troops was: 'Support the actions. We love Maggie for giving us the chance to kill some Argies. Just let's hope we get back in time for the World Cup and summer leave.'

The SS *Elk* was now a supportive friend to the *Canberra*, following us en route. As she was our ammo ship, full to the brim with all types of stores, her presence was a constant reminder to us that war was imminent.

I wrote home to Karon and my parents almost daily. The incoming mail routine had been quickly organised, but for many lads it was a morale-breaker. You would often see someone standing in the corridors moaning that he'd had a 'Dear John', or some other bad news. For the majority of us, though, the mail was just the boost we needed.

At home, the massive support had produced in hundreds of females a sudden liking for both the Army and Navy, and they all wanted penfriends. This amused us very much. The daily sackfuls of letters were dumped in our rooms and we picked out the ones we fancied. The whole platoon would gather in one room, grab armfuls of letters and retreat to our cabins. There we would first feel an envelope to see if there was a photo in it, then gather around the growing pile of snaps and pick the best lookers. Some of the lads, even myself, found some right beauties, though writing back to hundreds of women was out of the question. But I did write to a lady from Winchester who was very nice and after the war I visited her on a few occasions and we became friends. She had four kids and was very polite in every sense.

Naturally, not all the photos were of beauties, and the platoons took to keeping personal 'grot boards'. You could visit another platoon to view their board for the 'Ugly Pig Contest'. Some of the pictures that found their way on to the boards made you wonder if England had anything worthy of Miss World.

You would hear a scream of delight when someone found a 'grot' photo, and this would bring the rest of the platoon crashing into the cabin to look, making comments like, 'Fuck me; who'd love that beast?' or 'Pig in knickers!'

The photos would then be proudly stuck to the board, which was the nearest that girl would get to our hearts. We did, though, all pick penfriends to write to.

On Tuesday, 13 April, we sighted a Russian spy ship following us. The order came down that no one was to throw rubbish overboard as the Russians were picking up every bit for their intelligence. This brought me and Johnny to the bow the next day, where we secretly threw overboard a bagful of 'grot' photos. I said to Johnny, 'They'll look at those girls and forget about invading England forever.'

That same day, we started the many emergency lifeboat drills. The whole brigade were allotted places to assemble in the event of the ship going down. These drills always caused moans and groans from all the troops. The overcrowding on and around the lifeboats made the sinking of the *Titanic* look like a TV cartoon. You would hear some officer shout, 'Come on, lads, get in line. Play the game.'

Someone would crack back, 'Fuck off, Wodney, go play your game in the mess.' Or a lad, impersonating the voice of an officer, would shout, 'I didn't see the iceberg, sir!'

EVERYBODY LOVES A SOLDIER

The best crack shouted was a very good take-off of Surgeon Commander Rick Jolly. He would give an almost daily spiel over the intercom about one thing or another. We all believed it was so that he could hear his own voice. Up on deck one night at about midnight, someone imitating the Surgeon Commander's voice shouted, 'I say, there seems to be too many people crowding on the port side for lifeboats. Could you please move around to the starboard side now?'

Everyone looked at each other then turned in all directions, milling about. This in turn caused the officers on deck concern about the shifting weight and they shouted frantically for everyone to stand still. The troops shouted all sorts of things back at them, under cover of the dark night. About three-quarters of an hour later, the officers were still shouting for the culprit to own up. We nearly killed ourselves laughing at the senior ranks trying to look super-efficient.

Wednesday, 14 April. By now, we were running about fifteen times around the deck per session. The days were warmer, and we began to feel it. After our run, we would go straight up to the heli pad at the top of the ship and do body exercises for another hour. We exercised with logs, or performed sit-ups, press-ups and so on. We had only been at sea a few days, but it was all getting very boring. All the talk was: 'Are we or aren't we?'

However, Al Haig had finished his talks with the PM on that day, and the BBC World Service, which was fast becoming our only source of information, gave out the news that more Jump Harriers would be joining the task force. This was enough to make most of us realise that 'Our Maggie' wasn't going to fuck about.

As we passed the Canary Islands that day, we fired our personal weapons from the rear of the ship. The GPMGs were fired two at a time, each having roughly one hundred rounds through the barrel, so that we could balance them.

As on most evenings, I trooped off with Paul Reid and Steve Wake, both very good friends, to the early showing of the film in the cinema. Paul was a constant mate from our days in Germany and has remained one of my best friends.

Thursday, 15 April. After our morning run, we had our first Intelligence brief, which was attended by the whole company. A Marine officer stood up front explaining the ground and weather conditions on the Falklands. He started with a formal 'Hello, chaps. This will only take a small minute of your time', before rambling on and on. The only real benefit we received from the lecture, as one corporal pointed out loudly when we were leaving, was that we now knew we would be cold, so we had to pack an extra pair of gloves. The general attitude among the junior ranks was: 'Get the fucking senior ranks off our backs and stop the bloody officers all trying to be boss.'

The amount of rules and fart-arsing-about the lads had to deal with was bad enough for me to mention it in my diary.

That night the cinema showed *The Enemy Below*, an old submarine war film, which dragged out all sorts of cracks about Navy procedure. As the first reel finished, a lad shouted, 'Now watch how they run like fuck to the lifeboats, lads, and notice Wodney shouting, "Walk or you'll be on a charge!"' He was taking the piss, as everywhere you went on board there was some officer lurking in a corner, looking for a promotion for catching someone running.

After the film was over, the bar was packed as usual, with the battalion supposedly drinking no more than their two to three cans nightly allowance. In fact, the lads drank the bar dry within days and a special load had to be brought on to keep them happy.

Friday, 16 April. Our company had a swimming test. The tiny pool on deck barely held six people, but fifteen men crammed in, doggy-paddling. The test was really just a time-killer and the pool was so shallow that most of the lads were standing on the bottom, moving their arms to show the instructor that we were trying. The atmosphere was relaxed and no one was whinging about the possibility of going to war. Everyone just accepted that there were actions we had to follow.

Al Haig had arrived in Argentina for final talks with the idiots in charge there. In the bar that night, we were all on the same wavelength, thinking, Fuck the talks. Hope he fails. Let's go down there and sort it out.

Many of us, including me, missed home. When you suddenly find yourself in a position that may either eventually bring you home, or keep you away forever, you think all sorts of things. 'If onlys' are the big ones, but isn't life like that anyway? Writing home was for me a form of relaxation and a way of getting things off my chest.

That night, Tommo and Johnny came into our cabin, armed with two bottles of whisky. This was banned at our level, but many a Navy lad was selling bottles to a few of our boys in the know. Sitting around on the floor, we decided to play Yahtzee with the poker dice and get drunk. I had smuggled a few cans of beer from the guarded bar and the whisky became our chaser. The four of us got blasted to the point of vomiting. Next morning, my hangover was well worth it. GD was moaning like fuck: 'If I catch drink down here, someone will be on a charge,' and so on.

As Johnny said, 'Trouble with him is he doesn't know anyone to drink with in his mess.'

The following morning brought us into Freetown, Sierra Leone, West Africa. It was now Saturday, 17 April. The weather was hot and humid. We had some short but boring military lessons that morning, but, because we were now anchored up and looking at land, we could find distraction in the view for once.

As I stood with some thousand-odd troops, an English family came eagerly up to the pier, to wave a Union Jack for us. They had good intentions, but the patriotic feelings they had must have flown straight out of the window as soon as they got within earshot of us. They had not taken into consideration the average squaddy's humour. The flag and their good wishes were the last things we were interested in, once we spotted the daughter. She was dressed in a flimsy dress and her large breasts were more than noticeable. From us, looking down her cleavage, the general scream was 'Get yer tits out, love,' or 'Sit on my face, while I wave a different flag for yer.'

The whole family was there, little brother and all. They looked up at the troops gazing down at the main attraction. They tried to smile and pretend that they hadn't heard us, but you can't ignore hundreds of sex-starved men, shouting for nookie. After taking a spell of verbal abuse for the daughter, they slowly walked off, perhaps never to feel so patriotic again.

Out from the shoreline came some natives, paddling like mad in their canoes, which were full of African goodies.

About six canoes came to meet the troops; we called them 'bum boats'. As they stopped by the Great White Whale, the black guys looked and shouted, 'You good men want a spear or arrow?'

One lad from the Anti-Tank Platoon shouted back, 'Black bastard, we give seven point sixty-two up arse if no go away.'

This brought laughter from the troops on every deck. The black men in the bum boats laughed with us, oblivious to the insult. One of them shouted back, 'Anything plastic do good for me.'

A couple of lads below threw two containers at them for good terms. They became very excited at the – to us – useless gift. A Navy lad standing next to us said, 'It's like this every time we dock at places like this. They're so poor. The containers serve as water containers for the tribes inland.'

But the sick humour now led to coin-throwing. It began with a 'fuck off' gift, but they dived into the sea to fetch and retrieve the coins. It was amazing to see the clear outline of their bodies under water as they dived to the bottom. This game lasted for perhaps an hour, but we soon got bored because no matter how many coins you threw at them they retrieved them.

The intercom announced that anyone dealing with the bum boats would be charged, as they carried a high risk of malaria and other diseases. It was at this point that some lads below turned the fire hoses on the natives, which had a very good effect on them. The water was powerful and easily reached the boats bobbing beneath us. Crashing into the boats, it soon began to fill them. The locals frantically tried to paddle away from us, but the hoses followed them.

Two boats sank to their rims, sending us into fits of laughter. The group in another boat tried to paddle their half-filled and sinking vessel. The blacks were now angry and shouting, 'You bad white men, you bloody bastards.'

As they struggled in the water with all their worldly goods, a lad from the deck below us shouted, 'We remember your sneaky attack on Rourke's Drift. Now swallow that.'

The morning activities over, Johnny and I joined the huge daily queue for scoff. It always reached up two flights of stairs, along two corridors and ended in a small hallway. This occurred on both port and starboard of the ship, so that there were perhaps two to three hundred people queuing at all times. Many lads took to reading books in the long-drawn-out hour it took to get to the hotplate. However, the food was reasonable and not many complained. We would only baulk at the thought of the officers getting waited on, while sitting at their own tables: 'One law for the rich and another for the poor.'

After dinner, the heat became so intense that we sweated without even moving. Yet this didn't stop the forty-five minutes of running around the deck. The run, in shorts and trainers, was enjoyable, but you felt completely drained afterwards.

That evening was excellent. The run and the sweat made the bar the prime target for everyone and it was soon packed to the limits. The Marines had a jazz band that came in to entertain us. At first the lads said, 'Fuck the Marines' band, we don't need them,' as if they were alien beings, but the short-lived burst of hatred disappeared after the band played one hit. They gave it max for us and the fun turned into the normal inter-platoon singsong competition, each platoon having to do a stint. The music was readily supplied by the band.

As the night ended and I slipped between the sheets, the great ship lifted her anchorage from Freetown. By first light in the morning, we would be looking at nothing but sea again.

3

TALK ABOUT WAR

After leaving Freetown, we passed the next two days in relative ease. The only real hassles we had came from the officers above and the SNCOs issuing their silly orders. When really the best thing would have been to give us breathing space, our own sergeant was bent on fucking us around. His constant niggling got so bad that Tommo took him to one side and gave him a warning. He did leave us to our own devices for a while after that.

Our lectures were in the early afternoon now. The most memorable was by some very keen Marines who had been serving in the Falklands at the time of the invasion. Obviously, listening to first-hand experience was better than listening to some officer lecturing us on his personal beliefs all the time. However, an Intelligence officer from 'way up top' gave a graphic account of what the Argies were up to at that time. The intelligence constantly coming in was essential to all levels. What I remember most about this lecture-cum-brief was the officer standing proudly in front of us, saying, 'The Argentine Army is the best and strongest in South America.'

He told us, 'You will be in for a big scrap if it comes to war, gents, have no qualms about it. At the last recorded reports, the Argies have about nine thousand men in fortified positions around Stanley, the capital. But we also have good reports that they are underfed, morale is low and they have taken to eating horses and sheep et cetera, which they have been stealing from the inhabitants. This tells us that they are very undisciplined and goes to show that conscription is going to be their mistake.'

My immediate feelings were: 'Nine thousand fucking men, and we have only two or three thousand. What the fuck is the big brass up to?'

Al Haig extended his talks, which pissed off a lot of the guys, because the feeling was, if he succeeded, then all this bullshit was chess.

As we were propping up the bar that night, the usual scene now, the RSM entered and broke the news that our sister battalion, 2 Para, would be joining us and would be leaving Aldershot immediately. This was a morale-booster for us all, and there was a big cheer of approval. But, as one lad from C Company said loudly, 'Well, now we have nearly four thousand against nine thousand.'

His joke fell flat, but he had a point.

Next morning, heli drills in full kit were rehearsed with the Navy's Sea King helicopters, which were larger than the Army's. We knelt in our sticks. From kneeling, we ran to the doors, clambered into the helicopters and quickly shifted into position. We then debussed from the choppers. This was two minutes' work, but we had waited for two hours, in the tropical heat in full kit, for the lesson.

Tuesday, 20 April. I was up at 0630 hours for an early breakfast. Rawley and I went on deck to watch our arrival at Ascension Island. The island was British, but loaned out to the US Air Force. What was more important to us even than seeing land again was getting our first proper sight of the Royal Navy anchored offshore. The frigates and assault ships anchored there were watching us too. In all, there were about ten ships. But the sight of the mid-Atlantic island was the biggest shock for most troops. We had had a vision of palm trees and golden beaches. In reality, the island was nothing more than ninety square kilometres of ash, dust and rock. 'The pits of the earth,' Rawley said.

Fitness exercises were now held in the early morning, to avoid the midday heat. Plodding around the ship had become boring as our fitness improved, but the sweat ran from our bodies like water. We took showers after our runs.

The daily hassles were easing up and we were getting afternoons off. Sunbathing became the in thing while we were at the island. Whenever time was spare, it was common to see the upper deck crammed with troops plastered in lotion, 'getting the rays in'. One hilarious incident occurred when a lad from the Marines decided to cool off. After posing, he dived into a swimming pool which had just been emptied. His subsequent injuries are unknown to me, but the slagging that the Para lads gave the Marines afterwards was untold.

We had a daily ship's rag, which was printed with all sorts of jokes designed to raise morale. Its humour became increasingly directed against the brass and the jokes kept the junior ranks in fits. In earlier editions, the brass had put in their upper-crust jokes (which just made us yawn) but, when the editor let in slagging comments about those at the top, it became 'insubordination' and the rag died.

Mail arrived and this lifted morale. The penfriend mail was exchanged with great speed. The many letters from home for all the platoon showed support from everywhere. Perhaps it was still a game at home too.

Wednesday, 21 April. Because of the very hot weather, the ship's company rose at 0645 hours and fitness training took off first thing, the programme tightly packed, with different platoons taking over the deck for running every half-hour. The whole ship had to get through training before dinner.

During the time we were at Ascension Island, our routine was one of busy preparation. This involved not only fitness exercises but also lessons and loading. Then, on 22 April, we had a sudden change of routine. After doing a hard tab around the deck in full kit, we were taken on top and placed in orderly lines. Then, to our amazement, the area around us became like a scene from a war movie. Helicopters buzzed above us, landing whenever possible on their pads, or hovering and carefully lowering load after load of ammunition.

For four hours, we unloaded the ammo in chain-gangs. It was stacked below as well as on deck – all around us. For the first time in my army career, I was looking at, and holding, more ammo than you could dream of, from sixty-six-millimetre anti-tank rockets to grenades, as well as thousands and thousands of nine-millimetre and seven-point-sixty-two-millimetre bullets. That day, the SS *Canberra* took on board hundreds of tons of ammo. We were all very busy. It struck me how good it was to see the Army, Navy and Air Force all working closely together. If one day the button was pressed, my confidence would stay high, if everything worked like this.

In the short breaks from unloading, my small party went to the side of the ship to watch the activity in the bay. Navy ships signalled to each other, and landing-craft steamed from ship to ship loaded with all kinds of cargo. Most impressive were the choppers, hovering near us with cargo hanging, waiting in an orderly queue to unload. At the height of the operation, between six and eight loaded choppers whirred above our heads.

Having completed the unloading, we staggered back to our platoon sergeant to find him moaning that the cabins hadn't been up to standard that morning. This frustrated the lads. He was always coming out with pathetic comments at the wrong time. I know that the PC (platoon commander) had quiet words with him about this. But as Tommo said, 'It's properly shit him up, with all the ammo and nearer to war now.'

The PC gathered us for a quick brief and said simply, 'As it stands at present, we will be sailing south tomorrow, lads, so write home.'

This I did, without hesitation. The next morning, however, the brief changed and we reverted to normal routine. The false-alarm 'we're going now' chats became a regular thing after this, doing nothing to raise morale. That same morning, Rawley and I heard the BBC World Service report, 'The SS *Canberra* has now left Ascension Island.'

Rawley and I looked at each other and I said, 'Jesus Christ, what the fuck's going on back home for them to say shit like that?'

Rawley grinned. 'Next we'll hear them say that we're going to land on the Falklands tomorrow,' he said.

This was very near the mark. At a later date, when 2 Para entered Goose Green, the radio had told the world before the event. This, and some previous encounters with journalists on board, made for a massive lack of trust between the Forces and the press. We had an hour-long brief in our cabin, ordering us not to talk to any member of the press under any circumstances.

The press had had great treatment from the mess, although we had not really met many of them. They had officer-style treatment and, as most lads agreed at that time, 'Fuck them, anyway – just another type of snob.'

I can remember having to do some SF drills on the top deck for the cameras. They came around all nice and chatty, asking ridiculous questions for the papers back home, and most of the lads just cold-shouldered them, on orders from above.

Johnny commented that night, while we were playing Yahtzee and drinking whisky, 'I should have said, "Hello, old chaps, how about telling my missus to write?" – that's more important than "How long have you been in the Army, soldier?"'

Sunday, 25 April was a day to remember. The first news we had was that a Sea King chopper had damaged an Argie submarine. Minutes later, we heard that the island of South Georgia had been retaken without a single loss. That news was excellent. Some lads now hoped the Argies would withdraw from the main island. The corridors around the ship erupted with shouts of excitement. This is how the task force on the *Canberra* heard the news of the South Georgia episode: no brief, no BBC, just a very strong but correct 'rumour control', as they call it.

TALK ABOUT WAR

The next two days were boring. On 28 April, an air block was imposed around the Falklands. Rumour after rumour ran around the ship. No one really knew the score, or what tomorrow would bring. You had only to walk out into the corridor and say to the first bloke you saw, 'Have you heard, mate? The Argies are thinking of coming to Ascension Island to meet us, because they're fed up with waiting,' and this would probably then start a rumour.

The lack of intelligence and of positive action by the brass were beginning to get to the lads. In an effort to keep the brigade happy and get the troops more motivated, we took to the beaches on 29 April. Our platoon was now split into three teams, one team for each company. Each team consisted of six lads with two SF guns. As usual, I went to my former B Company and took control of the five guys under me. Tommo and TP were C Company, Johnny and Rawley, A Company. Christ knows how I ended up on my own with five Toms, but I really preferred it that way. The way I looked at it, if any mistakes were made on the big day, it was better if I took the blame on my own, rather than with two NCOs.

We spent the morning being briefed by 4 Platoon, to which I was attached. My company was split according to this procedure too, so the Mortars, Anti-Tanks and Signallers were with me too. Support Company supports each other company.

We carried out a small, quick exercise that was basically practising a beach landing and capture of a make-believe position. The landing-craft drills and beaching practice were really for 3 Para. Our usual role was strictly parachuting into battle. Who would have thought that, in our first battle since Suez, we would be pretending to be like our old enemies the Marines?

No ammo was issued, we simply put on our webbing, 'cammed' ourselves up and then joined the B Company queue in the galley, waiting to climb into the landing-craft. After what seemed to be an hour of waiting and fucking around, my turn came. I reached the door by the side of the ship and looked down into a half-full landing-craft bobbing up and down in the water. It could take a hundred and twenty men at a squeeze. Armed with my SLR, webbing and the bloody life-jacket, which was more of a burden than a help, I watched as the craft bobbed briefly towards me and then away again.

'It's an art to climb into these fuckers,' said a Navy lad, holding my arm, as I half-jumped, half-stepped into the craft. With my legs slightly apart, I attempted to balance myself. Watching the lads kicking and cursing as they jumped into the craft was funny only up to a point. Nearly everyone agreed that if the brass had said, 'You can either parachute on to the Falklands, or beach-land it,' we would all have wanted to jump. As Steve Ratchford said to me, 'If I had wanted to be a Cabbagehead, I would've joined them instead.'

Steve and Taff were with me for the exercise. Both were good lads – just as well because our experiences ahead were to be heavy. Once our craft was full, we took off towards the beach. Almost everyone turned to look at the *Canberra*, which towered over us, while the remaining troops looked down at us. The huge ship stood out from the small fleet in the bay.

We turned again and watched the beach get nearer. About thirty to forty metres from the shoreline, the big ramp at the front of the landing-craft was lowered forty-five degrees in readiness for the first 3 Para beach landing. The craft struck home, the ramp dropped and B Company stormed the beach, spreading out across the sand and charging the imaginary positions. I heard a sergeant shout at some lads who were laughing, 'Stop that, you cunts, and take it seriously.'

Running up the fifty metres or so of beach in soft sand in the incredible heat was much fucking harder than we had thought. We dropped into a hole by a small road, sweat pouring from our bodies. The Company moved around, running here and there. The OC then called out, 'Endex.' The whole thing had taken perhaps half an hour. The team under me had been very lazy and later, in a debrief, I went potty. However, it is only practice that brings out these faults, and it showed the day's drills were really needed.

Sitting on the beach, we waited for our lift back to the ship. The view of the fleet anchored in the bay was really impressive. The task force now had about seventeen ships waiting to move south. The SS *Uganda*, a hospital ship, had just joined us.

Climbing back on to the *Canberra* was just as big a hassle as climbing off the bloody thing. Back in the cabin, both Rawley and I found we had collected enough sand to make a sandcastle. It fell from our webbing, our boots, even our hair. I washed and showered, then joined the queue for dinner. Intelligence that night said it was almost 90 per cent sure that we would be going in, but nobody believed anything any more.

The last day of April, a Friday, we spent at sea, refuelling. For roughly nine hours, the *Canberra* sailed with the auxiliary ship alongside her, topping her up with fuel.

The next day we were up at 0430 hours and ashore again by 0600 hours. This time, the entry on to the landing-craft and the subsequent beach landing were better performed.

We clambered on to a one-tonne and got a ride over the rocky, hilly terrain to a firing range that had been set up for the day's shooting. The road was winding and we were sticky with the heat. When we reached the range, we took up positions along a one-hundred-metre front and proceeded to balance the SF guns, each of the three barrels in the kit. Our targets were oil drums, some six to eight hundred metres away. Unknown to us, the beating zone, further on, was a bird sanctuary. Flocks of birds were soon flying everywhere. The Mortars took to keeping them in the air.

The island was really one big dustbin. The ride back to the sandy beach was completed in minutes, and we were told we would be having an hour or two to relax. Most of the lads went skinny-dipping. It was far too hot for lying in the sun. The seawater was beautiful, clear and warm, with fish swimming in it.

We returned to the ship at 1730 hours and managed to catch the latest news: the RAF had bombed Stanley airfield. We hadn't realised it at the time, but on Ascension Island we had actually seen the Vulcans landing after their mission. I had managed to take a few photos of them as we passed the airfield. At first we took the news for lies, as the rumours were still unreliable and even the BBC news couldn't always tell us the truth at that time. But afterwards we felt it was good news that things were warming up. We didn't know it then, but that mission was one of the trickiest and longest ever for the RAF.

The following day, 2 May, saw the Navy bombard enemy positions on land and the RAF succeed in shooting down two Mirage fighters. But for me that Sunday morning was most memorable for the lie-in we had. The sergeant left us alone for once and we got up at 1000 hours to spend what was for us a day off, sunbathing on deck oblivious to the fact that the war had started down south. As we relaxed by the pool, Johnny remarked, 'Well, the Navy have had their little fun. Wait till they sink the fuckers.'

On 3 May, the submarine HMS *Conqueror* sank the *General Belgrano*, with the loss of around three hundred lives. When this news was first brought to us, we were sceptical, thinking, Yeah, OK. Once the news was official, it wasn't greeted with total enthusiasm. In the bar that night, most of us were solemn. We now knew that war was inevitable.

Although the sinking of the *Belgrano* was a shock to us, no one regretted it. The fact that the ship was outside the territories didn't matter. Our attitude was: 'Go to their ports and sink the rest of their navy before it comes to meet the troops.'

Later that day, we joined a queue for the issue of Arctic clothing. It consisted of wind-proof top jackets, wind-proof trousers, quilted trousers and jacket, and socks and a thick cap, also quilted. All this kit was new to us, but every bit was to be essential in the coming cold.

Our time was now free. Sometimes the lads would go to the rear of the ship, where a lad we called Ghost had invented a new game: fishing for trigger fish. These little bastards were like giant piranhas. They were so greedy for any type of food thrown to them that you could catch as many as you wanted by simply chucking out a line and hook. The fish were about the size of a paperback book, with teeth the size of your fingernails. They would bite into the bread rolls we stole from dinner and swallow them as if it was their last meal. In this case it was, for we would bring them up to our deck as quickly as our hands could pull them in. Once a fish was thrashing about on deck, we would poke it with our bayonets or stamp on it. The fishes' scales were incredibly tough, and it wasn't unusual to see a lad pushing the bayonet in as if he was really doing someone in.

Sport with the trigger fish was a good pastime for the lads when they were bored, and Ghost was much praised. Countless hours were passed fishing. We were only getting our own back. It was said that a lad painting the side of one of the ships in the bay off Ascension Island had fallen into the sea and half his leg had been eaten by the infamous trigger fish.

The night of 4 May, while we were playing bingo in the bar, news came that HMS *Sheffield* had been hit by an Argie Exocet and was sinking. The loss of a harrier jet was also reported. The news hit the troops on board like a sledgehammer. Until now, everything we had heard had been in our favour. South Georgia had been retaken, the Argies' submarine patrol boats had all been hit, even their inland positions had been bombed by the Navy and, now, the *Belgrano*. Sinking the *Sheffield* was the first of their strike-backs.

Morale in the bar that night swung from an incredible high to an almost sickening silence. Everything stopped, until the ship's captain came on the intercom to confirm the news. Four or six Navy lads, who had taken to drinking with us because of our shared dislike of the Marines, sat quietly in one corner. Total disbelief was written on their faces. One of them came to the bar.

'How can a Type Twenty-Two frigate get hit?'

Types and makes were unknown to us, but the lads' grief was shared by everyone on the *Canberra*.

4

THE GREEN LIGHT

The day after the *Sheffield* was hit, we knew our wait was coming to an end. The atmosphere was quiet and a morale-booster was now much needed. The only thing possible for the task force was revenge. The sinking of the *Sheffield* had hit us as if we had lost a personal friend. Tension mounted, frustration showed in everyone's eyes.

We all thought the same. What's the fucking brass up to? Why can't we go in now? Why don't they at least tell us what's going on? A million reasons for wanting to move flooded our minds.

The fitness drills were now carried out in full kit, and pounding the decks in the heat was gutty work. The queers from the Merchant Navy, the stewards, always came on deck to watch. It was not uncommon to see lads blowing sarcastic kisses at them or dropping their trousers, to flash at them in passing. It was all in good humour and the queers would shout back, 'Oh, you naughty boys' or 'My, my, aren't we a big boy then?'

Obviously, some of the stewards liked living dangerously and would try to score. The lucky ones got the good news, 'Like a beating?'

On 6 May, we sailed south at 1700 hours. Now the lessons in fitness and morale took on a new urgency. We were on our way to do our bit. Our SF GPMGs were mounted around the ship, playing an anti-aircraft role. As we got nearer our destination, our platoon became, with other gunners, the anti-aircraft team. Everything was set up in teams in each company.

The next day Support Company changed its anti-tank Wombat teams into SF teams alongside us. My team split up and I then had only Taff and Steve Ratchford with me. Joining me from the anti-tank teams were Johnny Crow, 'Skiddy' Skidmore and Kev Connery. I had known them all for some time from my time in the battalion, so the change wasn't a big deal. If anything, the change was for the better. Skiddy was a corporal, so he took charge in some ways, with me as second-in-command, although throughout we never looked at each other in terms of rank. All six of us were to stay in B Company.

Saturday, 8 May. That night I got blasted. I felt like getting pissed, so Johnny and I ripped into a good session. Trouble came when I found a lock-in and sat drinking with some Marines and a few lads from C Company. We finished the beer around 0100 hours and I took to the corridor to stagger back to my cabin. As I passed the intercom room, I saw two RMPs sitting there, trying to look smooth, chatting to a young woman, one of the fourteen or so on board. One RMP was a fat-looking wanker in my eyes and

I turned to him as I passed the door and said, 'You fat lump of shit.' Then I slammed the door and walked off.

Both RMPs came out and screamed, 'Come here!'

'Bollocks!' I said.

They started to chase me down the corridor. I ran down two corridors and into my cabin. I stripped off in seconds and leaped into bed. Seconds later, I could hear them going into each cabin. Reaching ours, they walked in and said, 'Hello.'

What a pair of wankers, I thought, as I lay pretending to be asleep. No way was I going to be nicked now.

Rawley sat up and murmured, 'Who the fuck are you?'

'Oh, we're looking for a Para that ran this way,' they said.

'Well, this is a dead-end and we are trying to sleep, so good night,' replied Rawley.

After they had closed the door, Rawley waited a few minutes and then turned on the light.

'What have you done now, Vince?'

I told him with a grin that the fat wankers had annoyed me. We both laughed at the stupid incident. Tommo and Johnny came into the cabin. Johnny's comment was the same as Rawley's. 'What now, Vince?'

Still half pissed, I said, 'Why does everyone point to me?'

''Cause if it isn't you, it's TP in this platoon who likes trouble.'

Grinning, I asked, 'No harm in slagging RMPs, is there?'

Tommo disappeared and returned with yet another bottle of whisky from his unnamed supplier. The four of us sat up drinking until 0400 hours. It was a good thing the next day was Sunday and we had a lie-in. I could not have got out of bed the next morning even if an Exocet had crashed through my porthole. I sobered up around dinnertime.

Monday, 10 May. We had the first briefing that was of real benefit to us. It was confirmed to us that we would be going in, but not before 16 May. We received the latest reports in that briefing in the cramped cabin, which stated that over ten thousand enemy troops were in some sort of fortifications in and around Stanley. Our task force was about four thousand strong. The difference in strength caused us to look at each other with concern. I wondered if our brass really knew what they were doing. If the rough estimate of three to one was correct, could the British task force take on and win against the 'best army in South America'?

Later in the meeting, we got a feel of what might be the first British actions on landing: a possible bridgehead formation somewhere to get supplies ashore. After the briefing, the company went straight into a five-mile run. Back to the routine.

The BBC World Service news on the morning of 11 May brought laughter from all the lads.

'There is still hope of a political solution to the problem,' said the newscaster.

Johnny giggled. 'Perhaps we are going to sunbathe in the ice and snow on the beach-head.'

The BBC news and reporters were becoming a pain. Trusting a reporter was now considered to be like talking to the enemy. Arctic kit was issued and packed. The last hopes of a possible heli-borne assault by the Paras were dashed in the briefing of the day by the platoon commander. We had hoped that we could save face and arrive into battle from the air, instead of clambering on to those bloody landing-craft again.

The evening was passed playing bingo in the bar.

Rawley, laughing as usual, cracked, 'Here we sit, on our way to war, playing fucking bingo. My gang at home won't believe this.'

All was quiet for the next two or three days. Rumours buzzed as usual, along with moans of 'Let's get in and go home.'

The main info we picked up suggested a possible move on 20 May. Our nerves now started. The move south was steady and without any real complications, but the further south we went, the further we were going in. Somehow, I and many others still didn't quite believe the war was going to happen. We were lost in our own thoughts on many different subjects. Home became secondary now. I thought about the 'ifs' and 'whens' of our arrival in the exclusion zone and of the landings and battles to follow. Home was not in my immediate thoughts. Survival was.

On the morning of Saturday, 16 May, two twenty-four-hour rations were issued to us for packing, although many of us never unpacked them. Speculation was now rife as to what the landing procedure would be. We were still very much in the dark as to what was happening. But within the next twenty-four hours all the bullshit, rumours and personal beliefs were corrected by the platoon commander.

'Gents,' he said, 'it's the green light.' In his hand, he held his orders from the CO and OC of the company and then, on 17 May, I heard for the first time the name Port San Carlos. This was a small farming community on the west coast of East Falkland. History was about to be made and the tiny community was not even aware of the coming invasion, nor were the forty-five Argentinean troops billeted there.

The platoon commander broke down the orders for the gun teams, assigning them their tasks. Steve Ratchford, Taff McNeilly and I were teamed up with Kev Cannery, Johnny Crow and Corporal 'Skiddy' Skidmore. Our allotted move was to Company B, 6 Platoon.

At a briefing with 6 Platoon's commander, Skiddy and I listened to the invasion plan, taking notes for the remainder of our section. We would be cross-decking to the assault ship, HMS *Intrepid*. Landing-craft would deliver us to a beach called Sandy Bay. We would move up through the settlement to a place called Windy Gap. There, B Company would become the forward line of defence in 3 Para's bridgehead. About five kilometres inland, we would meet the expected counter-attack, if it came at all, with an air attack almost certainly coming in first. The platoon commander of 6 Platoon explained all this quite calmly. 'Good luck, gents. This will be over in time for Airborne Forces Day, if we're lucky.' Airborne Forces Day is the first weekend of every July in Aldershot and is an annual parade of the Paras past and present.

When I left the briefing and entered my cabin to brief my half, the lads looked at me with wide eyes, in a way that told me they didn't want to hear anything but good news.

'Well,' I said, sitting on the floor. 'This is going to be one hell of a fucking exercise.'

'What's happening now, Vince?' asked Taff.

'Well, look at it this way, if we can tab five kilometres inland up this fucking hill,' I said, pointing to my small photocopied map, 'then dig in ready for their counter-attack within hours of landing, we should be OK. If we survive the landing, aircraft bombing us and the fucking weather, we can rest at Windy Gap.'

Taff and Steve looked at me and asked, 'What place?'

'Windy Gap,' I repeated. 'And by the looks of the area on this big detailed map, it *looks* windy, too.'

After my briefing, including the details for 3 Para's, A Company's and C Company's positions, the platoon packed their kit into their webbing ready for the expected green light.

The packing of kit was a careful and complicated operation. All kit for the webbing was packed into the usual polythene bags. The rations were broken down and squeezed into the mess tins in the kidney pouches. Socks became cushions for the straps. I wrapped my socks in poly bags, then taped them on the inside of my belt, as padding. My washing and shaving kit, 'as little as possible', was packed tightly into a poly bag and wrapped in a third of a torn towel. Packing and repacking to make our webbing as comfortable as possible, we began to psyche ourselves up for the days ahead. It was nerve-racking beyond belief. Yet morale seemed remarkably high throughout the ship, though the laughing and joking among the lads was partly to cover the fear. Not that anyone thought that death was going to hit him. That was for the guy you were talking to.

The platoon sergeant was an incredible pain to us all. Nag, nag, nag, all the time. Our patience is all that saved him. Don't get me wrong here. We had all served long enough to respect and obey without question, but the guy acted like a wet fart. There, in the middle of the Atlantic, we began to ignore him. The platoon was glad of one thing: he wouldn't be with any of the gun groups on the day.

On Tuesday, 18 May, we entered the Falklands Zone. The GPMGs were mounted on the decks above. My team and Tommo's had the sundeck. There, on the first day of our war, we loaded the guns with belts of ammo in readiness for the first expected aircraft attacks. Wind and cold whipped through the layers of clothing we wore.

After two two-hour stints on the decks, we were called below. Our guns were being replaced by the Navy's. In the corridors of the huge ship that had been our home for nearly six weeks, everyone was extra busy. With our weapons on our shoulders, pushing our way through all the running troops, I saw Paul Reid.

'Paul,' I said, 'what the fuck's going on now?'

'Going in early, Vince. Didn't you know?'

'Fucking brilliant, ain't it?' I replied. 'There we are on the decks with the brigade preparing to fuck off and leave us.'

Paul grinned. 'See you in Stanley.'

When we reached our cabins, the platoon commander and sergeant were waiting for the platoon to arrive back from its tasks. Once we were all together, the platoon commander said, 'Well, lads, we cross-deck in three hours. Get ready now, OK?'

Ammo was dished out to each man. In all, I had six magazines of twenty for my SLR and a belt of over one thousand rounds for the gun. New bandoliers were given out in which fifty rounds were to be placed, but we managed to push and squeeze a hundred into them.

Morale remained high, but our nerves showed as we clambered around the cabin in a frantic panic to get ready. When we had finished, there was nothing to do but sit down and wait. Waiting was the hardest part. I can remember Rawley, Johnny Cook and myself sitting in the cabin for up to an hour without saying a word. It was just eye-talk with smiles.

Tommo opened the door – I can't remember at what time. 'Vince, B Company is moving into the kitchen for cross-decking. See yer.'

My nerves disappeared at once. I now had something to do rather than sit. When I placed my webbing on my back, it was so heavy with ammo and personal kit that I thought the buckles were going to bend. It must have weighed sixty pounds. When I picked up the bandoliers and put them over and around my neck I thought my knees would buckle.

Weapon in hand, standing at the door, Johnny looked at me and said, 'Vince, with all that weight, let's hope the landing-craft doesn't sink, 'cause then you won't be going anywhere except the seabed!'

'That's all I need to hear,' I said.

We grinned and then smiled, as we said our farewells. 'See you later, twats.'

My team joined the long line of B Company lads. Slowly, the queue reduced. As I reached the door at the side of the ship, the wind slapped my face with unexpected force. The landing-craft bobbed around fiercely in the choppy sea. A Navy lad grabbed the webbing at my back.

'When I say, "Jump", you jump, OK?' he said.

The craft, half-full and wet with spray, came bobbing back to the side of the ship.

'Jump!'

In a flash, I jumped, then fell into the craft with my webbing, bergen and SLR. The weight was incredible. At that stage I thought, I hope they don't expect us to tab far with this little lot.

An hour later, I was half-soaked and fed up with watching all the other poor fuckers falling into the craft.

We set off for the *Intrepid,* about three hundred metres from us. Watching was all we could do. So cramped were we that if anything had happened it would have been like watching a brick sink.

The arrival and sight of the rear of the *Intrepid* was the start of my war, a war in which my struggle for personal survival was to begin, but also for the survival of my friends and the task force as a whole.

5

WELCOME TO SAN CARLOS

The intercom bleeped into life, requesting all members of 3 Para, including our B Company, to assemble in the galley area. Climbing off the bunk far below the water-line of the *Intrepid*, my gun team and I put on our already overweight kit and clambered up the small staircase towards the assembly point. I'd always thought the Navy had the life of Riley, but the conditions on that ship made us all appreciate land. Never since that day have I had a bad word for the Navy. The crew, young and eager, acted as perfect hosts during the short time we were on their ship.

When I reached the galley area, I was pissed off to see it crammed with Paras and Marines, slowly filling a gully in front of what seemed to be the sort of turnstile you get at a football match.

The CSM of B Company, Johnny Weeks, handed us all two grenades each. Further along the queue, we were also given two mortar bombs each. Steve Ratchford turned to me and swore in my ear, saying that we were to be 'donkeys for every bastard going'. I must admit many of us couldn't figure out how we were to steam up the beach (as in the films) with the amount of kit that we had to carry. Each person was by now carrying about a hundred and twenty pounds. The CSM shouted for us to squeeze up to allow more troops in. Those already in the gully moaned and groaned as we pushed up closer together. An officer standing by a door shouted that we were to hand over the mortar bombs once we landed.

'Fuck me,' said Taff. 'That takes the cake. Carry their kit ashore and hand it to them once we've landed.'

A lad from the Mortars smiled and said, 'Wrong platoon, mate. Don't think we carry everything, do you?'

Looking all pissed off, Taff sat on his kit waiting for another stupid order.

The area now looked like an overcrowded tube train. The troops had pushed so close together that you could count the blackheads on your neighbour's face. I sat on my kit, observing the order to 'Keep all noise down, no talking.'

I looked around me at the hundreds of cammed faces, all with big, wide eyes. Each face told its own story. Each soldier had his own thoughts of the coming battle as the lads quietly sat about waiting. Always waiting – the story of all soldiers. Myself, I couldn't help but think that it was still a joke and that we wouldn't be going ashore. My stomach was in knots and the nausea was hard to control. The nervousness running through me was the worst of all. Waiting, waiting for that fucking green light. Many of the lads talked quietly among themselves, probably trying to calm their own nerves. Steve Ratchford rabbited away in my right ear. I don't remember a single word he said. 'Doc' Murdoch sat facing me, pulling faces like a comedian.

'Fuck off, Doc,' I said. 'I've got the jitters.'

'We've all got to go somewhere, Vince. Don't worry.'

Sadly, Doc was to die on Longdon.

It was like waiting for the green light on a para jump, but worse. All the lads had wanted to parachute in, or at least go in by helicopter. Going in on landing-craft was an insult to us. I tried to sleep, without success. Taff managed to nod off and his head rolled from side to side and back and forth. He looked like a puppy dog in the back of a car.

A shout from the same officer as before brought us back to reality again.

'Listen in: 2 Para have only just landed, without a fight, though one of their guys slipped and broke a leg while embarking into the landing-craft. We are now some time behind schedule, so we must be quicker in the movements now.'

'Fucking brilliant,' whispered a Marine.

'Shut up, Cabbagehead,' whispered a lad from B Company. 'You aren't ashore yet.'

The Marines slowly left the mess hall, the first to embark and 'do their bit'. Slowly, B Company and its attachments shuffled towards the side door. I stepped out into half-light, on to the pathway leading towards the small landing-craft to which my gun team had been assigned. The OC of B Company and about twenty others clambered into the craft. As we squeezed in, the Navy lads waved for the craft to be lowered into the sea. The smell of the motor didn't bother me. The cold, fresh air that hit my face felt good after all those smelly, sweaty hours crammed together in the mess hall.

The frustration of waiting and all the hassles of the last six weeks disappeared as we watched, in stunned silence, the battle for Fanning Head to our left. Fanning Head was the Argie OP near San Carlos. The SAS had mounted an attack there, to allow our landings to go ahead without interference. The tracer rounds and naval bombardment on the tip of the bay brought us abruptly into the real world.

'Jesus, look at that. It's like a firework display,' shouted a lad at the front of the craft.

'Shut up and face the beach coming up.'

We hadn't noticed we were moving towards the beach. All heads had been turned to watch the battle.

'Sir,' said the young radio operator, 'messages coming through say there's a tank on our beach.'

'What?' screamed the OC.

The word 'tank' had caught everyone's ears. We all looked around and tried to peep over the side to see if a tank did exist. 'Sit fucking down,' shouted a sergeant. The craft swayed as we all sat down. 'Get a GPMG up front, now,' he shouted.

A young lad who had been sitting in the middle of the craft was manhandled to the front. He placed his GPMG on the ramp in readiness. His face was a picture. It had a look of 'What am I doing here?' that said it all.

The OC was busy screaming down the radio 'net' for confirmation of the tank. After all, a machine-gun against a tank was not good odds. The OC passed the handset back to the signaller, looked up front at the gunner and asked him why he was there.

'A tank, sir,' he replied.

'What tank?' screamed the OC.

'On the beach, sir.'

'You twat,' said the OC. 'It's a *tent*. Get down.'

So nervous were we that we couldn't help but giggle quietly at the balls-up. To say that that gunner looked relieved would be an understatement.

The cramped conditions inside the landing-craft became unbearable. Trying to stand up with all our kit was impossible. Sweat ran down through my hair. My mouth was dry with nerves. I was longing to land now, even if we had to fight. Six weeks of sea was enough for any Para. I could just see over the side of our craft. Five to six other landing-craft were moving alongside us.

Very impressive, I thought. And at least we're not the only target.

Fanning Head was still blazing, as the order to prepare for landing was screamed by the craft-handler to the Navy lad up front. The engine of the craft slowed as we reached our landing spot, Sandy Beach, according to the map. The ramp was lowered and we stood there enveloped in sweat, the adrenaline surging, waiting to launch our attack. But we were greeted by a stony beach. The image of storming it disappeared in a flash. Two hundred Paras hobbled off the landing-crafts. The stones and the kit we carried would have made it impossible to run, even if we had needed to.

We deposited the mortar bombs about thirty metres ashore and began to make our way towards the small settlement. The settlement, roughly two kilometres away, consisted of about ten houses. Later, we heard that forty-three Argies had fled the settlement on seeing our arrival.

We reorganised ourselves for the coming march. The weight of full SF kit and ammo was the heaviest we had ever had to carry. Slowly, we marched, sweating and puffing, over terrain that was to become a constant pain in the arse throughout the campaign.

Within fifteen minutes, Pete Gray, a sergeant in B Company, screamed, 'Air raid red.'

Everyone fell to the ground and looked up. Clear sky, nothing. 'Where's the red, then?' shouted some lads.

'Up there somewhere,' came a sarcastic reply.

'Point your weapons upwards anyway. Make it look as if we're doing something,' I said to Steve and Taff.

Whoosh. Three jets passed overhead before we could even fart.

They screamed into San Carlos Bay to attack the task force's shipping. There was a rattle of small-arms fire, then our missiles screeched into flight at the enemy. It was like watching a slow-motion movie. One of the jets disintegrated above a ship and the sea was showered with its remains.

'Wow, what a turn-on,' laughed some lad.

'Shut up, you twat. Just fire if they come this way.'

Within seconds, another two or three jets whizzed past, with a few token shots from us – too late, of course.

Over the bay, where 2 Para were tabbing up the hills, a Pucará flew slowly into view. It seemed like a snail compared to the MIGs. A rocket flew out from the surrounding hills and hit its wing. The plane spun around and tried to manoeuvre away, then disappeared from view over a hill.

The Navy fired everything they had at the jets. Some were hit, others flew off without a scratch.

C Company moved up into a large group of hills called Settlement Rock, while A Company moved into the settlement of San Carlos. We in B Company had a long uphill tab towards Windy Gap. We were to be the first line of defence for the beach-head attack about to be staged at San Carlos. Tons of kit and troops were expected to land after we had secured the settlement. Windy Gap was about six kilometres inland, a bloody hard uphill slog.

When we passed San Carlos, two Gazelle helicopters had just been shot down by some of the fleeing enemy. Word very quickly went around that the crew had been shot in the water while trying to swim ashore. Our anger brought home the reality of war and introduced us to the type of enemy we would be fighting. I personally felt that, if we had caught those responsible, we would have killed them for the cowardly act. But weren't all Argies cowards?

Resting every few kilometres, we made our way to our position. My back was killing me. The sweat ran through my helmet and down my back like water. We wobbled up the hill swearing at everyone. 'Not very happy teddy bears,' as we used to say.

Three-quarters of an hour later, we stumbled into Windy Gap, where the wind indeed shot through the small valley. Sitting on the hill, using my webbing as a back-rest, I looked back at the route we had marched. What a shitty place it was. It looked worse than Dartmoor and the Brecon Beacons put together.

Within a few minutes, the cold wind was digging through my clothing, and as my sweat dried it produced a shiver all over my skin. I struggled to stand up with all my kit and my weapon in my hand and looked for Skiddy from the Anti-Tanks, who, together with us, would form B Company's SF teams. It had been decided long before that the Wombats wouldn't be used, much to their disappointment. Skiddy,

Kev Connery and Johnny Crow, now with us, would form the gun teams for B Company.

They were sitting slightly behind me. I walked over to them and found Kev was already making a brew.

'What now?' I asked.

'Fuck knows,' grinned Skiddy.

We both agreed to set our guns about fifty metres apart and dig in. Looking at the area on the hill where we were, we decided that the valley and dead ground ahead of us was the most likely attack area for the Argies.

We got out our shovels and started to dig a trench in our different positions. However, at no more than a shovel's depth, water began to seep in. Taff stood laughing and Steve flopped to the ground, while I threw my shovel away in disgust. We all sat, making another brew, watching the small hole fill up. Skiddy, watching our progress, laughed, as he was having the same trouble.

To crown it all, rain started to fall. It was like having a bucket tipped over us. We sat there, on a bloody hill thirteen thousand kilometres from home, in our wet-proofs in the rain, wind and sleet, with an air attack in progress and our trench filling with water. What a lovely war. But we were still laughing.

The OC and his band of followers marched over to us. As we stood there with the rain lashing us, he decided that the gun positions weren't correctly sighted. Map out, binos out. The gang of leaders decided we should move further down the hill, on to more of a slope, overlooking a valley. Our present position would then become the area to our left.

Kit packed, weapons on shoulders, the two gun teams marched off to our new positions. These were a little better. We had a peat bank behind us, so we could blend in better with the terrain. The rain had stopped, but the wind screamed through our clothing. Because of an overweight webbing fighting order, no bergens had been carried on the landings. Promises that they would be delivered to our positions later that day were now broken and we couldn't have carried that much kit in one go anyway. With last light creeping in fast it now seemed that we were in for a shitty night.

A meal was cooked by the gun team's chef, Steve. We packed all our kit away and set our SF gun on its FPA. I'd be a liar if I didn't admit that, sitting on that hill, I wished that I was back between clean sheets.

Our shelter that first night consisted of a poncho placed on the ground, stacked in four corners with peat and another poncho laid on top and weighted down with large stones. Webbing was used as head-rests, as cowboys use their saddles. We lay on this bed in our Arctic clothing, our feet wrapped in black poly bags, and settled down for the fourteen hours of Falklands darkness.

Guards sat behind the SF gun, two hours on, four off. There was no sleep to be had, what with the cold and rain, ponchos flapping all over the place and everyone restlessly changing positions all the time. It was a great first night.

6
AERIAL OVERTURE

First light was a relief. We could move and do something. Having crawled from our cold, damp position, we stood up and ran on the spot, thumped each other on the shoulders and banged our feet together, to bring life back into our half-dead bodies. Breakfast and a brew finished, we set about improving our disgusting position.

A few hours later, some stores arrived, four-by-four wood to use in constructing the bunkers that seemed to have been copied throughout B Company's positions. Trenches were now a thing of the past, because of the wet and boggy ground.

Skiddy, Kev and Johnny finished their bunker well before us and sat back watching us slave away at something that resembled a kids' camp in the woods. Four platoon officers came around on inspection, seemed happy with even our poor construction and disappeared over the hill again.

ggling with drizzle, rain, sleet, wind and boredom was our next task. As we sat making a brew three hours after daybreak, 'Air raid alert' was being screamed over the hill.

Jumping to our positions, we unlocked the SF gun and looked up, waiting.

'Here they come!' shouted Kev, pointing into the far distance.

By the time we had looked in that direction they were on us. We fired as much as we could, in front of the coming enemy aircraft, hoping the rounds would hit. They were gone in seconds. We stood up and watched them dive into San Carlos Bay below.

Grabbing my camera, as I always did, I watched a Seacat score a hit on one plane. We could hear the rattle of gunfire even from our positions. The planes flew round and attacked again, then headed towards us. Within seconds, they passed over us, through a barrage of small-arms fire from B Company and away into the safe distance.

They attacked again later that day, from another direction. We could only watch and pray for the safety of the Navy.

Pete Gray gathered the NCOs around him for a daily brief and informed us of things we weren't interested in, but also informed us that A Company and C Company had had a 'blue on blue' some time earlier. Apparently, both companies had patrols out looking for the Argies who had escaped on our landing. One patrol had spotted the other and asked for mortars on their 'position seen'. In turn, the other company asked for artillery on the first company. So a battle began between A Company and C Company, both firing small arms at each other. Within minutes, the operations officer in charge realised the error and radioed for a cease-fire, but not before three to four lads had been badly shot up, two of them suffering head wounds. The ops officer was temporarily removed from the task.

Standing there, listening to stories of this type of balls-up made us wonder about the outcome of the war. Fortunately, the incident was the worst error 3 Para were victim to.

The last meal of the day finished, we settled down for another night of cold, wet stag (guard) duties. While we were sorting out the duties between us, Taff spotted light flickering about three hundred metres in front of us, across the small valley. Shouting to Skiddy, we quickly relayed the sighting to Pete Gray and the chain of command came into action. We set our SF guns on to the still-flickering light and waited. With the ammo lying beside and attached to the gun, we sat trying to build up a mental picture of what could be out there. Argie patrol? Perhaps an attack? The platoon, slightly behind, watched and waited with us.

'OK, OK, what's going down here?' asked the platoon commander.

'That light,' I said.

'Strange. What the fuck's that, then?'

'You tell me, sir, but we're waiting to shoot if you wish.'

'Wait. I'll find out.'

The minutes passed by. An hour passed by. Nothing.

In the end, the PC came trotting back to say he wasn't really sure.

'But Intelligence say they have lost a Marine patrol somewhere.'

You're telling me it's either Marines lost in our line of fire, or perhaps the Argies?' I said.

'Yes, that's about all, Corporal B.'

I walked over to Skiddy, to inform him of the mess-up. 'Looks like we'll have to wait till it moves.'

All that night we watched that fucking light flicker in front of us, as we sat waiting to fire. The threat wasn't as bad as we thought. It was just the unknown.

First light found us still by our guns, watching and waiting, very cold and thoroughly pissed off. Out of the early-morning mist came a batch of Marines who had sat on the hill all night after their officer had got them lost. We all stood there grinning and making sly remarks. Not one man replied: the humiliation of it all was too much. I often wondered how and why the incident happened, but, above all, did they kill that officer? Because we could have killed the lot of them.

The next air attack flew in to our right, down the valley, just above the water-line of the river that led to San Carlos Bay, now nicknamed 'Bomb Alley'. Again we fired, but with little hope of hitting these fast targets. The enemy aircraft banked away and headed up through C Company's area. Watching them, on the hill, had been the Artillery's Blowpipe teams. Their NCO was away at the time, about one hundred metres in front of their position, having a crap. We could just see him trying to pull up his white longjohns and denims, when his partner fired the missile. Whoosh. It screamed into life, trying to attach itself to the heat of the aircraft.

We watched the missile go, swaying, then stop in mid-air, just like an early film of rocket exploration. It started to plummet to the ground just above where their NCO was trying to dress himself. We watched him trying to run, his trousers half-down, across that terrain. It was like a comedy show. He dived into the grass as the missile hit and exploded very near to where he had been crouching. By now, we were rolling about in fits of uncontrollable laughter.

'The age of technology!' screamed Steve.

The bergens and resupplies of compo arrived, much to our joy, later that day. That night seemed like luxury. With the stag system now brought down to two hours on, ten off, shared between our two gun teams, we had plenty of kip. The warmth of the sleeping bags brought new life to us all.

The third day passed in the same way as the previous two. We waited for news of what to do next. The air attacks continued and we admired the bravery of the enemy pilots. They were hit from every angle, but still continued to attack. Some of us wondered whether their land forces had the same attitude. If so, we would be in for some hard battles.

Orders came down that we were not to fire any more small-arms rounds at the enemy aircraft as this was unnecessary wastage. So we sat and watched the Navy slog it out, much to our anger. However, on the last attack of that day, an eighty-four-millimetre anti-tank rocket was fired and some lads still shot at anything that moved, just to feel they were doing something constructive. So much for orders. The last plane to fly over us was hit by small-arms fire. Pete Gray screamed that it was hit by him. The plane smoked badly and slowed, before spiralling over the distant hills.

In front of us was a small pond. Skiddy and Kev had

watched a gaggle of geese sitting on it, trying to elude the war and the unaccustomed activity around their home. We decided that, during the next air attack, we would kill them for fresh meat. Three planes flew in together. Not one shot was fired at the enemy, but plenty at the geese. Not one of us hit his target. We all looked at each other and couldn't believe we'd missed. The geese flew away, seemingly laughing at us, no doubt feeling safer on the enemy side of the island.

'That takes the biscuit, missing enemy geese as well as the aircraft,' roared Kev.

The next day, Steve was washing the mess tins out in the pond when another air attack came screaming in.

'Stay there, Steve,' I screamed.

Looking up, having only half-heard, he stood and walked towards our positions with his hand cupping his ear to try to hear me. We all dived to the ground as the first air attack of the day roared towards us. It was a Mirage, lower than normal, so close you could see the pilot as he fired a short burst of cannon fire at Steve, who by now had decided he would be better off behind the gun than armed only with dirty mess tins.

The enemy rounds missed by miles, but their thundering fire brought home the seriousness of it all. Steve stood up when the plane had passed, looking up nervously, then picked up his mess tins and walked back to us. He looked a bit shocked. He threw the mess tins at all of us and said, 'You can fucking clean them next time.'

Sitting in the bunker, Taff and I kept grinning at each other, until we burst out laughing at Steve, who still looked hacked off. 'Fucking leave it out, you pair of kids,' he screamed.

He calmed down and, much later, giggled with us.

On about day five, we went back into the settlement for R & R. What a joke that turned out to be. Although we were the furthest forward of the troops, it was decided to let us rest away from our dangerous position for twelve hours. What got us was the fact that we had all been quite happy in our bunkers, away from the hassle of officers and too many chiefs. All the same, we stumbled back the six kilometres to the settlement, with half of B Company. We passed one of the burned-out Gazelles that had been shot down on 'D-Day'.

When we reached San Carlos, everybody appeared to be running about doing their own thing. The arrival of B Company seemed to cause an upset to the routine, but not for long. We grabbed an all-in airborne-style stew from the cooks and were given some hot water to wash in. Many of us chose to wash our private parts and change our underwear.

We then moved into a sheep shed, to be greeted by the sight of two hundred lads, all trying to pitch their sleeping bags for the night.

'Brilliant,' whispered Steve, 'we've a great little bunker sat empty up the hill.'

'Looks like we've got some nice cushioned wooden floorboards for the night,' added Taff.

'Let's grab a corner,' I suggested.

Lying on the floorboards, we looked up at the shed roof, wondering why we were there. Only the type who could sleep through anything slept that night.

At first light, we were all glad to get out and make our way 'home'. We arrived, sweating after the extra uphill trek, to see Pete Gray gathering the NCOs for the daily

Intelligence report. Taff and Steve went off to make a brew, while I came up alongside Skiddy to hear the latest.

'Well, lads, bad news,' said Pete. 'The *Atlantic Conveyor* has been sunk.'

'How the fuck did that get hit?' asked someone from the rear.

'You tell me.'

Pete wasn't a happy man, nor were we, for the ship had been carrying the Chinooks and luxury kit like tents, overboots and so on.

Some bastard should fall for this, we thought. All that kit on one bloody ship.

Bad news of our choppers being sunk hit us sorely and many of us were still thinking about it when Pete announced the next info.

'No choppers, so the big wigs have decided we start walking a.s.a.p. Like today.'

Pete gave us a breakdown of what was happening: 2 Para were to march on Goose Green; 45 Commando were to head north to a settlement called Douglas; we, of 3 Para, were to take Teal Inlet.

Within an hour, all kit was packed tightly away, last meals and brews demolished, weapons oiled and ready and bunkers evacuated. We made our way up to the prominent part of Windy Gap, where most of the battalion was gathering. The CSM of B Company was organising which kit we were to carry and which to leave. No tripods for the SF guns and no sleeping bags, no bergens – all unnecessary weight was to be left. We repacked our kit. The bergens and tripods were centralised for a later pick-up. They were to be choppered forward, if a chopper became available.

AERIAL OVERTURE

We all felt pissed off about the *Conveyor* being sunk and the prospect of the coming tab. We now knew that the march would be about fifty-five kilometres. But we were all glad to be moving, breaking out across the island, on the offensive.

We set out at about two-thirty that afternoon on what was to be an epic march for the regiment.

7
DONKEYS

With the GPMG, webbing order and ammo slung over every part of our bodies, we tabbed, or rather hobbled, as fast as we could.

Once over the first hill we started to march around the side of an adjoining hill. At this time, the Marines were walking alongside us, ready to break northwards towards Douglas settlement. Unlike us, they carried full kit, bergens and all.

Within thirty minutes, we had a short break, to let the stragglers catch up. A young Marine was propped on his back beside me, with his Bergen as a support.

'You lot have the right idea,' he said. 'No fucking extras. We look like donkeys here.'

I couldn't help but agree with him but thought to myself that, while we may move faster, we'd be the coldest at night. At that time, I didn't know we'd be marching flat out all the way, day and night.

Our march over the terrain was slowing, within an hour of starting out. But we tabbed on until the sweat ran from every pore of our bodies. My head was down, my arse was up and my shoulders ached with the weight of the ammo.

Skipping, sliding, sometimes walking, we pressed on. When I looked about me during the occasional short breaks, I could see the lads strung out in one big line, all following each other, like sheep. We call it the 'battalion snake': a continuous, meandering 'S' wherever you look.

The first river was more like a stream. We hobbled across on as many stones as we could find, to avoid wet feet. But dry feet were a short-lived thing because we soon came to low ground and, once over the small river, the terrain became a bog. Our DMS boots, made of compressed cardboard and leather, were not best suited to combat that terrain. Within a few metres of the river, they squelched into the smelly marsh and had to be dragged out. The marsh lasted about a kilometre and a half before we broke uphill.

Over that hill, around another and down into a valley, we came to a wider river. This time, no stepping stones. Just very wet feet and denims, as it was about knee-deep. I struggled to keep balance as I crossed. Wet feet, fine, but I wasn't going to fall over. I felt the freezing-cold water slop into my boots and soak my socks within seconds of stepping in. Gritting my teeth, I walked across the river, to see C and D Company lads sitting all around. The CO was walking among them, giving encouragement.

We dropped to the ground. Skiddy and Johnny changed their socks. I slipped out of my sweat-soaked webbing to join them. Taff sat quietly to our side, while Steve threw on a quick brew.

'Air raid red, air raid red,' screamed the signaller.

With no boots or socks on, we grabbed our weapons and as usual waited to hear where the attack would come from. We heard the scream of the approaching enemy aircraft, from the direction we had just marched. It came into view, but banked away from us southwards, totally unaware that 80 per cent of 3 Para sat there reorganising themselves.

'I reckon if the bastard had seen us he'd have known we are on the offensive and heading towards Stanley,' someone commented with accuracy.

As far as we were concerned, his banking away was good news.

We received new marching orders from above. Each company would follow another. The lead company would permanently have a point section feeling the ground for the battalion behind them. Last light was creeping in as we kitted up and sorted ourselves out into the battalion formation. We kept close together in the enveloping darkness. Keeping the men together was now just as important as reaching the settlement of Teal.

In less than an hour, our bodies were struggling under the weight of kit and ammo. The GPMG seemed to weigh a ton. We swapped it over on every short break. Within the first two hours of the night march, orders were passed slowly back along the length of the battalion that we would be stopping for fifteen minutes in every hour. Some started clock-watching. Our boots and wet socks were becoming unbearable to march in, rubbing badly on the feet of most, if not all, of us. Blisters and sprained ankles added unexpectedly to the injury toll.

Slowly, the battalion ground to a halt for its third rest

within two hours. Taff worried me greatly. He was hobbling badly and his thin frame was too light for the kit we were carrying. Steve and I had taken his turn with the GPMG twice within an hour.

The battalion now closed up into two lines, marching alongside each other. This helped some, because you could moan at whoever was marching beside you, which took your mind off the increasing agony of the march.

About three-quarters of an hour after darkness had fallen, we had marched about twenty kilometres. We marched at about two and a half kilometres an hour after leaving Windy Gap – a fair rate, over that terrain.

Our next stop was by a hillside. C Company had just split off to our left, putting about a hundred metres between us. However, the two-line march continued. Taff was by now causing a big gap between me and those behind me. Knackered though he was, I knew the lads would be getting fucking mad if he didn't catch up. It meant less time to rest, because, when you caught up to where the others were sitting, they were on the move again.

'Taff, move up, move up,' I screamed.

'I can't, Vince. I'm fucked.'

I was losing my rag. I could see he was out of it, but I couldn't stand the fact that he was going to let us down before we'd even got there. Taff was trying to keep up and mumbling out loud that he could do it if only we were to slow down a bit. But this was impossible. Nobody could tell the lead elements to slow down. The gap got bigger, the swearing got louder. Taff wasn't the only one to feel the strain. Many of the lads were struggling. At last, exhausted, we stopped on the slope of yet another wind-swept hill.

Taff shook uncontrollably. He had bad cramp and lay there, totally out of the game. I informed the medics. Phil Probets, the company medic, came over, as we were busy rubbing Taff's legs.

'What's up, Vince?' asked Phil.

'It's Taff. Look at him, he's gone completely.'

Together we sat him up and tried to revive some spirit in him, but with no joy.

Steve was sitting beside us when the unusual order came from the CO, 'Brew up a hot cuppa and make a snack.' This shocked a lot of us. Theoretically, it was a no-no, sitting in the middle of an advance in the open, in pitch dark. Practically, though, it was the best order yet. A welcome brew was what we needed. The CO was obviously aware that the lads were suffering from the speed of the march.

Within seconds of that order, little lights from our hexie burners started to appear all around and soon the brews had been thankfully drunk. While Steve had our brew going, I tried to get Taff motivated, still to no effect. I was getting niggled now because, although he was in my section, I also needed to see to my own sore and swollen feet.

We fed Taff some porridge and shared out the brew equally. To me, Taff looked as though he was about to die. His nine-stone frame wasn't strong enough for the rest of the march. Taff could run the Army's British Fitness Test in around eight minutes and was considered our best runner. This proves, as do other accounts I heard after the war, that the fitness of troops cannot be determined by how fast they can run. The Paras always pride themselves on tabbing with kit, and rightly so, but I learned a lesson on our first night's march. You must have body fat on you to waste, for the kind of long tab that we had embarked on.

On the side of the hill, the medics gathered together those who were holding up the speed of the tab. They were a group of about six lads, whose conditions varied between exhaustion, sprained ankles and severe blisters, the last caused by the poor quality of our boots.

As we started off without Taff, I was mad because this left only myself and Steve Ratchford to carry the rest of the kit. I was also worried about leaving Taff in the middle of nowhere. It turned out that the lads left behind at different rest points were left for three to four days to fend off the weather as best they could. We nicknamed the march the 'Do or Die'. We didn't mean that anyone would really die, but that if you were left you would feel like it. We slogged it out for another two or three hours of continuous hills, bogs, rocks, holes in the ground – everything that could possibly make you trip or get wet. On top of the bloody awful terrain, we had the rain, sleet, wind and freezing climate to cope with. Exhausted and near the point of collapse, we came to the first man-made thing I'd seen, apart from the small houses at San Carlos: a barbed-wire fence. There, right in the middle of nowhere, sat the fence, stretching far into the darkness on either side. Orders from above told us to rest up until first light. We had been marching for fifteen hours across the worst terrain you could imagine.

Steve and I attached our ponchos with bungies (elasticated hooks) to the fence, and Skiddy, Kev and Johnny bashed up the other side, creating a tent-like accommodation. It rained hard for the remaining four hours of darkness. The wind blew the rain in on us as we all lay trying to rest in the 'basher'. But although we were all exhausted, someone's snoring soon broke into my thoughts and outside, around the basher, little whispers could be heard, with other voices shouting for silence.

I closed my eyes, dreaming of a bath, clean sheets and a letter from home. I didn't mind the rain as it hit my face. The chance to rest was welcome and I eventually managed to sleep. I was awoken by a nudge from Skiddy, who was already half-packed and ready to move. Steve and I crawled from our refuge and quietly packed our kit back into our webbing. The rain and cold had shrunk the webbing so that it was difficult to fasten. Cold and numbness had us swearing out loud.

We all crossed the fence eventually and the company gathered together to make for yet another hill. We tabbed over more hills, through more bogs and marshes. My legs ached more than I had thought possible. Steve was, if anything, better than me with the weight. Every time I started to struggle with the GPMG, he took it without complaining. Carry that weapon he could.

Kev turned to me after two hours of marching. Indicating Steve, he said, 'He's knicky with weight, isn't he?'

I grinned and agreed, 'Without his help in carrying that, I'd be fucked.'

Full credit to Steve. I'll always remember his actions throughout that march.

My feet felt worse since the rest back at the fence. I was now hobbling badly. The weight we carried seemed to increase all the time. We climbed a large hill and from the summit saw many smaller hills and a plain of grass, stretching as far as the eye could see. Below us lay a river that had to be crossed. We could see the lead elements of

B Company crossing about eight hundred metres in front of us. The downhill march was, as always, easier than going up. Many of the lads, now low on food and water, stopped to refill their water bottles. Steve and I quickly filled each other's, to avoid removing our kit. Then we splashed into the wide river.

The water was just under waist-deep and we crossed with ease. I hated the feeling of the water slipping into my boots, even though my feet were already wet. When we reached the other side, the lads seemed to be standing about. Word from the CSM told us that, owing to our quick advance, we were now able to hold up for three or four hours. It was about three in the afternoon, so no move until 1830 hours, much to our delight.

Resting again, Steve and I got out our rations for a long-wished-for meal.

'Rice, peas and an Oxo cube are the remains of our pantry,' laughed Steve. Just that and a brew, but it went down well.

The wind dropped, allowing the rain in. We put a poncho over us. With only a small meal inside us, the hunger soon crept in again. My stomach felt hollow. The wind and rain drained me of life. Lying there, feeling near to total exhaustion, I couldn't even think of what was to come – the battle for Teal Inlet. My feet didn't exist any more; they were just two blocks of numbed ice attached to my legs. Tapping them together brought a pain that felt as if they would shatter and fall off.

Steve lay next to me. Lighting up a fag, he looked up through the rain clouds at the darkened sky.

'If we carry on at this rate, we'll all drop dead of exhaustion,' he murmured.

He passed the fag to me. I wasn't a smoker, but the smell seemed to bring a welcome sort of warmth, so I accepted it. I took a drag, then coughed and spluttered. Steve giggled beside me.

An hour or two passed. We drifted into sleep despite the rain and the feeling of total cold. When we woke, we saw B Company lads mingling and talking around us. I decided to check my feet over before we moved and try to restore some life to them. Steve said that he didn't want to look at his feet because they felt like they were falling off. I peeled back my wet socks, saw blood on my right foot and discovered that the nail of my big toe was hanging off. Numbness had masked what would normally have been agony. Clenching my teeth, I pulled the nail away by its remaining roots. I wrapped two plasters around the wound and put on my last two pairs of dry socks.

We had our last brew before next orders. Soon the shout went up to get ready to move. We were moving earlier than expected, to catch the last of the daylight. When I stood up my body ached from head to foot. I was minus one toenail too. I took up my kit and moved into line with the others, ready to go the last thirteen kilometres into Teal. So far, it had taken us about fourteen hours to march forty-odd kilometres. That was still good going.

We set off very slowly, spaced out in one long line. We hobbled over the hill in front of us only to see more hills and marshes. I began to become conscious of my toe, and the more I thought about it, the worse it felt. However, the thought of dropping out at that stage seemed a fate worse than death and so I fought the pain. It *is* funny, looking back, but the further we went into the campaign, the less I thought of my home or family. I wasn't thinking of Queen and Country either. I thought of myself and the lads around me. Letting the side down was my biggest fear. That fear kept me walking.

8

'KNOCKING ON THE DOOR'

As darkness crept over us and we closed up together, the march seemed to pick up speed. The lads tabbed as fast as they could. Kit changed hands constantly along the battalion snake. We were annoyed by the lack of info coming down the marching line to tell us where we were and how far we had left to march. However, at last light, we hit a fence line, which told us that we must be near to civilisation. A Company split off from us and headed in a different direction.

'We must be near now,' said Steve.

'Wouldn't count on it, Steve, the way we've been donkeying around.'

After about half an hour, we stopped and the leading troops marched past on our right.

Someone in front of me shouted, 'Who the fuckin' hell's leading this show?'

A voice from the darkness called back, 'Me.' It was the voice of the second-in-command of the battalion.

Tittering was heard all down the line.

We followed the fence for two hours. Sweat soaked our clothing. My feet ached beyond belief. All I wanted was to rest. Steve and I continually swapped the GPMG between us, from shoulder to shoulder. My webbing was much tighter than normal, as the wet had shrunk it to fit my body like a glove. In consequence, I suffered webbing burns on my hips and the base of my back. Sweat continually soaked our clothing.

We came to a fourth river, smaller than the rest, and stumbled across it in the dark. The cold water mixed with our sweat to cause yet more sores on our feet. We were now about one and a half kilometres from the settlement of Teal Inlet. The agony of the marching disappeared quickly as it became clear that the tasks of battle could soon confront us.

We were just north of the settlement when we were given a firing position. We placed the GPMGs, Skiddy's and ours, together. We loaded and cocked the guns. In the darkness, we could just see the line of the battalion spread out over the hill, the men looking down, waiting for some sort of action. The sky was clear and the moon shone. It was like a pleasant evening of military exercise at home on the common. But the cold wind and the real ammo attached to the GPMG told us different.

The nerves and excitement I was experiencing at the thought of perhaps having to fire my weapon in anger for the first time slowly disappeared as the time ticked away. One and a half hours of lying in the cold with the wind shooting through us was all the action we had that night.

Much to our relief, a whisper reached our ears that there would be new orders, as the Argies had left, withdrawing elsewhere. D Company, who had been operating in the settlement, had marched in before us, just 'knocking on the door'. The settlement had had its Landrovers stolen by the Argies holding guard over the place only hours before we arrived. Our lead troops were brought into a house and given a cuppa and an update on the Argies, who had apparently come and gone as they pleased, stealing whatever food and goods they wanted. The civvies were very happy to see us, at first.

At ease, we moved into the settlement. My only thought now was to settle down and get some sleep. The battalion came streaming into the settlement from all directions. Some of the lads accompanying officers were lucky enough to be bedded down inside some of the houses. Steve and myself sat in what seemed to be a garden. Jimmy Morham found us to say that he and some of Support Company had found a shed unoccupied and would we like to join him. So our first night at Teal Inlet was spent crammed in a small sheep shed with members of our own company. We talked briefly among ourselves to sort out who was on guard. Sleep came within seconds. I slept in my Arctic clothing with the now cherished black poly bag wrapped around my feet.

With first light came the smell of hexie burners, as morning cuppas were brewed around the small shed. The welcome smell and smiling faces made the fifty-eight-kilometre march seem almost worth it. Light beamed in through the cracks in the shed, allowing us to see clearly not only each other but also the sheep shit which we had been lying in all night. We were caked in it. As we opened the door to leave, our smell turned a few heads. We moved out to find where our positions would be. Once the shit dried, it brushed off and added to the camouflage provided by our dirty uniforms.

Steve and I found B Company's position. The company was busy reorganising itself into a defensive position to one side of the inlet. Our gun and Skiddy's were placed overlooking the two tracks most likely to be a threat. As we positioned the guns, the first of many orders hit us.

'A full slit trench will be dug, stag systems doubled, rations and water delivered within the first few hours.'

Much of everything that happened around us was fully expected, now that we were halfway to Stanley. The Falklands were half ours. Choppers came in, hugging the terrain, sweeping in to dump their underslung loads of military equipment within seconds, then zooming off for more. The blast from the whirling of their blades chilled our faces, as we helped to centralise the bergens and kit.

Having sited our trench positions, Steve and I started to dig in. After the long march to Teal the feet of all the lads were playing up badly. As I had a toenail missing and only a plaster covering it, the pain shot through me as I trod on my shovel. Steve looked at me with a grin and said, 'This is going to be fun.'

The digging was very slow. The ground wasn't very hard, but the injuries to our feet slowed us. The agony of digging forced us to break off frequently. However, we had our bergens and tripods with us now and the thought of crawling into our sleeping bags as a reward for finishing our trench pushed us on.

Johnny and Tommo came over for tea and chatted about the goings-on. We found out that some of the platoon had dropped out on the march. More importantly, though, Mick Coleman, one of our gunners, had just been shot in the leg

– not by the enemy but by a knob in A Company. Weapons training seemed to have been the guy's weak spot. He had left the mag on when cleaning his SMG and the weapon had fired a short burst into our lads. Mick was the only one that got hit. We were bloody fuming, since he was much liked in the platoon. Losing him to a stupid ND was not the best news of the day, though more bad news was to come.

The CO and his band of followers inspected the lines later that morning. We thought they might instruct us to move our trench or something – the usual thing – but we were still thinking as though we were on an exercise. The CO looked grim as he approached the six of us taking a tea-break.

'Listen in, lads,' said the RSM.

We looked at him, wondering what was coming.

'During the march, 2 Para attacked Goose Green and Darwin settlements. After a long battle, the regiment liberated the settlement, with the loss of eighteen lives, including their CO, Colonel H Jones. Many have been wounded and a casualty list is being drawn up. They captured hundreds of Argies. The war is now a different concept, for the enemy are believed to have shot down members of 2 Para showing a white flag. More information will be given once known.'

The CO half-smiled and proceeded to the next line of partly dug trenches.

Skiddy, Kev, John and I looked at each other with open mouths. The thought of eighteen members of 2 Para dead outweighed the victory for us. I, for one, couldn't have given a shit about Goose Green or anywhere else on the island at that time. It was the thought of losing our mates in the sister battalion that worried me. My mind flashed back to the Queen's, the pub in Aldershot where we all used to meet up for a session on the beer. Divvy Richards, Russell (wounded), Billy Baker, Paddy Sullivan, Tam (killed), Big Jack Rapier, Paul Dale, Quincy, Geordie – the list of my closest mates in that battalion could go on and on. It was their lives I was worried about now. With hindsight, we can see that in military terms it was a typical shock battle, with all the characteristics of the Parachute Regiment – swift and hard.

We hobbled back to finish our trenches. The small gathering of Paras that had grouped around the CO were all lost in their own thoughts.

By mid-afternoon, our water began to run low. Steve was happy to carry on digging the trench while I trotted off to a nearby house for water. I knocked at the door and a woman, the first I'd seen in a friendly context for weeks, looked down to see me clutching six empty water bottles. I must have looked like a beggar. She smiled and beckoned me in.

'Where you from, then?' she asked, as if I was a lost child.

'Aldershot, love,' I replied.

'I know you're from Aldershot, you all come from there.'

This wasn't the first or the last time I've had to explain to someone that I actually did live in and come from the garrison town of Aldershot. People could never work out why I wanted to join the Army, coming from the same environment as my work. The woman giggled once she grasped the thought that these things did happen. In 3 Para alone, at that time, some fifteen lads came from or near Aldershot.

I filled my water bottles and was ready to go. I felt like an alien and that I shouldn't abuse the woman's hospitality any longer. There was a knock at the door and four to five other lads appeared for the same reason as me. We were now all crammed in her kitchen and she made her way to the stove to make us all giant cups of coffee. She was totally friendly and warm towards us. That coffee was the best I've ever tasted. I sipped it slowly, not wanting it to be finished.

Meeting the woman sparked a new feeling inside me. Then and only then, as I drank her coffee, did I begin to believe, as well as think, that the war was right. Strange that I should remember an incident like that. If I ever meet that lady again, I wonder if I could tell her that those fifteen minutes in her house helped me through the war.

When I got back, Steve was finishing the trench and looking pissed off. I thought it was because I'd been away too long and felt guilty, but this idea was short-lived.

'While you were away, Vince, we caught Chaderton hiding behind a bush eating a bloody big pile of jam sandwiches that he'd been told to share out among our lads. He'd eaten the lot, Vince.'

'Bread, Jesus, bread – and that bastard's eaten our rations?' I screamed.

'Yeah,' he replied.

Johnny came over, as I was contemplating ways to kill Chaderton.

'Sorry, Vince, you've heard,' he said.

'Yeah, and it's the last he'll eat after I've smashed his teeth in.'

'He's been dealt with. Leave it for now.'

Johnny walked away. His only task had been to come and cool my temper.

Within our platoon, we never forgave Chad's selfish act.

What his eating those sandwiches meant for all of us is talked about to this day.

With the trench finished and the stag system sorted out, we settled down as the night crept in. Huddled in the trench, Steve and I made the biggest compo scoff we could muster together with our rations. As we swallowed the last dregs of a hot cuppa, we both smiled with contentment. The warmth of the trench made us doze, but our feet needed sorting out before we turned in. Fresh socks in my hands, I looked at my shrivelled, blue and bruised feet. The wet boots and socks had taken their toll of blisters. One blister was the size of my palm. There were six in all to complement my missing big toenail. Some people may think I moan too much, but at the time I complained only to my trench mate, who in turn moaned about his aches and pains.

The condition of our feet was becoming a major problem for the battalion. An old complaint suffered by troops during many wars was afflicting us in a modern war: trench foot. Our boots, badly and cheaply made, coupled with our old-fashioned socks with puttees, caused this condition. It was characterised by a dull, thumping ache all over the foot, with blueness at the edges. Some say it is similar to frostbite, which some lads also got. The constant wet and cold would make the problem even worse before the war ended.

I wrapped and dried my feet as best I could and put my boots back on. We all slipped into our sleeping bags and our exhaustion put us to sleep before we knew it.

9

SORE FEET

'Corporal B, Corporal B,' a voice whispered into the trench.

Steve and I came round together. I looked up to see 4 Platoon's officer looking down at me.

'Yes, sir,' I replied.

'Vince, isn't it?'

'Yes, sir.'

Being asked your first name wasn't unusual between officers and men in the field.

'Sorry, old boy, bad news for you.'

In my half-sleep, I couldn't think of anything worse than being woken up.

'Orders from the boss. We're pulling out at first light and marching to Estancia,' he said.

'Estancia? Where the fuck's that?' I asked.

It was another thirty to fifty kilometres away, towards Stanley, we learned. Steve and I looked at each other, as we sat in the bottom of our trench, too numb to speak. I broke the silence first. 'This is getting fucking stupid, Steve. March here, dig there. We're dropping down like flies and now more. Do-or-die marching without resting.'

Steve laughed at my moaning, his teeth shining in the dark.

'What are you so happy about?' I said.

'Just the thought of more pain for the cause.'

Pain – Jesus, was he right. My feet would die before me, I thought.

As I drifted back to sleep, I thought of my old corporal, who trained me: Corporal Derring. We hated him for his hard methods. He used to say, 'Pain doesn't matter, the mind does the work.'

He was right, so right. His voice was screaming in my ears now, four years later. It was going to be mind over matter. There is wisdom in the Paras' training methods. I thought briefly of my parents, who over the years had had a rough time with my slobbish attitude. I had been in and out of all sorts of trouble before joining the Army. I said to myself that, if I died with a bullet in the head, at least it would be better than worrying them into an early grave with my attitude, but to drop out now and be branded a wanker would be unbearable. I owed a lot to everyone – my old NCO, my parents and, above all, to the lads around me. A Para team cannot work without everyone giving their best. It's the lads you fight and work for; you come second. A fresh outlook in the next stage helped me push myself that little bit more.

The morning was freezing, with snow lightly covering the ground. Winter in May. The bad weather was coming in fast. Tactically, we had to get in sooner rather than later. With our kit packed, webbing on and bergens stacked and centralized for delivery, we sorted ourselves into marching order. Standing to one side of us was a civvie, ranting and raving at one of our SNCOs about the condition of his garden, now that trenches had replaced the neat lawn.

'Sir, the Cabbageheads will fill them and will be staying to occupy them. Please calm down.'

The man wouldn't listen, complaining and threatening was his last wish, so he was punched square in the face and sent flying backwards on to his arse. Some of the lads who were finishing off brews spat out their tea, laughing.

'Get on with your work,' screamed the SNCO. We all looked away. The SNCO was much admired in the regiment. We began to think what it was all about. Just that one civvie made the morale bad. Perhaps he was a member of the infamous Falkland Islands Corporation.

The order came to get ready to move out. We put on our damp webbing and grouped up ready, with weapons in hand. The Marines were just staggering into the settlement, hours behind their schedule, looking worn out and still carrying full kit. We were now a full twenty-four hours ahead of them. We moved around the settlement and passed, lying on the ground, a spreadeagled Argie who had been caught by D Company. I looked at him with interest; he was my first sight of the enemy. He was like any of us – only his uniform was different.

The March was slow and laborious. The pain in my feet returned with every step. For the next few kilometres, we went up and down small hills, and the settlement quickly disappeared behind us.

Jimmy Morham walked behind me, whispering about the amount of kit Steve and I were carrying. He was pushing his lads to keep up. I couldn't help noticing how much thinner his face had become. Did we all look like that now?

A Scorpion tank, on tracks, came past us. The commander was looking out for anyone struggling hard. He pointed to me and shouted, 'Jump on.' I grabbed the GPMG from Steve. A ride up the coming big hill was an offer I couldn't refuse. Steve shouted to me that I was a 'slimy bastard', so I grabbed him and pulled him with me. The ride was bouncy and we struggled to hold on to the vehicle. The long line of our troops going up and down the hills spread out for a couple of kilometres.

About half an hour later, we stopped. Wishing to stay on board but knowing it was the turn of others, the five or six of us on the tank jumped off without having to be told. Others clambered on, thanking God for this luxury. How we all wished that we had had the choppers.

We came to a small wooden bridge where the lads were stopping for a tea-break. Rumours that we would be staying there for the night proved false. Orders for a night march hit our ears within minutes of stopping. However, the lie-up in that spot was to be two to three hours. We would wait until dark before we moved on.

Ian McKay stood laughing with his platoon. We sat down with them and brewed up. Suddenly, a small fire broke out, caused by someone's hexie stove igniting the grass. We all just sat there, looking at it. Ian grinned, but ordered it extinguished.

'The fucking Argies will think we're sending an Indian smoke signal, you twats. Get it out,' he shouted.

We all laughed.

Sheltered from the wind, Steve and I lay in the sun. It felt warm for early winter. Half-dozing, we all lay there, waiting for last light. We didn't know it at the time, but we had just crossed over the Malo Hills. To our right, the SBS had taken out a small group of Argies hiding in a house.

At last light, we stood up, glad of the rest we had had from the day's marching. We joined the long line of 3 Para marching towards the mountain ranges that were beginning to appear in front of us. I wondered how much further we would march before we had to fight.

Our few hours' break had restored us somewhat, but the next few hours were designed to undo all that. The pace was hard, very hard, compared with the past stretch. Closing up was automatic on a night march, but gaps still appeared. Some senior members of the battalion told those leading to slow up for the weaker ones, but to no avail. We went on like this for hours. The sweat poured off me, and my feet had ceased to exist, so that I stumbled, hobbled, trotted. Whatever I could do to keep up, I did.

We came to a halt at around midnight. We'd been tabbing for six hours. Apart from the two hours' break before last light, we had been continuously tabbing. We flopped to the ground. I was totally exhausted by now and prayed that the brass would lie up for the rest of the night. My prayers were granted. Orders swiftly came back along the line of the battalion to 'bash up' for the night, with follow-up orders that we would not be marching until first thing in the morning. We looked at each other, wondering why.

We got up and moved into some sort of defensive position. Kev Connery, John and Skiddy were to our right, Johnny Cook was just south of us. He came over to explain that we would be staying put for half the next day. An officer from battalion HQ gathered a few of us around him.

'We are now within the enemy's artillery range. The CO has ordered that we will dig shell scraps for protection. No movement, like walking around et cetera, until ordered tomorrow. Mount Kent is just to our front, which the SAS will deal with later.'

They did, with a back-up from 42 Commando. Hardly any Argies were there, as they had been airlifted out to help at Goose Green.

Skip and Tommo were laid up with us in our little area. I heard Skip mumbling in the dark about having to dig in.

'Skip, is that you?' I whispered.

'Yeah, come over.'

I found him knee-deep in a peat shell scrap, finishing off this improvised sleeping position.

'Tommo's over there somewhere, playing boss.' He commented that the rest of our guys who had dropped out of the tab were not happy with all the kit we'd had to lug. 'Portable donkeys, are we?'

'You're telling me. I'm fucked. If I hadn't had Ratchy with me, I'd be dead somewhere out there. Ratch has been brilliant. Guts or what?'

I didn't mind admitting that Steve had helped me mentally and physically.

Tommo came over and we were all pleased to see each other, our platoon having been split up since cross-decking from the *Canberra*. We were all anxious to see each other. I told the others about Taff dropping out early on in the tab. I was worried about him and told the lads so. Tommo told me that those who had dropped out were being airlifted up to Teal after we had left. Feeling happy about that, I returned to Steve Ratchford and told him that all was OK with the lads left behind. Now I could moan about Taff, knowing he was safe.

Lying on the damp ground, I looked at my poor feet again. The blisters were red-raw and bleeding and my other big toenail was going the same way as the first. Please don't fall off, I thought. The agony of having two big toenails missing would surely kill me off.

Steve and Tommo looked at my feet, wondering if I would be able to carry on. I found a bandage hidden in my webbing and cut it up to make small dressings for my blisters and toes. I thought that fresh air would help. Leaving my boots off that night was to be my worst mistake so far. After a freezing-cold and sleepless night, the morning light showed me two swollen feet and the hardest-frozen pair of boots imaginable. I cursed myself for being such a dickhead. Putting those boots back on was agony.

After brewing up and eating the last of our compo, we lay there in the showers of rain and snow, waiting for orders. How we wanted our sleeping bags for warmth. My faithful black poly bag was now just about ruined. I went for a crap but it wasn't worth it because of the agony of constipation and the cold wind whipping around my backside. Kev Connery thought I was pulling faces at him.

We waited there until 1600 hours before moving off slowly, tabbing across small streams and countless small hills. We could just see Estancia in the distance but it never seemed to get nearer as we plodded towards our next goal. We marched for about four hours until the whole battalion had rendezvoused. By the time we reached this point, I was nearly crying with pain. My hips had bad webbing burns and my feet were two raw blobs. As I slumped against a peat bank, Jimmy Morham murmured that I looked like death warmed up. I felt like it, too.

An officer walked down the line informing us of developments at Estancia. Were the enemy waiting this time?

'They've buggered off again, lads. We'll be moving *in* and around the houses come early morning but we'll be marching the last kilometre and a half and securing a defensive area around it.' He walked off.

I was glad that the Argies had run again but I wondered if I could tab that last bit. Perhaps it was knowing that I had only a kilometre and a half to go that enabled me to succeed. All the same, it felt ten times as far.

Tommo, Skip, Steve and I put up a poncho in the middle of some open ground about a hundred metres from a building. We could just see its outline. We drew straws to see who would be on stag duty first and who would sleep in the middle. I slept on the short straw and the wind rushed through the side of our pathetic basher.

First light brought with it the misery of the rain lashing down on us. Soaked to the skin, we slowly dismantled the basher.

'Grenade!' shouted Steve.

We all looked at him in dismay , as if he had flipped. He lay on the ground, covering his head. I wasn't sure if it was for real, or a sick joke. Others half-crouched on the ground and some looked at them as if they were pricks. The seconds ticked away. Nothing. Tommo got up and picked up the webbing. He put his hand into the pouch and pulled out the grenade in two parts. The primer and grenade had come apart. Feeling stupid, Steve reprimed the grenade as we slagged him off.

SORE FEET

The rain belted down as the company advanced into Estancia from all angles. Many troops had been there all night and had picked the best places for bashing up already. The CSM ordered us into a large, new-looking shed. We clamoured for a good spot and brewed up, scoffing the last of our rations. Ian McKay dished out a bread roll to every man – our first bread in two weeks. It is impossible to explain how it feels to eat fresh solid food after eating watered-down Arctic rations for a long time.

We dried off as best as we could, and then came a foot inspection by the company medic. My feet being bad, I was ordered to the main house to see the battalion doctor. I joined a long queue in the rain that eventually led me into a back room where the doctor was treating five guys at a time. As we entered, we were told not to touch the wallpaper as they had waited nearly a year for it to be delivered. I couldn't help but think what a stupid request it was, seeing the lads around me and their condition. After my inspection, I was given an aspirin and fresh plasters for my toes. I was told I was in a bad way with trench foot, but to carry on. I wasn't bothered about this, because I wasn't going to go sick even if ordered. I hobbled back to the shed and waited around with the rest for new orders.

10

A WAITING GAME

Estancia House, which we had just liberated, consisted of the main house, a small barn, a large shed and a small shed at the back of the house. Troops milled around the place as the rain stopped. Within hours, our bergens arrived by chopper and I was able to put fresh socks on my sore feet. I had now used up all my socks. The old ones were stinking and damp. I put my old socks over my hands, like gloves, to try to dry them over an oil-drum fire. Many others did the same.

As I chatted to the lads around me, I became aware of our physical state. On the *Canberra*, we had laughed at the stories of Argies being reduced to eating anything and looking like tramps, but within two weeks we looked like a rag-and-bone army. Our faces were drawn with the loss of weight, our uniforms matted and soaked, our boots were damaged and we were hungry for solid food. Despite all this, morale was very high, in the reassuring knowledge that we had marched and taken most of the island without a battle or loss of life so far.

Late that afternoon, we were ordered up the hills surrounding Estancia to secure it defensively. All the companies were dispatched from the house, leaving Company HQ as a base. We now had a few civvies to drive their Landrovers for us but no choppers for 3 Para at all. It was a foot-slog and 'rover march up the side of Estancia Mountain. It was last light when we piled off the 'rovers and sorted out our defence positions. We dug shell scraps but, yet again, we had no bergens. We were told they had been dropped off, and spent the next two hours stumbling around in the dark trying to find them. Many lads jacked in the search and slept in their clothing until first light. However, we located our bergens and, armed with our kit, settled down into a stag system with Skiddy's team.

Dawn came amid a storm of rain and sleet. Not wishing to crawl from our sleeping bags, Ratch and I lay under our poncho listening to the rain. We were enjoying the rest too much to move.

'Corporal B, Corporal B.'

'Fuck, I've heard that before,' I said to Ratch.

I peered through the side of our poncho and came face to face with 4 Platoon's PC again.

'Don't tell me we're moving again, sir, I'll crack,' I said.

'You are, we're not,' he smiled. 'Skiddy's gun team stays here. All machine-gun teams are to be down at Estancia a.s.a.p. for new orders.'

I flopped back and faced Ratch, who had covered his eyes with his hands.

'Don't say fuck all, Vince, please – just leave me to think who I can kill now.'

A WAITING GAME

The rain lashed down on us as we packed our kit. Skiddy, Kev and Johnny grinned as they watched from their position. We hobbled off, leaving the other half of our team on the hill. The walk downhill to the settlement was a pain. Last night, we had been told to go up the hill. 'Up, down, on the bus, off the bus' – that's the Army.

When we reached the settlement, we found the rest of the gun teams all together, gathered around our PC, who had been getting sly chopper lifts across the island. As he greeted us, I told him I now had a new name for him: 'Taxi Mike'. As usual, he bit. Our platoon sergeant, GD, was with him, whom we called 'Duff Gen'. GD was good at barrack-room soldiering, but would he rise to the challenge of the real thing? We would take Mike Oliver, lieutenant, rather than Sergeant GD any day, because he was visible throughout the conflict. We all liked the PC because he didn't hassle us as if we were army cadets. This may seem petty, but the ability to work together is paramount in a platoon.

We shuffled together and were informed that we would be marching straight on to Mount Longdon that night. The battle was about to begin. We had no time for last letters or anything else. We packed our kit and were briefed and ready to go within two hours. The battalion formed up and marched uphill again, spilling out of the settlement towards the summit of Estancia.

The route we took was atrocious. We crossed a rock field of some sort. The rocks were sharp and jagged. In four hours, we covered only three kilometres. Sweat ran down us like water. I stopped at one stage to tear off my soaking longjohns. Eventually, we reached the summit and at last light the battalion was gathered in their own areas, ready to march over the hill towards Longdon. B and C

Companies were going over the hill as we reached it. We set off within fifteen minutes of reaching the summit. We had gone only a few metres when we heard a chopper banking away from our lead elements.

We came to a halt as the order 'Turn back, turn back' hit our ears.

'What's the fucking matter, now?' someone shouted.

'Just turn back and do as you're told,' screamed an officer. Just on the other side of the hill, out of view of Stanley, the lads had been ordered back. Why?

Shortly after, we learned that the Cabbageheads running the show hadn't agreed to our advance. They didn't think that we should take the risk of going into battle on our own. The chopper, reputedly with Brigadier Thompson on board, had stopped our CO's advance to contact. This left the battalion fuming. We had been pushed hard by our CO, but we were ready and eager, longing to push in first. At our rank, we have no say in the running of battles; we just respond to orders. But, it should be known, at that point we had a far better mental outlook in warfare than the Craphats – that is, any soldier who is not a Para – who couldn't, and didn't try to, understand our regiment's history. The Paras should never be led by Craphats. We had to suffer the humiliation of being told that we couldn't do what we knew we could do. We all felt bad for the CO, who was hard and strong and would always talk to the lads. He was perhaps the best CO I've served under.

We heard later that the Marine brigadier had wanted a joint assault on the Stanley mountain ranges, a brigade attack, and that his troops had not been ready. He told our CO that we had out-marched his men and were showing him up with our ability in warfare.

The lads gathered about, waiting for new orders. The unexpected withdrawal hadn't been good news for us. We sat around waiting, yet again, for something to happen. Suddenly, the air around us disappeared and an explosion hit the area. Three or four Argie shells crashed within a hundred metres of where we were sitting. Molten shrapnel lit up the dark night.

'Get on to the Scorpions and head back to the settlement, lads,' shouted the PC.

Without waiting for another word, the gun teams clambered on to the vehicles. My feet were near the exhaust during the thirty-minute drive back down the hill and this dried out my boots – the only good thing to happen that whole day.

When we reached Estancia again, the place was half-empty of troops. We fought like cat and dog to get a good bash-up place. Earlier, I had seen 9 Squadron using some oil drums. I headed for these, and Ratch, Chris Dexter and I had a comfy place to sleep that night.

The following morning was foggy. There was no movement around the base, just a few lads chatting here and there. I clambered out from what we had christened our 'hotel'. We had the best basher there: oil drums and an old car bonnet with a poncho draped over the top. It provided near-perfect protection from the weather.

I needed a shit badly. Armed with my SLR, I wandered away from the lads, into the fog. I dug a small hole and crouched down, relaxing away from the tourists' eyes. Suddenly, I heard, 'Yep, yep, yep, yep, here, here,' and out of the fog came a herd of sheep. They came right up to me as I pulled up my denims. A sheepdog growled at me, then a settlement farmer walked into view.

'Hi, looks like you needed that,' he said, nodding towards my hole.

'Yeah. Sorry about the place, but you can see there's no public loos around.' All the time I was thinking, This is stupid. Here, right in the middle of what is going to be a battlefield, I'm chatting to a farmer and his sheep.

'You hungry, mate?' he asked in what sounded like a South African accent.

'Yes,' I smiled, as I finished dressing.

Suddenly, he grabbed a sheep by the neck, cut its throat and within a minute had skinned it. He hacked off one of its rear legs and handed it to me. He picked up the rest of the carcass and walked off singing. I stood there holding a warm sheep's leg, in the middle of a field, in the fog. It felt weird.

When I reached the basher, the lads were up and about. 'What the fuck have you done now, Vince?' laughed Johnny.

'A farmer gave us some fresh meat.'

'Liar, you killed it,' said Ratch.

'No, honest, it was given to me.'

Nobody would believe me, then or now. We chopped up the leg equally among us and had fried lamb for breakfast.

The next few days passed with no real news about anything. Johnny and Rawley managed somehow to find a tent, and we lived and looked like campers on holiday. Johnny took my place on a recce on Longdon one night, as my feet were still in a shit state. Further inspection of my feet by a doctor confirmed my trench foot and the toenail of my other big toe had to be removed. I now had no big toenails, trench foot and drying blisters. I didn't report sick again for fear of missing the last push into Stanley if I were casualty-evacuated out. The PC and I got together and I explained that I'd have to be dragged to the chopper before I'd be left out. The PC had a quiet word with the doctor, who answered to the effect that it was my neck and washed his hands of me. I spent the last days before the battle caring for my feet as though they were a baby, giving them as much air as possible to dry the wounds. I succeeded in adequately restoring them.

One night after stand-down, Johnny and Tommo crawled into my basher to tell me, 'The farmer has hung up a cow and some sheep round the back.'

By now, we'd had orders not to loot the meat, but the temptation was too great. Tony Peers and I, armed with knives, sneaked into the yard to be greeted by the sight of 9 Squadron and other 3 Para lads hacking at the corpses of the sheep. We split the meat up and hid it. Next morning, the shit really hit the fan. Only skeletons were left hanging on the meat hooks. Searches were made among 9 Squadron and around the general area. It was pathetic to watch those lads being searched for meat. We hid their meat for them until their sergeant cooled down.

The meals we had that night tasted better than Mum's Sunday dinner. The engineers of 9 Squadron were a good bunch of lads. As they were always attached to the Paras, we knew many of them as well as we did our own. Sadly for them, they had what we thought was the hardest platoon sergeant ever. His attitude was unremitting. All 9 Squadron hated him and so did we. What a pity he survived.

The next day, our platoon sergeant borrowed a farmer's motorbike to go and look for two missing barrels belonging to one of our gun teams, which had been reported missing but were later found by Dave Hughes of the Mortar

Platoon. He wasn't seen again for the rest of the day. Early that night, he came back, limping and pushing the bike. He reckoned he'd had a fall from the bike, somehow. Tommo and Johnny heard the OC politely telling him to fuck off after he told the doctor he couldn't walk. The platoon was embarrassed by his actions and tried to avoid him.

'Sergeant D, get a shave,' the RSM shouted at him.

He limped off and as he passed us he shouted at us, in turn, to shave. He managed to get out of being our platoon sergeant in the coming battle and got the job of ammo resupply. As a platoon, we were happy with that outcome.

Dicky Absolon (later killed and posthumously awarded the Military Medal) and Gerry Phillips were having a brew with us one morning after a hard night recceing the objective.

'It's like an ants' nest up there, Vince,' they said. 'Argies everywhere.'

Being part of D Company, led by Sergeant John Pettinger, they had spent many hair-raising hours crawling among the positions on Longdon for Intelligence reports. Nobody wanted their job. Extremely successful and professional, they and many like them had helped to build a model showing the Argie bunkers and possible minefields. During the week we waited, the model showed that Argie strength on Longdon was growing by the day. It was thought the enemy had between three and five hundred troops with anti-personnel mines, radar, mortars, one-hundred-and-six-millimetre rifles, point-fifty-calibre machine-guns and enough ammo and supplies to last for a long siege. Hearing this first-hand made our stomachs churn.

A WAITING GAME

That night, as I lay in my sleeping bag chatting to Ratch and Chris, the ground suddenly shook and rumbled like an earthquake. The area lit up in a flash accompanied by the loudest bangs we'd heard so far.

'What the fucking hell was that?' shouted Chris.

'Don't know, but we're not going out there to see,' I replied. Outside we could hear some guys shouting and running about but generally everybody stayed put. Next morning, Intelligence told us that Argie *Canberra*-bombers had dropped their load not three hundred metres from us. If they had hit us, the battalion would not be around today. We spent the day digging full-scale trenches. Better late than never.

As we were milling around a peat fire with 9 Squadron, a chopper came down from one of the mountains. Some nosy lads ran towards it and quickly brought back the report that some of the Marines had had a blue-on-blue contact that night. A returning patrol had stumbled on a mortar-based team asleep and had shot them as they lay in their sleeping bags. There were three to four dead. Whatever we felt about the Marines, we were sorry for them that day.

On 10 June, we had orders that something was going down soon. We stripped our weapons thoroughly, and oiled and greased them. The PC issued fifty rounds per gun for SF balancing. We needed to have our barrels working without gas stoppages. Bob Geddis immediately balanced his gun by firing across the water inlet into the sea. Tony Jones was just setting his up when the QM came screaming over and ordered us not to waste ammo. We pointed out that the guns needed balancing, but as it turned out there was a major fuck-up with all the guns in the battle: only two out of six worked. Fifty rounds through each might have saved lives and would at least have provided better firepower for the battalion.

Late that day, the PC came round with new formations for the coming battle. Support Company would now be a fire-based team, one SF gun working alongside a Milan team from the Anti-Tanks. These guided missiles would be used as anti-personnel weapons. I was to take charge of Bob Geddis's gun with Sas, our worst soldier. Ratch went off with Johnny. I was happy with Bob, but I argued about the change, as I always contested orders that seemed to me to be backward. I pointed out that Ratch and I had gone so far together that we wanted to go the rest. In the end, though, the whole platoon was swapped around. Why?

My new gun team teamed up with Ginge McCarthy, Pete Hedicker and little Phillip West. We sat together and worked out our routine and methods for the battle procedures to come. We were told that the Wombat side of the Anti-Tanks Platoon, Skiddy, Kev and Johnny Crow, would help fill in the gaps in the rifle companies. Rations were given out, and Tom Smith, the *Daily Express* photographer, was still trying to swap sweets for other items of food.

That night, we lay there knowing this was perhaps to be the last night under the basher. We lay thinking and wondering.

At first light, we saw the CO and the OC in deep conversation, down by the company HQ, pointing at the model of Longdon, which had now been uncovered. It was shaped like the mountain itself. A gut feeling told me we were on our way. Breakfast over, we chatted and made brews. Still nothing happened. The only distraction we had was the sight of a lad walking back towards our lines covered in human shit. He had sat on a plank over the pit that had given way and he had fallen in. The sight of some officer holding his nose and telling the lad to clean up was too much for us. We laughed as the poor lad tried to get replacement kit for the afternoon.

The PC came down to us and *we* gathered round him eagerly. He stood, faintly grinning at us.

'Spit it out, sir,' said Johnny Cook.

'Orders in half an hour. Tonight, lads. Green light. See you by the model in half an hour.'

11

'GENTS, THIS IS IT'

The following account is based on my own experiences during the battle for Mount Longdon. To the best of my knowledge, everything I have said is true. It is not my objective to trumpet any military achievements, or to stand in judgement on the rights and wrongs of actions carried out in battle. This is now history and can never be changed. My aim is to try to express my feelings, and those of some of my friends, as we experienced those critical moments of life and death.

I am no great military commander or leader. I was just an ordinary soldier from the ranks. In battle, I found that I had forgotten many basic things: home, our cause, even my own being. What became paramount was survival – nothing else.

When we read a good story, we tend to imagine ourselves as the hero or heroine. We say to ourselves that he should do this or that, believing that we could play the part better. I am not suggesting that, in order to understand what follows, the reader should dig himself a hole in the garden in mid-winter. But, while curled in his armchair by the fire, secure, perhaps he might remember a time when he was cold, wet, hungry and near to exhaustion. Only then will he come close to the full reality of what we experienced.

Standing around the model of our objective, the members of the newly formed fire-based team waited for the last Intelligence reports to flesh out the OC's orders. The morning was cold and lightly frosted, and the ground was starting to warm under our boots, which trampled the allocated spots as we awaited orders.

Now, after eleven days, it would seem that the green light had been given for the attack. Major Dennison approached the model and the fifty men awaiting him. His confident smile and his humour had been a constant morale-booster to his company. There before him and us lay the large model: the earth moulded to show every nook and cranny of the terrain; small, but prominent, white markers showing the positions of the Argentine bunkers; small twigs marking their machine-gun positions; white mining tape indicating possible mine-fields. Silence surrounded the area as the boss came to a halt by the model.

'Gents, this is it.' His smile signalled relief, encouraging thoughts of a quick victory and home.

Using a long stick to point out the positions, he started to deliver the orders.

'Here is our base line, gents. We will be giving support

fire for B Company throughout the battle. They are the first line for the assault.'

Looking at the model, his stick going from position to position, he explained the layout of the CO's orders, which he had broken down for this company to understand. B Company would be assaulting first, hoping to capture the heights with a silent approach to their objective. C Company was to be held in reserve, then moved forward through the battalion to capture Wireless Ridge, the second phase possible only if the first had been successful. A Company would assault from a given flank once the heights had been secured.

The delivering of orders lasted for some time and it was not until the OC was happy that he had given a full explanation that he threw open the floor to questions.

'What's going to happen if we fail to take the heights?'

The group turned and looked at the sergeant who had broken the ice with the first of many 'ifs' and 'buts'.

'Failure isn't in my vocabulary, Sergeant,' said the boss, smiling.

Everyone felt his confidence, as if we were all one. Many questions later, all answered with serious humour, he recapped the orders.

'Remember, they have the edge. Their bunkers are well prepared. Morale is low, but equipment they do have. All I will say now, in closing, is "prisoners".'

Everyone looked at the Intelligence officer who stood close by.

'Gents, as we are well aware, the Argentines demonstrated at Goose Green their total lack of regard for human life, in the gunning down of 2 Para while accepting their surrender. They cannot be trusted, so, as far as our objective is concerned, it may be in your interests not to think about chatting to these fellas until later. Get my drift?'

No one said anything; it was more than obvious that the enemy were in for the kill too. We had talked between ourselves about the white flag issue long before these orders. No one was keen to accept the enemy's word any more.

'Well, gents, scoff up and get ready. Move out at 1400 hours. Good luck.'

I was deep in thought. His 'good luck' was something we would all need.

Sitting by our basher, we started to make the 'last supper', as Johnny put it. All the weapons were now well oiled and ready, ammunition squeezed into every spare hole on our webbing and bodies, water bottles filled. We ate and then finished packing our equipment tightly together.

Few spoke during those last hours of waiting. We were wrapped in our own thoughts. It was hard for me to think of anything but the coming night.

Tommo and Johnny came and sat beside my basher. This small damp corner surrounded by old oil drums had been my only refuge for the last eleven days. Sitting in a small circle, we talked of the battle facing us.

'Well, I remember Dicky A telling me that the whole area was like an ants' nest up there, though the orders seem as if there was nothing to worry about,' I said.

'You're right, Vince,' said Tommo, 'but we have to trust the Intelligence and brass on this.'

Johnny passed the brew to me, smiling, and said, 'Might be the last time trust comes into it now.' He laughed. His

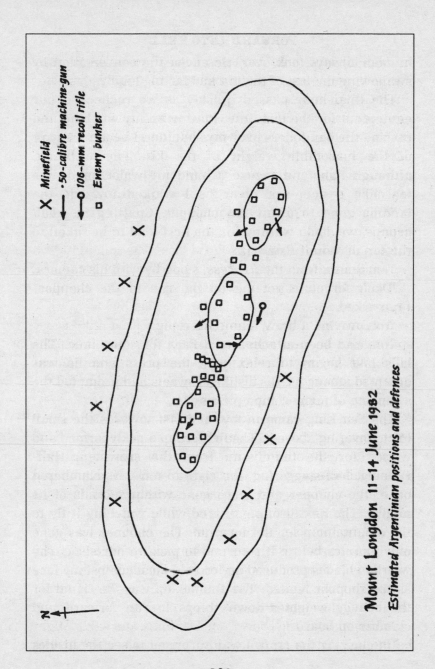

Mount Longdon 11–14 June 1982

Estimated Argentinian positions and defences

Key:

X Minefield

→ .50-calibre machine-gun

⊸ 106-mm recoil rifle

☐ Enemy bunker

N

humour always took over. He ended the conversation by swallowing the last of the tea and farting loudly.

The final hour passed quickly as we rechecked our equipment for the last time. Putting on my webbing and placing the bandoliers over my shoulder, I became aware of the incredible weight of the kit. The webbing, although tight and secure around my waist, made me feel like a deep-sea diver as I walked towards the landing zone to await the chopper. Chatting in small groups, we stood waiting for the first load to be taken to the top of Mount Estancia.

Tom Smith, from the *Express*, stood by with his camera.

'Don't forget to get me on the run to the chopper,' I remarked.

'You owe me a brew,' came his reply.

Tom had been attached to 3 Para for some time. The lads had begun to relax with the press and he was accepted among us. His dislike of sweets had prompted the swapping of many compo pieces.

The Sea King came in low and fast towards the small inlet, hovering above it. The first group quickly formed and waited for the thumbs-up from the crewmen. Half-running, half-staggering, the eight to ten guys clambered on to the chopper and were gone within seconds of its arrival. The next group gathered while watching it fly to the mountaintop for the form-up. The chopper was gone only minutes before it returned to pick up our stick. The whirling blades produced an ice-cold blast against my face as the chopper landed. The thumbs-up was the signal for the heavily weighted-down troops to run forward and clamber on board.

On entering the craft, I was surprised to see the insides

completely ripped out: there were no seats or safety harnesses. Ten guys squeezed into all the available corners. Sitting by the window near the door, I watched the ground and the remaining troops grow smaller. I was leaving behind me not just a small inlet called Estancia, but perhaps my last glimpse of life as I knew it.

The chopper hovered and landed in what seemed seconds, and the pilot thumped it on the ground without any hesitation or regard for the usual rules and regulations of the MOD. We spilled out on to the rough terrain and pulled our heads in to avoid the cold wind as the chopper zoomed away on its next task.

Moments later we all stood up to see other members of our battalion walking about, talking and pointing out the different tasks to be completed. Tommo and Johnny joined us in the last load from the chopper and, sitting on the side of the hill, or rather mountain, we chatted for what were to be the few remaining minutes of spare time.

Lieutenant Mike Oliver, our PC, came up to us. 'Corporals Cook and Bramley, come with me.'

We followed him to the very edge of the hill, which meant skylining ourselves to the enemy, for they could see Mount Estancia and Mount Kent next to us, both now in our hands. We stopped behind him and wondered why he had brought us so close to the enemy's eyes. Placing his binos in my hands, he smiled and said, 'There you are: Stanley, our ultimate aim.'

Looking to where he pointed, I could see the small town about twenty kilometres away. Lying before this was our first objective, Mount Longdon, which began about twelve kilometres away.

At less than three hundred metres, starting from the

side slope of Mount Estancia, lay one long area of what was, in fact, dead ground, which rolled into our objective where it rose up again to form Mount Longdon. Handing the binos to Johnny, I couldn't help but remark, 'Sir, we have Longdon to worry about first and, to tell you the truth, that *does* worry me.'

Johnny was busy looking through the binos, and joking that he hoped the pub wouldn't close before we got there.

Lieutenant Oliver grinned at us. 'No worry. As you know, I'm with you and we're lucky in the fact that we're giving support.'

Johnny said, 'Well, support or not, I feel that Vince is right but I also say that I now need a shit.'

We looked at him and laughed. I looked at Lieutenant Oliver and confided, 'See what I've got to put up with. You've only had us for four months. I've had this character round my neck for three years now.'

The binos were back in the PC's hands now, as we watched Johnny trot off back to his kit to sort out the 'tracing paper' the MOD supplied as toilet paper.

Steve and Taff were sitting with Bob Geddis, making a brew. As we reached them, they looked up and asked, 'What did he want to show you?'

'Stanley and Longdon.'

'Well, what's it like?' asked Steve.

'From what I saw, it looked like a dump.'

'Dump or not, it's where we're headed,' remarked Bob.

Rick Westry clambered over to sit with us and share the remainder of the brew.

'Well, how are we feeling?' I asked.

'Fucking stupid question,' said Taff. 'What do you think we feel like?'

His remark was said as if he was upset, which made us all look at him with wide eyes.

'I personally feel that this is the right place to have my last wank because it's turning me on, but because I know you'd all be watching I've given it a second thought.'

Throughout this time on the top, waiting, the constant humour never ceased to make me laugh. There we were, halfway round the world, about to embark on a life-or-death crusade, with six hundred troops cracking sillies. It was almost certainly a way of masking fear, fear of death itself, or at least the unknown. When I look back now, I not only remember waiting with shattering fear, but also the humour that overcame it.

A small convoy of tractors and civvy Landrovers pulled up beside the main bulk of waiting troops. The Mortars Platoon unloaded its cargo of mortars and the Milans, the latter each costing about six thousand pounds. In the age of technology, these small sophisticated guided missiles were being dragged across the hillside strapped to wooden pallets.

As the unloading of this equipment took place, a light booming sound was heard from the direction of Stanley. No one took any notice of the continuing sound and carried on working. Some guys were chattering in little groups.

The first shell to reach us took us by surprise. The sudden rush and suction of air, and the distinct whistle, made the troops duck their heads as it crashed into the ground about a hundred metres away. More shells landed in roughly the same area, bringing an uneasy feel to the air around us.

The atmosphere changed in seconds. Had the

Argentineans placed a spotter on us? No one knew, but the officers suddenly started to shout loud verbal commands for the troops to split up, to cease bunching. Within minutes of this sudden artillery attack, a whole new concept seized us: reality.

Sitting by Rick, I mentioned Johnny's idea of a crap – it was now in my mind, too. I got up from the damp ground and strolled over to the other side of the hill, about fifty metres from the forming battalion. I found a small batch of rocks and, placing my weapon beside me, carried out the usual human function. Rick came up behind me and squatted a little way from me. While we were chatting, I suddenly noticed a guy in the valley below. There he was, walking along, seven hundred metres from us, as if he was out for a Sunday stroll. Rick shouted to him; both Rick and I were out of sight of our company. The guy stopped and looked up in our direction, where he must have seen us waving. He immediately waved both of his arms at us then carried on walking towards Stanley. To be sitting in this absurd position, first chatting while artillery shells landed the length of a football pitch away, and then waving and shouting to try to stop what looked like a Sunday walker in the valley, seemed too ridiculous for words.

When we got back to the platoon, Rick mentioned the solitary walker to the PC.

'Oh, it's probably the Argentines' artillery spotter. If he's going towards Stanley, there's nothing to worry about, is there?' He smiled and walked off.

Tommo and Johnny both looked at me and Rick and said, 'Yeah, yeah, what next?'

The conversation was interrupted by the OC calling everyone in for a quick change of orders.

'Well, gents, I'll make this snappy, for those shells are near the mark. Firstly, our SAS boys have reported from their little nest somewhere over this hill that Mount Longdon is experiencing a lot of activity at the moment. By this, I mean reinforcements. Last reports were about another company, strength one hundred and twenty, so, contrary to our estimated hundred and fifty men on there, we'd better think more along the lines of two to three hundred, OK?'

'Yes, sir,' we all murmured, as if this was quite a normal thing.

'Good,' he said. 'No change of direct orders, plans the same. The CO feels very confident still. Right, go back to your positions until move-out time.'

Back in our little corner of sanctuary, we made our last brew. Steve Wake joined us and we swapped a few simple messages for home. It was becoming more and more nerve-racking, this time to ourselves. Steve chatted for some minutes before he was called away. As I sat on my webbing, the padre came over and stood there in his uniform, trying to be cheerful for us. The guys handed him their various messages for home. Johnny and I stood up to chat with him.

'Sir, just a little favour,' I said.

'What's that, Vince?' he asked.

'If the worst happens tonight, could you jack it up for me to be buried in Aldershot and not here?' Grinning, I also said, 'Could you ask Karon to put a bottle of Bushmills Irish whiskey in the coffin with me?'

He gave me a stern look, which changed to one of agreement when he realised that I was serious. 'Yes, no problem,' he replied.

The padre, Derek Heather, had married me to Karon

only six months before. He had married many of the lads in the battalion and I for one didn't envy his task of having to be the bearer of bad news. Johnny chatted hurriedly with him and Tommo joined in. The time was nearing and the atmosphere was growing tight.

'Mount up, mount up!' shouted a sergeant from platoon HQ. Suddenly, my nerves became uncontrollable, my knees shaking as I stood and my stomach churning as it had never done before. Not even the feeling of my first parachute jump can compare with the nausea that surged through me. My mind was blank with fear and the prospect of death. Shaking, I put on my webbing and adjusted all my kit comfortably for the coming tab.

It was almost dark. Our silent approach, attack and tab were now in Stage One. The battalion set off from their places at their own speed; all would have to be in position by 1200 hours that night. H hour was 0030 hours.

Lying before us was about twelve kilometres of ground and a river. The time was about 1700. This seems like plenty of time to reach the starting line of our attack. However, what must be taken into consideration is the nature of the ground and the amount of kit that we had to carry. My kit alone weighed about a hundred pounds, possibly more. Many lads in our group had to swap kit throughout the march – a machine-gun for a tripod, for example. Milans, being bulky and awkward, went from shoulder to shoulder. As the last daylight faded, I could see the thin line of troops disappearing into the darkness, struggling with their kit and the terrain, and there, in front of us, the lights of Stanley presented an eerie view. To see Stanley's houses all aglow with cosy fires seemed an unnatural sight, almost make-believe.

As I stepped off, three or four local civvies stood by their Landrovers and tractors, all wishing us luck. As Tommo reached them, one turned to us and said, 'Makes me sick, all this waste. I tried to come with you, but your bosses wouldn't let me. I really wanted to help you more.'

I smiled, the whole group smiled. I looked at the man and said, 'It's not a waste, whatever happens tonight. Just remember you did help, OK?'

'How?' he asked.

'Your tractors and Landrovers have been a lifesaver while we were tabbing this island. Now it's our turn to do the rest.'

Smiling, Johnny piped in, 'Not only is my mate right, but with the mentality of some of our bosses you'd be better off watching the game from here.'

This short and simple conversation was over in seconds and the civvies watched us disappear into the darkness.

Within a thousand metres of setting off towards the objective, sweat was running down my forehead. Jesus, I wanted a rest. The weight of my webbing was cutting into my shoulders, the bandoliers cutting into my neck. By resting the SLR on my webbing, I could reach up and pull the straps from my neck to help relieve the agony they gave me.

About three kilometres into the march, we stopped. I sat down quickly and swapped the bandolier straps over to my other shoulder, longing to rest for those vital five minutes we were given. But, within seconds, whispered orders to move passed along the line. Struggling to my feet, I hobbled under the weight and stumbled over the ground.

Every kilometre seemed to grow longer, and nobody spoke now. The deadly silence hung over the advancing troops, each man wrapped in his own thoughts of the coming battle. Who would survive, who would die? In the silence, the occasional grunts of the lads cursing their load were very audible.

My own thoughts of the weight I carried and the march were overcoming the fear. Again, the feeling of occupation, of doing something practical, wiped out the misery of standing around and waiting. Waiting, the soldier hates. Now we were on our way, the fear was there, though obscured by this quick, hard march.

The second break in the march came after about seven kilometres. This time, like many others, I just fell to the cold, damp ground to capture those glorious moments of rest.

Unbeknown to us, we had at this stage reached the river. It had been an earlier idea of the 9 Squadron boys to bring up some girders to lay across it, but they were forced to abandon this plan. Some of the forward recce lads from 9 Squadron and our D Company had tried, much to its credit, though unsuccessfully, to search for a shallow crossing. It wasn't to be, and for us it wasn't to be a dry night! Those fucking rivers – no other word can I find to describe them – meant wet feet and in our boots the wet mixed with the cold, letting us know that we were in for extra misery. (Strange, now, that I should remember the wet feet and a small river crossing.) The Murrell Bridge to our right lay some two kilometres away. We expected it to be mined.

12

EXCHANGE OF FIRE

As I sat on the damp, semi-frozen ground, half-lying and half-propped up on my webbing, a moment of peace was shattered by the whistle of three or four artillery shells whizzing over my head. The explosions came from not too far behind where we had just advanced from. The artillery opened up behind us: British shells exchanged for Argentinean. Our barrage lasted for a couple of minutes, restoring an uneasy silence among us. One or two more enemy shells came back in our direction within minutes, the tit-for-tat seemingly picking up. There we sat in the middle, listening for what could be a deadly hit. The ground shook behind us, sending shock waves into the air, until the whole barrage ended as it had begun. Nothing. No booming sounds behind us or in front.

The twin peaks of the Two Sisters lay to the right and rear. We had penetrated well into No Man's Land. Two Sisters was the objective of 45 Commando, while 42 Commando were to take Mount Harriet. All this would happen simultaneously for 3 Brigade at 0030 hours. I kept looking at where we were going to be, three or four kilometres further in. It made me feel even more vulnerable.

As the last of the shock waves disappeared, the march was no longer a hassle or a burden, simply because reality was on us again. I leaned over to Pete Hedicker and half-whispered in his ear, 'What's the fucking hold-up now, Pete?'

'Rumour has it we've reached the river. Mind you, I wish they could find a dry crossing tonight – the last thing I want is wet feet again. They've taken me days to dry out.'

The conversation ended and I leaned back on my webbing, grabbing the most of the extra minutes. We had now spent five minutes waiting, and the cold air was penetrating our bodies, the sweat from the tab drying.

I looked up and the sky was clear, with not a cloud in sight. I sat in a trance, trying to ignore the nervous turmoil of my insides. A shooting star caught my eye. It raced across the dark sky, disappearing as quickly as it came. I thought to myself, That spent years reaching here, all for a few seconds of life. Crazy. I wished upon it all the same.

Little Phillip West sat next to Pete, whispering that we were moving. Ginge came up to us. 'Right, lads, about twenty-five metres and we cross the river. Any probs?'

We shook our heads and I passed the message on to my gun team. Bob Geddis and Sas got up with me. We stood for a moment, then followed the snake of troops heading to the riverbank. On reaching it, I was happy to see that it was only five metres wide. A sergeant from 9 Squadron stood by the bank. To help us, he had a couple of his troops in and around the route across. Nine Squadron's help affected me greatly. The sergeant and the guys on the other side were saying, 'Sorry, lads, we couldn't find anywhere shallower.'

They lightly manhandled us across. Stepping on some stones, I prayed I would reach the other side with dry feet. I managed about five or six dry steps, then in I went right up to my thighs. I cursed to myself. I could feel the water seeping into my damp boots and through my socks.

Once the support team were across, we set off again, tabbing along the river line for about a hundred metres. Suddenly, the line of troops I was following were dropping to their knees. As I reached my secure halting position, a stream of more troops came out of the darkness. Standing up, we realised that we had bumped into B Company tabbing to its start line. At this stage, we were all parallel to each other, with only a metre or so separating us, as everyone came to a halt again.

Beside me stood a dark figure. I stepped forward and whispered, 'Who's that?'

'Doc. Is that Vince?'

'Yeah,' I replied.

He looked at me. Through his heavily camouflaged face, I saw his teeth grinning.

'What are you grinning at?' I said.

'I'm grinning at this fucking show. At this rate we'll be late and then the Cabbageheads will have something on us.'

In the pause, we stood looking as the others filed away into the darkness.

B Company was now almost at its start line and we were only two hundred metres from ours. Doing a complete 'U' turn, I followed our line, stumbling. Trying to keep sight of Pete Hedicker was in itself becoming a task and the weight of the ammo was cutting into my shoulders again. We came to a halt and Lieutenant Oliver came down the line. 'Corporals Cook, Bramley.'

'Here,' I whispered.

'Good, follow me.'

We came to a peat bank. Our company was splitting up, getting into position. Lieutenant Oliver crouched down with us when we came to the final stop.

'Right, we're now on our start line. Set the guns up quickly. We have about fifteen minutes.'

Looking to my right, I saw for the first time the steep slope of Mount Longdon's rear, only three hundred metres away. The objective still didn't look much. I looked at it, trying to pick out points from the orders, and at the same time getting the GPMG placed on a good spot on the bank. Finally, I managed to put the tripod into the high mount. The gun slid on and Bob Geddis tucked the tripod legs in. I loaded the GPMG and slowly cocked the weapon, instinctively trying to make no noise. The long belt of ammo hung from the machine-gun waiting for its eventual expenditure. The silence of the night had an eerie effect on me, but, with battle imminent, all we could do was sit, watch and wait.

My stomach tightened and, with five minutes to go, my legs began to shake and my whole body felt numb. Was it the cold from my drying sweat that was causing me to shake, or fear?

I had long been resigned to the fact that, if this was the end, then so be it. Was I lucky to be in this position, or unlucky? I had no doubts about our actions then and still don't. Resigning myself to possible death was easier than I thought; the waiting was the only pain. As those final minutes passed by, I didn't think of home, nor did I think of my family. I didn't think of death or myself. All I remember, and very clearly, was thinking about B Company's lads going in first. I had so many friends going up that slope ahead of me, taking the brunt of the attack. I can remember crossing my fingers and half-praying for them. It was too late now to think of my family or examine my conscience. All that mattered now was survival and victory.

Behind me, Captain Mason was struggling to establish radio contact with battalion HQ. The strict radio silence was still in force. The message came to him to get off the net and wait. In the stunned silence that followed, Corporal McCarthy whispered, 'This guy's a complete knob.'

This little hassle quickly forgotten, we turned back to the slopes of Mount Longdon, watching and waiting. You could have heard a pin drop in those final seconds. Our eyes were almost popping out of our heads, straining to see the opening shots.

'Sir, sir,' whispered the radio operator.

'What?' asked Captain Mason.

'CS24 has contact.'

We turned our heads back again to the sight of an unbelievable display of tracer rounds. The area was like a shooting range, tracer rounds ricocheting in all directions. At times, the noise of the battle would seem to pause as if nothing had happened at all, then it would burst into life again. I remember saying out loud, 'Get in there, get in there,' willing the lads on.

It was an easy time for me, lying by my gun, but it had also to be the most frustrating ever. It was like a football match when you want to join in and help your side.

'Sir, sir,' shouted the radio operator. His loud mouth didn't matter now, but minutes ago he would have had a fist filling it.

'What now?' shouted Mason. Jesus, was that man arrogant.

'CS9 wants you.'

Mason grabbed the handset – one moves quickly for the CO.

'CS76 here.'

The conversation took seconds. Mason thrust the handset into the radio operator's hand.

'Pack up, pack up,' he said.

We all looked at him in surprise.

'What's up?' shouted Lieutenant Oliver.

'Pack up, I said.'

'Fucking hell, why doesn't he tell us the rest of the message?' said Johnny.

We gathered all our kit together as quickly as possible. The GPMG and tripod were dismantled, the ammo linked together and thrown round our shoulders in seconds rather than minutes. Sitting in a half-crouched position with my SLR facing the objective (not that I could use it, not knowing our own positions) I and the others watched the slope and the tracer rounds. We also kept turning towards Captain Mason to see what he had up his sleeve.

Small groups of men formed circles around their commanders and, when radio silence broke again, Lieutenant Oliver rushed over to our position.

'Right, listen in,' he said.

I felt like saying, 'I was anyway', but the time for joking was over.

'B Company has had to change its tactics a bit. Corporals

Bramley's and Cook's teams will follow myself and Captain Mason into A Company positions, while Corporals Tommo, Rawlings and Peers will go to another task, OK?'

Johnny looked at me as if he knew I was just about to ask what was happening. Johnny's look told me to keep quiet and I did. Mason came up to where we were crouching down in a small semicircle. He simply shouted at us to follow him and not drop behind, then leaped up and was running in the darkness.

'The bastard,' said Bob Geddis. 'We have all this fucking weight and he's gone.'

We quickly followed him, running and stumbling over the thick tufts in the ground.

A lad from the ACC who was ammo bearer for us all fell over in front of me. He was carrying two sandbags full to the top with seven-point-sixty-two link for our guns. I helped him up; my own weight didn't seem to matter. Lieutenant Oliver came running back.

'What's the hold-up?' He looked angry.

'Sir, you're gonna have to tell Captain Mason, we're the ones with the heavy kit here, he's going too fast.'

Captain Mason was six feet four plus, with bloody long legs.

'Give me a bag to carry,' Lieutenant Oliver said. Placing it on his shoulder, he ran on again.

We had run about two hundred metres. We were all still together but now the run had become a fast stumbling walk. The noise of the battle continued to our right now, as we moved around the slope. Suddenly, a zipping sound whipped across my face. I didn't think anything of it as I walked and stumbled to keep up. Then, three or four more zips hit the ground in front and at my feet. Still I carried on.

As I was walking behind Lieutenant Oliver, we saw bodies lying all over the place. I thought, What the fuck are they doing, lying there? Jesus Christ, fucking lying there and we're struggling.

I saw a lad kneeling over a guy in a sleeping bag. I remember, as I got to them, just watching him. A low moaning was coming from the sleeping bag.

I had gone about twenty paces when several more zips hit the ground, sending a small shock wave all around me.

'For fuck's sake, are you completely nuts or what?' some guy shouted.

'What?' asked Lieutenant Oliver.

'Do you know a sniper's picking at us?'

We stopped, frozen solid in our tracks, then fell to the ground, our small column now joining the bodies lying all over the place. We had walked into A Company's form-up, where they had been stopped by a sniper. Lying there, it hit me like a sledgehammer: the zips had been missing me by inches. I lay there thinking, You fucking idiot, Vince.

I cursed myself all the time we lay there, blaming myself for an unprofessional act, but then I'd never been shot at before and my mind had been so occupied with moving that the zipping sound seemed unconnected with the battle.

As we lay there, Lieutenant Oliver urged in a low voice, 'Pass the word back a sniper has us in his sight. We will crawl to the bank ahead, OK?'

'Yes, sir,' I replied.

Once the word had gone along the column, in which I was near the rear, we crawled on all fours, those zipping sounds still thumping into the ground around us. After about ten minutes of crawling – bloody hard work with all the kit we had – I looked up to see a peat bank about twenty metres in front of me. Sitting behind it were about twenty guys all looking at me and the others. I lay flat on the damp, freezing ground. Raising my head in the direction of the raging battle, I could see the tracer rounds still ricocheting in every direction. I was about to get up and run the last few metres, when a bullet zipped into the ground by my fingers. I flopped down again, having raised myself only slightly. I lay there for a few moments, not daring to move.

The others behind me had cottoned on to the danger. I was now so alert that I felt every ounce of energy in me was acting on my behalf. I raised my head only and there sat my audience and Johnny, grinning. I couldn't believe it. There I was, pinned down with four others by a sniper, and my mate's there, all comfy and grinning. I lowered my head, looking at the ground and shouted, 'What are you fucking grinning at, John?'

Almost in a laugh he shouted back, 'You don't know how silly you look lying out there. Why are you talking to the ground, you pleb?'

Still facing the ground, I yelled back, 'Because that bastard up there may just see my breath in this cold air, OK?' Even I was seeing the funny side to it now.

Our banter was abruptly stopped by the PC.

'Corporal Bramley, this is neither the time nor the place to have a chat. Get over here with us, now,' he said in an agitated voice.

'Sir,' I shouted, still facing the ground. 'This guy up there is quite good and …'

My excuses were interrupted by him again. 'You are no use to man or beast lying there. Now get here.'

Now I was mad. 'I'll not even be beast if I move, for Christ's sake.'

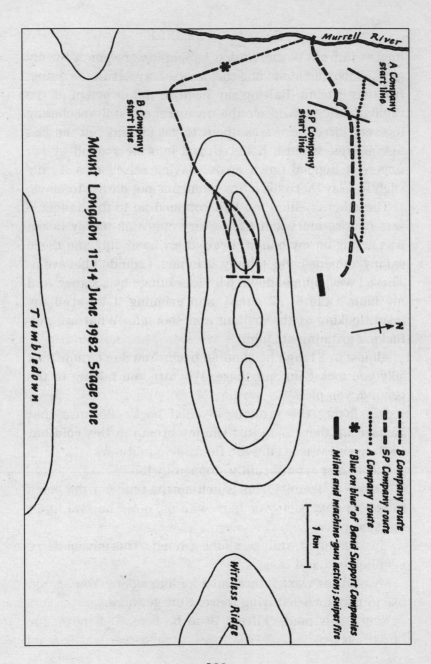

Mount Longdon 11-14 June 1982 Stage one

Murrell River

A Company start line

SP Company start line

B Company start line

Tumbledown

Wireless Ridge

N

\- - - B Company route

\- - - SP Company route

.... A Company route

* "Blue on blue" of Band Support Companies

▬ Milan and machine-gun action; sniper fire

1 km

Top: The twenty-three temporary graves at Teal Inlet for the dead of 3 Para.

Bottom: The funeral at Aldershot for the repatriated dead of 2 and 3 Para.

Top: Marines and Paras looting in Port Stanley.

Bottom left: Left to right: Lt Mike Oliver, me, Pte Tony Jones, Cpl Johnny Cook.

Bottom right: Homeward bound. Celebrating Airborne Forces Day on SS *Norland*. Left to right: Joe, (?), Kev Connery, Johnny Cook, me, Paul Reid, Billy Baker.

Top: Human faces of war. Taff Williams surrounded by Argentinians who gave themselves up in Port Stanley.

Bottom: Prisoners clearing up.

Top: Two helmet-topped SLRs mark the spot where Doc Murdoch and Geordie Lang were killed.

Bottom: Tony Jones (left) and Bob Geddis entering Port Stanley. The Red Cross buildings were in fact ammunition depots.

Top and bottom: Bodies awaiting burial. The Argentinians were buried on Longdon.

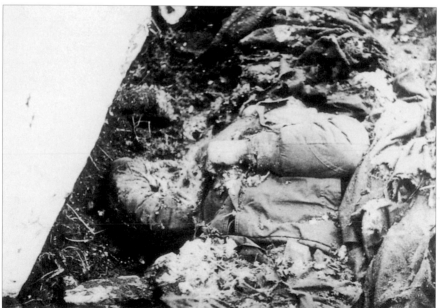

Top: Cpl Pete Thompson (left) and me pointing at the wound from the bullet that killed this Argentinian.

Bottom: The mutilated victim of a shell attack.

Top: Young Argentinian soldier killed by a collapsing bunker.

Bottom: Charred remains of an Argentinian killed by a phosphorus-filled grenade.

Opposite, top: Argentinian prisoners.

Above: Rick Westry (left) and me with two Argentinians found hiding in a bunker.

Left: First aid post for 3 Para at the base of Longdon. L/Cpl James (centre) was wounded in the back and foot.

Top: Me on a captured 81mm mortar position.

Bottom: View from my machine-gun position along the ridge of Longdon (about 1,000 metres).

Top: Me with Kev Connery shortly after the battle.

Bottom: On the hard-won summit of Longdon.

SF machine-gun tracer lights the sky during the battle for Longdon.

Top: Gun positions in a bunker at San Carlos Bay. Left to right: me, Ratch, Taff.

Bottom: Boarding chopper to fly to the summit of Mount Estancia for the assault on Longdon.

Top: Left to right: Pte Dominic Gray, me, (?), Ben.

Bottom:The machine gun platoon, 3 Para. Back row, left to right: Pte John Skipper, Pte Stewart, me, Sgt Deaney, Cpl Johnny Cook, Lte Mike Oliver, L/Cpl Tony Peers, Cpl Thompson, L/Cpl Mark Hawlings, Pte Chris Dexter, Pte Tony Jones. Front row: Pte Steve Ratchford, Pte Taff McNeilly, Pte Robert Jeffries, Pte Chaderton, Pte Dave Chambers, Pte Rick Westry, Pte Billy Knight, Pte 'Rats', Pte Bob Geddis, Pte Mick Coleman.

Top: On Ascension Island.

Bottom: One of B Company's gun crews. Left to right: Steve Ratchford, Taff McNeilly, me.

Top: Heading towards the South Atlantic aboard the SS *Canberra*.

Bottom: Landing-craft drills on Ascension Island.

A pause came, with whispers from the bank. All four of us had been lying there for some fifteen minutes.

'OK,' shouted Captain Mason. 'Just crawl slowly and see what happens.'

I lay there thinking, What a fucking joke – crawl slowly and see what happens.

The five of us started a very slow crawl. My mouth was dry. We all expected the ground, or even us, to be hit now, but nothing happened. Those twenty metres to the bank seemed like the longest tab I'd ever done. On reaching the bank, I flopped beside Johnny, half-lying across him in my relief. I could feel him vibrating beneath me. Looking up, I saw he had his hand across his mouth to muffle his laughter.

'You bastard, Cook,' I said. 'Remind me not to give you a hand if you want it.'

'It's not that, it's your face, Vince. Talk about a look of shock or "what am I doing here?"'

Glaring at him, I said, 'It may have escaped your notice, but I don't make a habit of being shot at every day.'

The lads on the bank were a mixture of A Company, ACC bearers, our own fire-based team and some others I can't remember. I sat back against the wall of the bank, between Johnny and Bob Geddis. Every now and then, an ACC lad would pop his head up, or put his helmet up on his rifle to test the sniper. All the officers sat to our right and were not watching this.

I thought to myself, This doesn't happen. This is a comic, or John Wayne stuff. But, there he was, happy as a pig in shit, testing for bullets. The trouble was the sniper was still firing at him, at all of us.

The battle was raging on the hill. Artillery shells were

landing there, adding to the ricochet of the bullets. If you slowly raised your head, you could watch the free firework display, because that's what it looked like. The odd shout could be heard, and the odd scream, but it was the sound of rifle, machine-gun and artillery that dominated the night.

After about an hour, we were all getting pissed off with this fucking sniper. Something had to be done, and quick. He was holding up a hundred and thirty men. The radio operator was busy listening to orders from battalion HQ and spelling out changes verbally to the PC and Captain Mason, changes that would affect us.

While this was going on, I could smell cooking. I leaned my head round the corner of the bank, where the smell came from, and saw four guys crouched around a mess tin brewing a cup of tea. Johnny and I slid in beside them, smiling, as if they had suddenly become our best friends. They looked at us. 'Yeah, yeah, "Can we have a sip?"' they said.

In a while, the brew was shared around. It tasted beautiful. My one and only sip seemed to revive me completely. However, once back in our positions, I was aware again of how cold my feet were. They seemed just like two blocks of ice stuck on the end of my legs.

One and a half hours had gone by and the PC was sitting with us, when suddenly Captain Mason crawled over to us.

'Right, I want the best gun for the job,' he said.

Lieutenant Oliver looked at me and Bob and said, 'Get your gun ready.'

I looked at Johnny, who was again grinning.

'Fuck off, Johnny,' I said, knowing that he thought it was funny.

'What did you say to me?' shouted Captain Mason.

'Not you, sir – Corporal Cook, I meant. A private joke.'

'Well, shut the joking. Come with me now.'

'But, sir, I would like to know the size of the task, for ammo reasons,' I said.

'Look, don't argue, just come now,' he replied. I looked at the PC for support.

'Mr Mason, he has a point. Where and how big is the task?'

Captain Mason crawled back, showing his disgust. 'Look, just grab, say, a thousand rounds and follow me.'

He crawled away. I looked at the PC and Johnny, when both put their fingers to their lips as if to say, 'Just shut up.'

Bob Geddis, Sas and I got the kit together and followed Mason into the unknown. At the end of the bank, I met up with Ginge McCarthy, Westy and Pete H. Again, I looked at Ginge as if to say, 'What's happening?'

He returned a look that told me he didn't know either.

'Right,' said Captain Mason. 'Look up to the objective.'

We did this.

'Now go one fist to your right of the highest height. You will see what looks like a shark's fin. See?'

Johnny and I placed our knuckles, clenched into fists, against the height, and found the fin.

'Seen,' we replied.

'Good. Now just below that is a bunker, and possibly the sniper that is holding up the advance of B Company. When we get the order, we will eliminate him, OK?'

We all looked at him.

'Well, yeah.'

'Right. Crawl forward about twenty-five metres. You'll find a small bank. Begin and set up.'

All six of us got our kit together and started to crawl forward from the safety of the bank. The crawl forward wasn't as slow this time, but then the thought of the sniper was always in my mind.

When we reached the bank, Ginge and I split up. He was about ten metres to my right. Bob Geddis and I set up the gun on its tripod, loaded it and cocked it ready again. This time I hoped we would fire it. I laid the gun on to the target and waited. The Milan team had also set up their piece and were waiting. The idea was to fire the Milan at the bunker and for our gun to fire about the area, wiping out any survivors.

The tension grew as the minutes passed. The battle had now taken a new turn. A point-fifty-calibre machine-gun was having a duel with one of the machine-guns on the hill. It was an amazing sight. First, you saw the stream of tracer rounds spill out from our gun on the hill, immediately followed by its rattling fire. The rounds would hit the area of the enemy gun, flying off in all directions. Some even seemed to be heading our way. The tracer rounds would only be ignited from one hundred metres. They would just fizzle out at eleven hundred metres, but would carry on unseen for at least another thousand.

Once our team had fired, the enemy would answer back, causing the same effect with its tracer rounds. We sat watching this for some time, willing our lads on the hill to wipe out that deadly gun.

Sometimes, when the tracer rounds seemed to make a direct hit, you would think, That's got them, but then the enemy would return fire.

As I sat there, I could only feel my knees – my feet had

become frozen beyond help. All the same, I continued to bash them together, trying to bring life into them, but it was no use.

I heard a noise to my rear. I couldn't think what it was. Turning around and looking down, I saw that Sas had fallen asleep. I couldn't believe it. There we were, ready to go on a fire mission, and this guy had fallen asleep. I picked up a rock and threw it at him, scoring a direct hit on his helmet, which brought him back to life.

'What the fuck are you on, Sas?' I said.

'Sorry, Vince, I just ...'

I stopped him dead. 'You do that again and I'll kill you.'

Bob shook his head in disgust and I was fuming.

Just then, Captain Mason called to us to get ready. I flicked off the safety-catch and Bob placed his finger on the trigger. I would elevate or traverse the gun if need be.

'Stand by,' shouted Captain Mason.

My feet were forgotten, my mind emptied of any thoughts. But my eyes were completely alive, staring at the area of the fin and possible target.

'Fire!'

Ginge let off the Milan. The rocket whooshed off the small portable frame and picked up its deadly speed – after a hundred and twenty metres it was at its deadliest. We were only about ninety metres from the target.

Ginge managed to guide the wired missile on to the target. The explosion ripped into the night, sending sparks everywhere. Bob pressed the trigger and our gun burst into life for a few seconds, then stopped.

'Stoppage!' screamed Bob.

I tried to lift the cover off the top of the GPMG, but the night sight was in the way. I ripped the sight from the weapon and threw it into Sas's hands. I cleared the gun and reloaded.

Bob was just about to fire again when a zipping sound ripped into the ground right in front of our tripod. We both ducked behind the bank. The enemy's bullets whizzed over our heads and around us. Ginge was laughing and shouted, 'They've seen you all right!'

'Fucking brilliant, isn't it? My big night and the bloody gun's packed up.'

Captain Mason shouted over from behind us, 'Reload, reload – CS9 wants another one up there.'

When I looked up, the area was alive with ricocheting again. Bob turned to me and said, 'Looks like we disturbed a bees' nest, yeah?'

Ginge reloaded and we waited again. One minute passed, two minutes. The area was bursting with gunfire. The snipers still fired at us but now we just looked up at the target area again and nothing seemed to bother us.

'Fire!' shouted Captain Mason again.

The Milan ripped into life and scored on the target area. Our gun also burst into life and this time carried on.

About four hundred rounds had gone through the gun when the order to stop came through. The barrel was smoking with its new energy. All went silent around us and the target area. Everyone watched and waited. Then the bloody sniper started again. The zips hit the ground more to our right this time. We threw ourselves behind the bank. I could see the Milan team doing the same. Captain Mason shouted for us to return and he crawled off back to the bigger bank. Bob and I pulled the whole gun and tripod up to the bank with us and dismantled it there. Ginge moved off first, followed by us. The sniper had finished with us, so it seemed, and was now concentrating on someone else, the rounds flying well above us.

When we rejoined Johnny and our PC again, both asked us what had happened. I simply said what we had done and 'That's all I know.'

The PC crawled off towards Captain Mason and the radio operator. We sat there for about fifteen minutes, before getting the order to move. We were told that the move would come in another fifteen minutes' time. But then Captain Mason said we were now needed for another task on the summit. With all our kit packed ready to go we sat back and waited again. A lad from A Company crawled past us and said to an officer near by, 'Corporal Hope is still out there and the medic's with him. Sir, he's got to get him out of there.'

The officer whispered back, 'No problem.'

Now it seemed we'd wiped out the bunker and the worst sniper. As we waited for orders to move out, my mind flashed back to the body wrapped in a sleeping bag that I had seen while I was struggling to keep up, while I was being sniped at. Many weeks later, I found out that Corporal Hope had been hit in the forehead by the sniper while walking behind the OC of A Company. The sniper had picked his target well: Steve Hope was the company radio operator. He died many hours later, having struggled to the very last. The medic who treated him, Lance-Corporal Chris Lovett, was later also killed by mortar fire. As I write, I recall how close I had been to death, how close all the support team that walked through the sniper fire had been.

13

ON LONGDON

We waited and, as always when waiting, the cold crept in.
I was banging my feet together to bring some life back into
them when a sudden racking explosion erupted about fifty
metres away. At nearly the same time, Bob Geddis and an
ACC lad sitting with him leaped up and jumped about
shouting. Both had been hit by molten shrapnel, but luckily
it was ending its deadly flight when it struck them and
lacked enough force to penetrate their skin. After about
four seconds, we grabbed them and made them sit down,
in case of a sniper. They got really niggardly, cursing and
moaning. About a minute later, three or four more
explosions occurred and this time we all threw ourselves
on to the damp ground. Captain Mason got up first and
shouted a quick order for us to dig in. This caused some
reluctance because we were waiting to move, but orders
were orders, so we started to dig in.

A corporal from the Mortars started giving orders for

some lad to move over, saying he was in his space. Next thing, the two guys were holding each other's collars, ready to fight, all over a piece of ground. Johnny and I giggled.

I whispered, 'Can you imagine this on exercise at home? Two guys fighting to dig in the same place – it's just not heard of.' (Every soldier hates digging in.) The brief friction ended with a joint effort, but it was unreal to watch them digging together.

We had hardly started when Captain Mason gave the order to hitch kit and follow him. We all quickly packed our kit on our backs and followed him out from the bank, in the order we were, in a well-spaced line. We left behind about fifteen guys, sitting in shallow holes, grinning at us and waving. A Company stayed put.

We walked first in the direction of the westerly slope of Mount Longdon, then in the direction of where the mortars or artillery had tried to hit us and lastly into the open for the sniper again. Captain Mason had no choice in this route. At this point, he had a difficult task: to get us to the summit as quickly as possible.

We had walked for about five minutes when a round whizzed past my nose. I flopped to the ground, like everybody else. A sniper had spotted us again. Minutes later, Captain Mason shouted for us to move on. I thought to myself, Fuck this for a laugh, why not go shopping as well? But we simply had no choice.

The sniper took spasmodic shots at us, but never scored – why not, we will never know. One thing I am 100 per cent sure of to this day is that he, or they, were brilliant shots, and deadly.

We reached the bottom of the hill at about 0030 hours. The battle had been going for some three and a half hours.

We came up to the FAP and walked past a line of guys lying there, moaning in half-silence. The medics were busy with all the wounded. There seemed to be about twenty-five guys, working and wounded, in the group.

We were sitting some twenty metres from them in the darkness and we could only just see the scene by the light of the moon. A sergeant from battalion HQ came over to us and Lieutenant Oliver and Captain Mason stood up to meet him.

'We have three confirmed dead at this moment,' he said, 'Murdoch, Scott and Greenwood. We know there are more but we can't get to them as yet.'

Their conversation continued around our coming task and that the RSM was coming to meet us. I sat in a trance; I couldn't believe that we had lost guys. Today, it seems crazy that I should think like this. Why? I can only put it down to the fact that I was still in my own little world of make-believe: we would win the war without anyone getting killed! The death of those three guys hit me like a brick, total shock. Murdoch, or simply Doc. Doc, who I'd been chatting with on the way to our start line after we bumped into B Company, now dead; Scotty, from the MT Platoon, like Greenwood, recently nicknamed 'Fester' because of his sleeping habits. My mind was a blank to the conversation around me.

Johnny nudged me. 'Vince, we're moving, mate.'

This woke me to the reality of it all. I was now fully alert, for surely there was more to come.

Standing on my wet, cold feet, with all my ammo over my shoulders, I followed the line of troops past the wounded towards the summit. What was going to happen? I didn't know, but I was bloody nervous walking up the slope.

After about fifty metres, we stopped, and everybody sat down, looking and listening. The crags in the mountain jutted out and looked sharp. We seemed to have hit a path of sorts. The sounds of gunfire were only about fifty metres away.

I could hear someone shouting, something like, 'Get the fuck back here, you twat, there's two Argies hidden that way!'

The atmosphere on the path leading up to the hill was eerie. The battle had cooled and there was much less fighting, but it was more than evident that it would continue throughout the night.

My personal feelings at this time were mixed. I knew that I had to get in there and 'do my bit', but half of me was saying, 'Get the fuck out of this madness.' This doesn't mean I would have got out, or even thought seriously about it – basically, it was just the same old doubt: What the fucking hell am I doing here?

Captain Mason came to a halt as I was thinking this and the whole fire-based team sat down for what we thought would be another wait. He then decided to see what was at the end of the path. He climbed on to a large boulder and stood there looking in the direction of the gunfire. Suddenly, a bullet whacked into the rock beside him. Amazingly, he carried on gazing – he hadn't even noticed, very like me earlier on. Corporal McCarthy, sitting below him, looked up at Captain Mason and shouted, 'Sir, you're being shot at!'

'How do you know?'

'Jesus, I just heard the bloody round!'

As Corporal McCarthy finished shouting, another bullet thumped into the rock again.

'Oh, yes. Looks like you're right, Corporal. Thank you.'

His thanks and answer were said as he leaped down. I must hand it to Captain Mason: either he was very cool or he just did not click. Everyone giggled. He had replied in such a typically relaxed manner, as if it was a daily event to be shot at.

Our RSM came out of a crag to our side. I always admired Larry Ashbridge as an RSM: he was totally dedicated to the lads, and in my eyes the best RSM I'd ever been under. This also goes for my OC, Major Dennison, and CSM Caithness – all very professional men. The RSM called Captain Mason over and a quick brief was held. We could hear the new orders clearly, as all of us were straining for every word.

'The OC and CSM are on the summit, waiting for your new mission. If you go with Craig Jones here, he'll lead you up there. Be warned, though, the Argies are still everywhere,' announced the RSM. He then disappeared down the hill at a half-trot, with his followers.

'Well,' said Johnny, 'this looks like fun.'

'Yeah,' I said, 'better not get too comfy up there; I can't see us sitting around any longer.'

We picked up our kit and slowly climbed through the crag to follow the line of troops. There were about fifteen or twenty of us at this stage.

Johnny was in front of me, when his foot slipped and released a deadly smell.

'Cooky, you dirty bastard,' I said.

'What? I haven't done nothing.'

'Liar, you just shat in my face.'

Private Jones stood helping us through the gap, laughing at Johnny and me.

'You're now going through the Argies' shithouse area. It seems this is where they came.'

It then became noticeable that the smell was everywhere and getting stronger. Everywhere there were mounds of toilet paper on small piles of shit. I tried to place my hands on clean rock as we climbed up through the crag. When we reached the other side, we trotted to catch up with the teams. It seemed amazing to me how they would always walk off and not wait for anyone.

We came to an open spot by some empty bunkers. Captain Mason told us to wait, so again we sat. I was searching for a good spot to sit when I saw Pete Hedicker, so I sat beside him and chatted.

'Got a good spot here, Vince,' said Pete.

'Yeah, let's hope they forget us for a bit.'

Pete looked at me grinning. 'You know we'd be in the Queen's now, don't you? I mean, it's the weekend.'

'Yeah, don't talk to me about a pint, I could murder one right now.' Johnny sat opposite us, banging his feet together to bring them to life. Bob sat with him.

'Bob,' I said, 'where's Sas?'

'Don't know, thought he was in front of you, going through the shitpit.'

My mind flashed back to where I had last seen him. I could remember him giggling about Captain Mason and the sniper, but since then no sign. I looked around me, but no sign there either. I whispered loudly, 'Sas, Sas.'

Nothing. Johnny stopped banging his feet.

'Oh, for fuck's sake, where is he now?'

Johnny got up and walked back towards the shitpit some fifty metres away. He had not gone far when Ginge called him back.

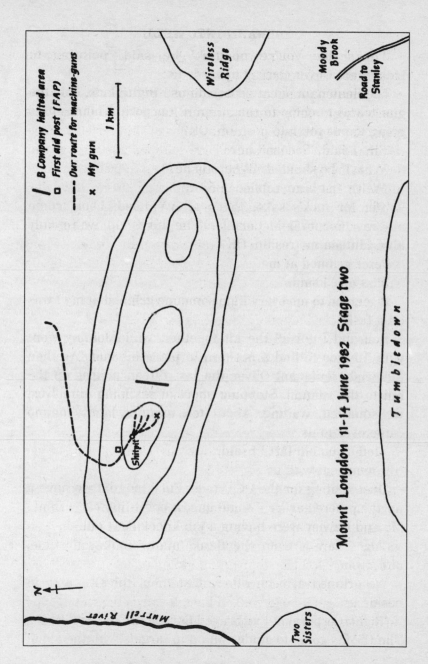

Mount Longdon 11-14 June 1982 Stage two

B Company halted area
First aid post (FAP)
Our route for machine-guns
× My gun

1 km

Wireless Ridge

Moody Brook

Road to Stanley

Tumbledown

Shitpit

Murrell River

Two Sisters

N

'Looks like you're needed,' he said, pointing to Lieutenant Oliver coming towards us.

The lieutenant squatted beside us. 'Right, lads, only the gun teams to come to the summit. Corporal Thompson is going to put you into position, OK?'

'Sir,' I said, 'Sas isn't here.'

'What?' he shouted. 'Where is he?'

'We've lost him,' replied Johnny.

'Oh, for fuck's sake, that's all we need. Look, come anyway. Corporal McCarthy, if he turns up we're only about fifteen metres up, OK?'

Peter grinned at me.

'Piss off,' I said.

It seemed to me every time someone grinned at me I was on a task.

Bob and I got all the kit together, while Johnny went with Tommo to find a position to place his gun. We then followed Lieutenant Oliver the last fifteen metres up the hill to the summit. Stopping short of skylining ourselves, we squatted, waiting. About ten minutes later, Tommo came over to us.

'Hello, you old fart,' I said.

Tommo sat with us.

'Just waiting for the OC, Vince. Fuck me, did we have a party up here earlier – some gun, a point-fifty cal, I think. Me and Rawley were having a job knocking it out.'

'Ah, I saw it from the flank, mate. Took your time, didn't yer?'

We grinned at each other. Just then, the OC came in beside us.

'Right, Corporal B, I've briefed Corporals Cook and Peers. The CSM is going to guide you on to targets with the aid of an NOD. We will be trying to knock out the bunkers before A Company do their bit on the flank. Everything OK?'

'Yes, sir.'

'Good. Corporal T, take them to the position you found for them.'

We got up and walked three or four metres to the right. Tommo got down on all fours and started to crawl towards the summit. We all copied him, as he had been up there long before us. No more zipping sounds for me, I hoped.

When we reached the summit, Bob sat to the rear while I slid in beside Tommo and Lieutenant Oliver. Looking across the hill, all I could see in the darkness was the crags jutting up and down along the top. In the far distance, Stanley blazed with lights. We could see vehicles going up and down the only road into town.

The stars were still out and it was freezing, a typical winter's night. I glanced behind us, at the battle of Two Sisters. The Marines' attack had been helped by a bombardment by our artillery. Their battle wasn't important to me, and only a few times that night did I glance their way. To our right across the largest valley was Mount Tumbledown. All quiet there.

14

NOTHING PERSONAL

'Right, Vince, there's your arc of fire. Nice, isn't it?'

'Yeah, but where's my cover?'

'Only this rock.'

Beside us was a boulder about chest high, covering me from the left only. To our right was an open space. I looked at Tommo, who said nothing.

The short straw, I thought.

'Right,' said Tommo, 'I'm off. See you later.'

Lieutenant Oliver beckoned Bob up and, with a great struggle, we placed the gun on the tripod again, this time in the low mount. I centred the gun, then loaded it and cocked it. I took off the safety-catch and we waited.

Bob was busy getting all the ammo linked up, while I watched to the front. Then, out of the blue, Sas came up. Standing right over us, looking down, he said, 'Vince, is that you? Got lost, mate.'

As he spoke, three or four rounds hit the large boulder

on the other side of my head. I could almost feel the vibes go through it.

'Get down!' shouted the PC. Bob was pulling on Sas's denims as he fell to the ground.

'Sorry.'

'For fuck's sake, Sas, you've just given our position away.'

He looked dejected.

'Look,' I said, 'do the ammo. Give it to me as we need it, OK?

'OK.'

The OC shouted across, 'You OK?'

'Yes, sir.'

'Good.'

He was about ten metres to my left.

We had got some of the ammo together when the CSM shouted.

'Corporal B, get ready!'

I waited for the CSM to give the orders to fire. The wait was longer than I expected and my finger stayed on the trigger, frozen, waiting.

As I sat waiting for the command, other voices came to my ears from among the sounds of battle. The voices of the wounded. Everywhere their cries pitched in with those of the survivors still struggling and screaming frantically at each other to move there or move here. But the wounded were unlike anything else. Their cries could be heard above the uninjured: their shouts were desperate. My mind went blank. My eyes were wide open with fright for them. My mouth dried as I lay there. The seconds seemed like hours. Their anguished moaning and crying is here in my ears now, as I write. No matter what I or the others did to try to ignore them, they seemed to grow louder and louder. I burned with frustration.

One victim, who I later found out was Baz Barrett, seemed so near, groaning and shouting, 'Help me, please don't leave me. For fuck's sake, help – I can't move.'

Someone further along to our left called out, 'For Christ's sake, I'm dying. Don't let them bury me here, please, please.'

I shouted out, 'Hang on, don't move, for fuck's sake, keep quiet!'

I started to crawl from my position, I wanted to help them. The PC grabbed my arm.

'Leave it, Corporal B, leave it.'

I looked at him. 'Why?'

'Because a sniper has already picked off about five or six guys that have tried to help. The Top says no more, OK?'

I slumped to the ground with a feeling of total helplessness. It was the worst feeling that anyone can imagine. As I tried not to think it was real, the cries continued.

'Oh, God, I'm hit in the chest, I'm all wet, please help.' The crying went on and on.

Some wounded guys had been dragged or had crawled away from the main impact area, only to be pinned down elsewhere. My mind seethed with anger.

'Corporal B, stand by!' the CSM screamed. The command to follow killed off all the cries and moaning. The weapon broke into a stream of fire at the Argentinean positions, three to five rounds bursting across the summit. The steady rate of fire continued as the CSM shouted across to change direction, using our tracer rounds as indicators. All six guns opened up. Our tracers ripped across the summit to the other end of the mountain, the bullets bouncing and ricocheting in all directions.

'Stop!' screamed the CSM. 'Corporal B, go right three clicks, up fifty mils.'

Bob removed his finger from the trigger and I quickly adjusted the weapon.

'On!' I screamed.

'Fire!'

I followed the CSM's orders, and the gun burst into life once more. After about thirty or forty rounds, he screamed again. 'Stop!'

He shouted to all guns in place, 'All adjust to Corporal B's target area.'

Our platoon guns locked on to their targets across the hilltop.

'On, sir,' came every reply.

The CSM then shouted, 'Bramley, you will traverse right. Corporals T and Cook, traverse left. Stand by, fire.'

We all fired together. Tracer rounds could be seen passing left and right, as we slowly moved the traversing drums in our respective directions. The flow of bullets parted like hair being combed. The summit came under a deadly stream of fire. Our gun rattled and thudded as the rounds were fed into the top slide. The bullets went to their targets and the empty cases fell below the tripod, the link spilled to the right of the gun and the cordite of the spent cases filled the air around us. The smoke whiffed off the barrels as we let about two hundred rounds pass through them.

'Stop. Everybody drop about sixty mils and go right seven, eight clicks.'

'On!' I shouted.

In the darkness, I heard one of the teams cry out, 'Stoppage.'

All was quieter for a few seconds, but my ears rang with the sounds of the GPMG. Then, once again, 'Fire!'

The barrel spat out the rounds again, the weapon fired steadily and with a good tempo. The empty cases piled up as Bob fired about four hundred rounds.

'Stop. What's going on over there now?' I heard another voice shout.

'Gun's jammed, sir.'

'Well, clear the fucker! Corporal B, your gun OK?'

'Yes, sir.'

'Good, go right five clicks and wait.'

I adjusted and waited. As I lay there, I felt Sas pulling my denims. I looked down at him.

'What can I do now?' he asked.

'Link up still,' I said.

'I've done it,' he said, passing me a handful of link. He had only linked up small bits, about thirty rounds in a strip.

'Where's the rest?' I asked.

'Here.' He passed up small bundles, not even linked.

I crawled down to him and grabbed his smock. 'Listen, you. I said "link up" not "fart about". I'm going to need this in a minute. Sas, I'm getting sick of you.'

'Fuck off,' he shouted.

We started fighting, there and then, fists flying, half-rolling about the hillside, trying to kill each other as if it was a Saturday-night brawl. Lieutenant Oliver rolled down beside us and quickly pulled us apart.

'I don't believe this, I really don't. The fucking enemy is that way, not here,' he said, pointing towards Stanley.

Sas and I went back to our areas of work quickly. This time he started linking the belts together. I got beside the gun and waited. Bob giggled beside me. Looking at me and grinning, he said, 'That has got to go into the history books, Vince. Who's heard of that before?'

'No worry, we're all on edge. I just don't expect to do two jobs at once and I've had enough of him for one night.'

Lieutenant Oliver whispered across, 'Corporal B, cool down. I know what you mean, but later, OK?'

'Yes, sir.'

Sas tapped my leg again. I looked back at him. He looked down in the dumps. 'Sorry, Vince. Here's your ammo now.'

'That's OK, Sas. No problem. Cheers.'

After taking the ammo, I linked the remainder on to the gun.

'Sas, how much more ammo have you got?'

'That's all of it.'

I leaned over to Lieutenant Oliver. 'Sir, we're nearly out of ammo.'

'What, how the fuck can that be?'

'That ACC lad has got to be back there with the sandbag load,' I said.

Lieutenant Oliver got up and went to the rest area. About three minutes later, a bag of ammo was dumped on Sas.

'Right, get linking. Quick,' the lieutenant said.

'Everybody ready?' the CSM shouted.

'No, sir,' came the answer to my right.

Two more teams had no more ammo; two guns had bad stoppages. Tony Peers's team had gone on another task. This left just our gun.

'Sir, we will need more ammo soon.'

'How much you got left there, Corporal B?'

'About two thousand rounds.'

'Right. I'll see to it.'

Within fifteen minutes, bodies appeared out of the darkness and started to drop ammo at Sas's feet. He was now very busy. Our gun had been firing for some ten minutes. The steady fire of the gun echoed around us. The bursts of fire had warmed the barrel so much that it glowed red-hot in the darkness.

The CSM continued to correct our fire after long bursts. Sometimes, we would hear him shout, 'Good shooting. Ah, that's got that lot. Right, quickly go two clicks right, down thirty mils. Good, that's got that lot – they're running all over the place.'

'Stoppage!' screamed Bob.

'OK, let's change barrels, now.'

I cleared the weapon and we moved the barrel without touching it. The glowing barrel sizzled as I placed it on the frozen grass. Immediately, the replacement barrel burst into life.

We'd been firing across the hill for about forty minutes. I can't remember the exact length of time – it could have been longer. The ammo was going down rapidly. The CSM screamed at us to get the gun firing again on our last target. We resumed firing as soon as the gun was cocked. Bob's finger was giving max on the trigger, the gun vibrating almost non-stop. I watched our tracer rounds bouncing off rocks about two hundred metres away.

'We've got them,' the CSM shouted.

Suddenly, the air around me seemed to disappear. I heard a loud 'whoosh', followed by a terrific explosion behind me. The impact shook the ground. My para smock was pulled up through my webbing and I lay there completely stunned for a few seconds. I hadn't the slightest idea what had happened. The air smelled of damp earth and cordite. I turned around to face Bob and the PC. We all looked at each other wide-eyed, shock on our faces.

Bob was the first to speak in those opening seconds. 'But what the fuck was that?'

'What was it, what was it?' I shouted.

Lieutenant Oliver screamed, 'Forget it, forget it! Keep firing, keep firing!'

Bob was on all fours as if trying to get up, shaking his head as if he'd been hit by a hammer. Lieutenant Oliver grabbed him and shouted, 'Stay there, stay there!'

I felt winded, my lungs drained of air. I coughed and spluttered. I could see only stars, as if I had unexpectedly been punched in the face. I lowered my head and grappled for the trigger. After a brief search, I found it and pressed it again. The weapon resumed firing, vibrating as normal. Only the gun had felt nothing.

The short bursts of fire carried on across the summit. Within a few seconds, the OC shouted across to us, 'Corporal B, Corporal B, are you all OK over there?'

His voice registered in my ears, but my mind was spinning, though the stars were beginning to fade. I shouted back, 'We're OK, sir.'

Bob and Lieutenant Oliver looked all right. We just looked at each other as the gun continued to fire. The shock on our faces said everything. The OC said, 'Corporal B, Corporal B, that was a mean one. Looks like they've got you clean in their sights now. Don't worry, keep firing.'

The gun carried on. I still hadn't realised the full impact of what had happened. All of us just went on firing. We had only about six hundred rounds left when the CSM shouted to us to stop.

While the gun cooled, we sat on our sides and looked at each other again, taking a brief rest.

'Sir, what happened?' I asked.

'Yeah,' shouted Bob, 'my fucking head is ringing.'

'I think they fired a rocket or something – not sure,' replied the PC.

A lad was stumbling behind us and walking around in a daze. (I now know it was Chris Dexter.) Someone shouted for someone to grab him and bring him to them. The voice seemed to come from about forty metres down the hill. A figure appeared from nowhere and guided the lad away. Bob looked at me and said in a worried voice, 'Vince, this is the pits.'

Pat Harley came up to the CSM in OC position and said in a quiet voice, 'Sir, Corporal McCarthy has been hit. Seems to be in a bad way.'

The OC replied, 'Go and see to it then. We have a job on our hands here.'

'I'll go with you and see,' Captain Mason said.

Pat and the captain went a little way down the hill and, in the dim light, I could see them busy over Ginge McCarthy.

'Corporal B, get ready again,' screamed the OC. All three of us turned our heads back to the target.

'Ready, sir.'

The CSM shouted, 'Up fifty mils, go right four clicks and fire.'

The gun erupted into life again and carried on firing. Its noise drowned out everything around us but, in the brief moments it stopped, we could all hear the zipping sounds hitting the rock and ground to our left and front. We knew the enemy were still trying to get us, but we couldn't move. I was glad when the gun was firing; it took my mind off the snipers.

When we had spent our last six hundred rounds we screamed out, 'Need more ammo, need more ammo!'

About one thousand rounds were thrown at us from behind. Sas linked and passed it to us. The ammo wasn't ours now, it was Argentinean. Some of the lads were searching empty bunkers now and bringing it up to us. The Argies had fired one tracer round, one ball and one armour-piercing bullet in every three rounds they fired. We had had one tracer and four normal rounds in every five rounds we fired.

The CSM shouted, 'Stop, stop.'

Worn out, we rested our heads on the ground. The battle had now been going on for some eleven hours. How long we had lain there firing I did not know.

The CSM came over. 'Well done. A Company is moving through to our left now. We've covered and given them all the help we could give. The rest is up to them. We can't fire any more – it'd get them, it's too close now. It'll be light in an hour or so. Pull the gun back and dismount it.'

'Sir, did we get any?' asked Bob.

'More than enough,' he replied and walked away.

Had we killed? We must have. I felt nothing afterwards – just relaxed. I hadn't seen our target: they had been hidden in darkness. We hadn't killed at the end of a bayonet, or through a rifle sight. We had killed with a spray of machine-gun bullets. It didn't seem personal. It was as if the enemy hadn't existed at all.

15
FORWARD INTO HELL

We dismantled our gun and evenly spread out our kit. The air was chilling. Everything seemed frozen and still. Just over the skyline where we had been firing earlier, rifle fire now dominated the night. Bob and I crawled back to where we had been. Against the skyline, we could see figures moving through the crags. A tracer round bounced off the rock: the second phase was well under way.

The air went still, then it was sucked up as if a small whirlwind had come. The 'whoosh' grew louder and louder. I buried my head in the dirt. About seventy metres away the ground exploded in a mass of earth, shrapnel and rock. Then another shell came over, this time further to our right. I looked down the hill as the shell exploded, and saw an unbelievable display of flying red sparks: deadly shrapnel. The ground shook as shell after shell fell behind us. The first minutes of the shelling were terrifying.

'That tells me they know they're losing,' shouted the OC.

His comment was briefly registered, before another shell pounded into the ground.

'Right, listen in, everyone, listen in!' screamed the OC. 'First, get into cover, get into cover now, quickly.'

I grabbed my kit, stood up and made for a base line of jutting rock about thirty metres away. Bob and the PC found a bunker and slid in. I wished that I had seen it too, for my new position didn't seem safe. I squeezed into the crag, which had a lip, like a cave. It covered me, though I was vulnerable on my left side. Shells were landing further down the hill as we all scrambled for protection. I pushed myself as far into the crag as I could. I thought to myself, Lie facing the inside of this rock, Vince. Then I thought I wouldn't see what was happening, so I pushed my back into the crack, laying my webbing over me, as if that would help. What a joke!

In the distance, a booming sound began that carried over the area. Someone screamed, 'Incoming, incoming.'

Sure enough, the air disappeared, there was a 'whoosh' and then the explosion killed any remaining peace. The shells came in thick and fast. I lay watching the red, glowing shrapnel flying by. Now the shrapnel was creeping up towards me, the explosions getting so loud I thought that they would deafen me. The shells were landing about fifty metres away. Four or five shells would hit an area in a salvo; the next batch about ten metres nearer.

The booming from Stanley could still be heard in the gaps between explosions in our area. As I lay there watching the shrapnel getting closer, I found myself shaking. Was it from cold or fright? My legs shook and I couldn't control them at all. The next salvo landed thirty metres away. I curled up into a ball as the shrapnel splintered the rocks around me. A piece of shrapnel landed in my little alcove, still burning with fury, sizzling into the dirt by my waist.

Four or five more shells landed around us and then it stopped, as if it had never begun. The air was misty, as though a fog had swept over us. I lay back, praying it was over.

In the half-light of false dawn, I could now hear shouting all down the hill. Some guys were screaming like mad. One voice went right through me – the scream of a man who knows he is about to die. All over the hill, people were shouting, 'Medic, medic.'

I was about to crawl from my hole when another shell hit the ground. I hadn't even heard it coming. I fell on my face and stayed there for a few seconds. Another shell landed nearby. This time a shower of dirt fell on my back. I crawled back into my hole and curled up again, waiting. My body shook uncontrollably. The shells landed in thick salvoes, the noise and explosions around me making my head spin as if someone were banging it against a wall. I willed it to stop, but the shells carried on landing around me. Then, this second bombardment within minutes ended as suddenly as it had begun. The last shell landed further down the hill. After a few minutes, many of us began to crawl from our hiding places. Standing on a rock, I looked down the hill. In the early-morning mist, I could see troops walking and running in all directions. Some guys were carrying wounded lads down towards the FAP. The screaming of the wounded was everywhere.

About twenty-five metres away, I saw a lad half-dragging himself down the hill, holding his leg. He had no webbing, no helmet, but his weapon was still in his free hand. I searched about me frantically. I had to help someone, but who first? I picked up and replaced my webbing. SLR in hand, I made my way towards the guy dragging his leg. As I reached him the OC screamed, 'Support teams on me, support teams on me.'

The lad looked at me with pitiful eyes. I recognised him from B Company. He'd obviously been wounded for some time, as the blood on his leg was now dried and dark. He rested against a rock. When I reached him, I crouched to look at his leg. I was about to help him when he said, 'You'd better go, mate. Your boss is screaming for you. Besides, it's your turn over there now.'

'OK,' I said.

Quickly turning around, I made my way to where the OC was standing in his original spot. As I reached him, with all my kit, Tommo, Johnny and a few others joined us.

'Where's the rest?' shouted the OC.

'I saw a few carrying wounded down the hill, sir,' said Tommo.

'For fuck's sake, we've a bloody task to do. How many here?'

Tommo did a quick head check. 'Eight, sir.'

'OK, follow Sergeant P. He will lead you to our new positions.'

Sergeant P stood there, his eyes showing strain. He was an excellent soldier, and many had great respect for him. As part of D Company, he knew the hill better than most, from previous recces.

'Right,' he said. 'Keep well behind me. It's hell up front still – they're crawling out of bunkers now, so watch yourselves.'

I quickly fixed my bayonet. I was standing right next to

Sergeant P when he turned on his heels and started to half-run, half-trot through a small gap in some crags. I immediately followed him. Tommo and Johnny were behind me as we all squeezed through.

I can remember the OC shouting behind us, 'Move, move. Their artillery will soon be here again.'

Sergeant P waited only for me to squeeze myself through the gap before he took off again. After we had gone about four or five steps, a hand dropped out of the rocks, grabbing at my ankle and denims. The shock of it made us jump. Instantly, Sergeant P was back with me. We both looked at my feet. Still holding my denims was a wounded Argie. His eyes were staring at me, pleading perhaps, full of sorrow? Sergeant P shouted, 'Step back, Brammers.'

I tried to step back, but the wounded soldier tightened his grip on me. I leaned back as Sergeant P pointed his weapon and fired two bullets into the man's head, the noise of his weapon echoing around the small gap. Tommo and Johnny were behind me now. The Argie's head bounced quickly as the two rounds entered him. His eyes rolled to the back of his head and his mouth opened to release a trickle of blood and saliva, which ran down his chin on to his shirt collar. At the same time, his hand gave up its grasp on my denims and dropped on to my boot. I flicked my boot as if I was playing football. His hand and arm dropped across his body and from his mouth came a low whistle of air, mixed with blood. All this took seconds, but it seemed a lifetime to me. Each detail remains with me today. The sight of this guy dying at my feet shocked me. But I was growing harder. Although shaken, I felt no remorse at that time. The deadly game of war lay at my feet; only I mattered.

The rights and wrongs of war can never be argued from the armchair. Decisions are made on the spot, questions asked afterwards. That lone Argie could have been rigged to a booby-trap, or even armed. The kill was done quickly and professionally. I felt that I should have acted as quickly as Sergeant P.

'Come on, move!' he shouted.

We all took off behind him. The small gap ended about five or six steps later and we broke out into a clearing. Across the skyline, I saw some guys walking through the mist, which was now lifting. They had fixed bayonets. In groups of two or three, they were searching around. Sergeant P and I stood together for several seconds, while the rest of the eight guys left from the platoon broke out into the clearing as well. A shell screamed in, landing just as we all hit the ground. As we picked ourselves up, Sergeant P shouted at us to move and we ran further into the clearing.

My first view of the surrounding area in the clearing was one of total bedlam. Bodies lay everywhere, wounded and dead alike. I could see four or five Argentineans clumped together across our pathway, twisted in their final positions, now beginning to rot. One had an arm hanging off. Another had half his head missing; the brains lay to one side, like spilled minced meat.

A bullet hit the rock above my head and I ducked – not that it would have made any difference. A member of B Company was firing a sub-machine-gun at the area where the enemy was still holding out.

Sergeant P screamed an order to follow him. As we trotted further into the clearing, we had to jump over the twisted pile of corpses. My mind never was, nor has since been, so alert. Adrenaline was rushing through my body so quickly that I felt I was floating with an excitement mingled with fear.

A little farther into this clearing lay three or four Argentineans, shaking visibly, close together on the ground. We half-ran, half-walked through a deadly, sickening area of death. They looked up as we arrived. All had been seriously wounded, and were moaning and crying. One held up his hands across his eyes and shouted, 'Mama.' I felt he thought that we were, or I was, about to shoot him. He went on calling for his 'Mama' in a low wail.

Some lads from B Company were pushing a few prisoners to join the three or four already on the ground. One prisoner held his head in both hands. As he was thrown to the ground, he released his hands to break his fall and I saw that his ear was missing. A gunshot wound was also visible on his left knee. It had been bandaged, but the bandage was loose and trailed from the wound. Blood ran down from his ear and from his leg. He hit the ground and began to cry like the others.

One Argentinean sat in a trance, his eyes wide and staring at nothing. Tears ran down his face, the only sign that he was alive. None of them moved; all looked like they expected to be shot by us. But we ran past. The whole area was littered with weapons, helmets, clothing, food and ammo.

After running through this clearing, I noticed some B Company lads covering and firing into some rocks ahead of us. A lance-corporal screamed, 'They're breaking!' He then fired off six or seven shots at what must have been fleeing enemy soldiers. Some others joined him, their SLRs echoing around the clearing.

My mind buzzed; my eyes searched and checked every

crag. I felt I was floating, as if it was all a dream. At the same time, I was completely ready to meet my own death. I felt that luck was the only way I would survive now.

A few bullets whizzed overhead and smashed into the rocks. A corporal shouted that Tumbledown was firing at us. We ran into a tight gap in the path and all came to an abrupt halt, as it was a dead end. Four or five bodies lay sprawled there, close together. This time they were our own men: the camouflaged Para smocks hit my eyes immediately. CSM Weeks was standing over them like a guardian, screaming at some of his men to cover the further end of the path and a small crest. The CSM and Sergeant P exchanged quick words. I wasn't listening; my mind was totally occupied with looking into the crags for the enemy. I turned and looked at our own lads, dead on the ground, mowed down when they tried to rush through this gap. I felt both anger and sadness. The CSM's face showed the strain of having seen most of his company either wounded or shot dead. That night's fighting was written in every line of his face.

We all doubled back into the clearing we had just run through. We spread out and waited for our next move. A wounded Argentinean lay to my right, about ten metres away. He had been hit in the chest and screamed as he held the wound. A lad from B Company ran across the clearing at him and ran his bayonet through him. The screaming Argentinean tried to grab the bayonet from him before it took his life. Our lad screamed, 'Shut up, shut up, you cunt!'

The enemy soldier died as the bayonet was withdrawn. The lad walked back to his seat among the rocks, as if nothing had happened.

To my right, three Argentineans were crying with their

heads in their hands. Were they the dead man's friends? At their feet, lay one of our lads, moaning in pain as a medic attended to him. I could see his back was peppered with shrapnel. I swung to my left and fell against some rocks. I now felt the shock of it all coursing through my body. I wailed softly, my throat feeling like I wanted to choke. My eyes watered and I shook my head to force myself into reality. But this *was* reality. I looked for Bob and Johnny. I couldn't see Bob, but Johnny was there, staring right at me. Our eyes met, telling each other that we felt the end had come.

A lad resting with his rifle pointed towards Tumbledown turned and fell into a tight ball, curling himself up as he hit the ground screaming, 'Incoming, incoming.'

We all dropped to the ground, crawling behind rocks wherever we could. The first shell went over us, on to the west side of the mountain. Then the shells started to creep towards us and one thumped into the clearing, hitting a rock about thirty metres away. The ground shook as if we'd been hit by an earthquake; shrapnel pierced the ground or bounced off rocks all around us. Grant Grinham screamed out as shrapnel hit his leg. Two of his mates were pulling him into better cover as the shells rained around us again. This time, when an Argentinean cried out, no one went to his aid. Soon after, Corporal Stewart McLaughlin was hit in the back by shrapnel. He was later killed by a direct mortar hit as he was being taken to a first aid post.

I lay there trembling, as the shells roared over us. Each explosion shook more fear into us. The barrage ended after ten or fifteen shells had landed on different parts of the mountain.

I crawled from behind my rock. I stood up, then fell

against the rock that some lads were running around as they tried to get the wounded lad out of this deadly area and to the FAP. In front of me, a B Company lad was sitting beside a wounded Argentinean. They rested together as if they were watching a game.

Jesus, I thought.

A sergeant shouted to the lad, 'See to him, will you?'

This broke his dream and he turned to the enemy soldier beside him and started to dress his wound with a field dressing. The Argie put out his hands, holding on to the lad for support as the bandage was wrapped around him.

I looked about me in a frantic search for 'Mick' (Dominic) Gray. I looked at all the remains of B Company spread out around the clearing. I couldn't see Mick and I remember thinking, Oh, no, not Mick, please.

I stood up and walked into the clearing, 'Anyone here seen Mick Gray?' I shouted.

No one answered me. I turned to my left and saw the elder Kempster brother, who sat leaning forward, his head resting on his rifle, both hands grasped around the gas regulator.

'Kempy!' I screamed. I trotted to his side and sat with him. 'Where's Mick?'

Kempster looked up at me, as I moved in beside him. His eyes were laughing, yet I could see that he was worn out.

'Hi, Vince,' he said, with a slight grin. 'Mick's been hit in the head. Lucky bastard survived it. He's gone to the rear now, skiving git.'

I felt an immediate relief. Thank God, Mick was OK.

'Thank fuck for that,' I said. 'You OK, mate?'

'Yeah.'

'Where's your brother, Dave?'

'He's been wounded, Vince. Bad, I've heard.'

'Oh, fuck, I'm sorry.' I felt bad for not asking about that first.

Three Para had many sets of brothers in and around the battalion. It was amazing that none lost their lives. Private (later Lance-Corporal) Gray survived million-to-one odds when a bullet hit his forehead without entering his skull. Instead, it travelled over his head, through his helmet, then out through the back. Dave Kempster lost his arm in a burst of rounds that took it nearly clean off. A lad with him lost a leg.

'Right, let's go,' shouted Sergeant P.

I patted Kempster on the shoulder and ran towards the sergeant. We followed him over a small hump to another clearing. We bumped into our OC, who tagged on. As we ran over this clearing, an Argie crawled out of a bunker. He looked like a mole, about to dart back if seen. We all seemed to fire at him together. Bullets hit him from about four weapons, including mine. He slumped in the entrance of the bunker, dead. What would we have done if he hadn't been holding his rifle? Was he thinking of surrendering? We ran on round a corner. There lay more dead Argies, three sprawled in a line. One had his weapon still in his hand, the breech with a bullet half-fed into it. His fingers were outstretched as if he'd tried to grab a grenade that lay there. I trotted over these bodies, as we all did, but I stopped briefly to pick up the grenade and place it in my smock. Once round this bend in the path through jutting rocks, we came upon a group of about five or six guys busy beating up a group of shouting Argies. A rifle butt hit one of them square in the face and he dropped to the ground. The others at once stopped shouting.

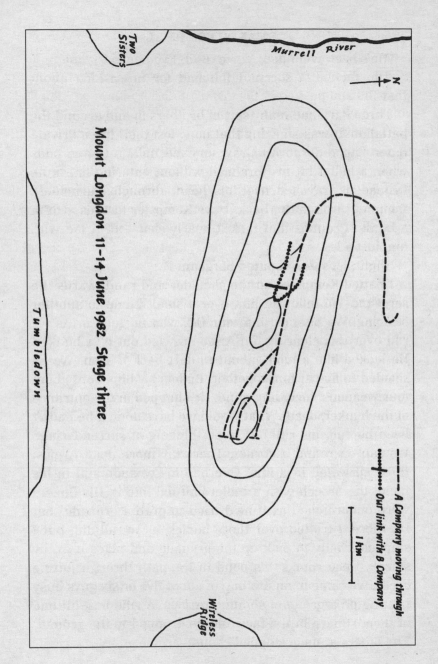

Two Sisters

Murrell River

N

Mount Longdon 11-14 June 1982 Stage three

Tumbledown

1 km

Wireless Ridge

------ A Company moving through

•••••• Our link with B Company

We stopped and placed ourselves in a small opening on the north side of the mountain. A guy from D Company grabbed and pushed at the group of Argies, shouting, 'Shut up, you Argies, or we'll top the fucking lot of you!'

The language barrier didn't matter. His tone said it all.

Nearby, another Para was sticking a bayonet into an Argie. He leaned on his weapon to make sure it went in fully. The Argie's arms flapped at his sides in a last dying act. (As often as not, the bayonet was jabbed into the eye, because of the thick winter gear the Argentineans wore.)

I felt physically sick and my stomach churned. I swallowed to fight the nausea. I didn't feel sick because of the sights of the last thirty minutes, but through the combination of shock and exhaustion.

Our group slumped to the ground and sat waiting. We placed the gun on its tripod facing the length and side of Mount Longdon. The gun cocked and loaded, we waited for the expected counterattack. Instead, we heard a booming sound from Stanley. The OC was sitting with Captain Mason and Lieutenant Oliver. He shouted across to our group of about ten, 'That's incoming, lads.'

We all stopped what we were doing and sat looking at each other in complete silence, listening.

Moments later the air rapidly disappeared around us, and the whistle of the shell in its final seconds of flight hit our ears. The shell cracked and exploded about six metres away. We had all thrown ourselves on top of each other in the little clearing. Another shell dropped a metre or two further to the right, then another. The bombardment that followed was much bigger than the early-morning one. The shells crept over the summit in a rolling barrage.

First, we would hear the booming from Stanley, then the whistle and rush of air would tell us roughly where the shell would land. We had now become able to judge the area of impact.

Each barrage started at the low part of the mountain, then crept up in salvoes of three or four shells. We would all prop our heads up to listen in between salvoes. Often the shells would creep past our area on to A Company's positions further along the summit.

We had centred our group about halfway along the mountain. The OC shouted at us to split up a bit, otherwise a direct hit would cause a heavy loss. Three or four Anti-Tank lads got up and ran to a bunker on the side of the hill as another salvo came rushing in on us. A shell crashed into the rock above the OC, sending shrapnel and rock in the opposite direction to us. He looked up at us as we all looked at him, expecting him to be dead, since the shell had landed only a few metres from us all. He shouted across, 'Well, that was a naughty one, wasn't it?'

We laughed, unanimous in appreciation of his complete calm. The shells came in for over an hour. We just lay there hoping, praying, that it would end soon. I lay looking straight into Johnny's face, who at times would poke out his tongue or do his grin again.

The shelling stopped, as usual as suddenly as it had begun. I stood up and saw Kev Connery crouched by a rock.

'Kev,' I screamed.

He looked over and smiled.

'Get your arse over here, you twat.'

He had started to walk towards us when two or three more shells hit home. We all flopped to the ground once more. The vibration of the explosions shook us and earth landed on our backs. We jumped up to see Kev running towards us. He jumped into our little opening.

'Jesus, fuck me,' he said. 'I've had a right night of it too.'

'Where's Johnny Crow and Skiddy, mate?' I asked.

Kev looked into my face and said, 'Johnny's dead, Vince, killed outright. Skiddy's been wounded. Only me left.'

'Oh, for fuck's sake. How?'

'In the attack, a burst of rounds hit Johnny square in the chest. I reckon he was dead before he hit the ground,' Kev explained.

We carried on chatting about the situation in general. Rick Westry was brewing up for us when we heard the booming sound again from Stanley.

'Incoming!' someone screamed.

'Not again!' shouted Johnny.

We were getting more scared with each bombardment. We hit the ground and fought to get legs, arms and bodies more comfy and secure than each other's.

'At this rate, they'll get us. We can't have luck on our side forever, you know,' I shouted, as the shells exploded around us.

I lay next to Kev. We both faced the mess tin, where a cuppa was brewing. A shell landed not three metres away, sending shrapnel and dirt in our direction. Rocks and earth fell around us, then over us, as if we were about to be buried alive. Both Kev and I automatically reached out to cover the mess tin and the water that was coming to the boil. The dirt landed on our hands and the brew was saved. Everyone burst out laughing.

'Talk about in a time of crisis let's all have a cup of tea!' Johnny shouted.

How in hell none of us got hit in that burst I'll never know. We drank a brew that was worth a million pounds, our first cuppa in nearly eighteen hours. We were knackered beyond words; but so alert and hyped up that we couldn't have slept if we'd wanted to.

I took off my boots and socks. The sight of my feet made me think of Scott of the Antarctic: blue-cold trench foot. I held my feet in my hands like a newborn baby. I powdered them, then took out my last pair of dry socks. When I put those socks on, I felt like a new man.

The battle was coming to an end, with rifle fire from A Company's position. I had to do something with my feet, even if the battle was not yet over. I had had enough of banging them together! Rick was sitting on a rock facing Wireless Ridge. The second part of our objective hadn't been taken, owing to the stubborn resistance we'd experienced all night. The enemy had put up a much fiercer fight than we had first expected, so that only Mount Longdon was captured. But Two Sisters and Mount Harriet had also been won.

Looking across the side of the hill, Ricky shouted, 'Here, look, there's Argies running all over the place down there!'

We jumped into position. I grabbed the gun, releasing the lever and locking the weapon on to the fleeing soldiers.

'Hang on there, you blokes!' some guy shouted.

I picked up a pair of binos beside me and scanned the view.

Bill Hayward, the battalion's sniper, looked through his sight to double-check. 'They're Argies, all right – must be ten or fifteen of them.'

I looked through my sight and saw them running. I fired twenty or thirty tracer rounds, showing a hit of some sort.

The OC shouted, 'Corporal B, there's no need to shoot lambs at the slaughter. Have a brew. Hunting tomorrow, yeah?'

I took his hint and sat back. Everyone grinned at me as if I was sick or something.

'Look, whatever you think, they're history now, so let's have a brew,' the OC insisted.

I wasn't callous. Tomorrow, they could be hunting us, I thought.

16
THE QUALITY OF MERCY

Tony Peers walked around the corner carrying a pistol, an Argie grenade pinned to him.

'Hi, John Wayne,' shouted Tommo. 'Where have you been?'

'Looting goodies,' he said, as he joined us.

I looked at Kev and he looked back: two minds, one thought. We stood up. 'Look, lads, I'm going for a walk now, OK? See you in about ten minutes.'

Everyone grinned. 'Yeah, yeah, see yer.'

The OC shouted over to me to join him. I thought he was going to say something about the shooting, but I was wrong.

'Corporal B, while you're on your travels, see if you can find us an Argie bayonet or something.' He grinned.

'Yes, sir.'

Kev and I walked up and over the hill. Ricky followed us, armed with smock order with every pocket filled with mags for our SLRs. We came to a clearing. Ricky was busy looking to one side of us when suddenly Kev and I heard moaning. We stepped up on a ledge and came face to face with a wounded Argie. Sitting beside him was his friend, who obviously wouldn't leave him. The wounded soldier had been shot in both knees, and in his chest and arms. Blood showed on all the wounds. His face showed no pain, merely pleading. His mate stood and put his hands up. No one had seen these two until now.

I pointed my rifle and bayonet and nodded towards the wounded guy. He started wailing and moaning, and put both hands together as if praying to me.

Kev pulled his pistol from his belt. 'Well, Vince, we either shoot them or help them. What will it be?' Kev lowered his pistol and looked at me.

I raised my rifle and framed the wounded Argie's head in the sight. The man looked down as if he was expecting death, knowing that he could do nothing about it. He wailed louder. I lowered my rifle. 'Kev, he looks like my neighbour. I'll help them, OK?'

'Yeah, OK. I'll go and find some goodies.' He walked off.

I motioned to his mate to sit on the other side of the wounded guy, while I placed my weapon to one side of me and went down to help. The wounded Argie's mate shook his head, looking at my rifle. 'Me friend, me friend, you friend, you help my friend, we all friends now,' he pleaded.

I looked at him and gave a small grin. He grinned back. I didn't trust him one bit.

The wounded guy started to cry. It was then that I felt sad, sad that I had thought of killing them and that we were all in this mess together. We had different views and different homes but there we were all together. I still hated the enemy, but just then, when that guy started to cry, I felt different. We all had to be hard, hard to the facts of what was happening to us: kill or be killed.

I unwound a bandage that was lying about and found the chest wound, a clean hole in his upper right shoulder. I plugged the hole and wrapped the bandage around it. His mate held him up while I dressed him. About ten minutes later, I motioned to his mate to pick him up. They were like a wedding couple crossing the threshold. I pointed my bayonet in the direction I wanted them to go and we walked off the hill.

Fifteen minutes later, we bumped into a group of A Company lads taking more prisoners down to battalion HQ. A youngster, who didn't know me, stopped his small party. I looked at him with these guys. All the Argies, about fifteen of them, lay face down with their hands on their heads. I gestured to my two to join those on the ground. The Argie who was not wounded gently placed his mate at the feet of the others. He then pointed to his private parts. I nodded yes. As the Argie was pissing, a familiar booming came from Stanley.

'Incoming!' shouted two guys on a ledge.

Seconds later, shells began to land further down the hill. The Argie stopped pissing and lay over his mate. I remember thinking, as I threw myself down, What a guy he must be, willing to take shrapnel and get killed to save his already dying friend.

The shells came up the hill, exploding in waves of three or four at a time. Three Argies suddenly stood up and started screaming. I threatened them with my rifle. We were all in the same boat, with nowhere to go. They lay down again, as two shells landed about twenty metres away. Shrapnel hit one in the back of the legs. He screamed in agony but not loud enough to drown the sound of the explosions all around us.

The next salvoes landed further on as the barrage rolled over the hill. An Argie and I leaped on the injured guy, who was wriggling in agony. The A Company lad in charge shouted at the Argies to get up and move. Some now didn't want to move because the shells were still landing up ahead. But they did when he pointed his rifle and bayonet at them. The Argies picked up their two wounded mates and carried them towards the FAP. I stood where I was.

My Argie was again carrying his wounded friend. He smiled at me and said, 'Dank you.'

They walked off the hill, away from hell itself. How ironic that their own shelling was wounding them, I thought.

I made enquiries much later about those two Argies. The medic remembered them for sticking so close together. The wounded guy survived and went home and should be fully recovered now. I wonder if he knows how close he came to death. Could I have pulled the trigger? I've asked myself this question a thousand times. Still I don't know.

I made my way back to where our team was stationed. I got there as Rick was sitting down. The OC was busy with orders.

'Vince, we're out of water. Got any?' Johnny asked.

'No,' I replied.

Just then, Captain Mason shouted to us, 'Have any of you seen Peter Hedicker around?'

'I saw him last night, sat with Ginge and West, sir,' I shouted. 'Perhaps Westy will know.'

Captain Mason looked at me with serious eyes. All the support team who were sitting there looked at Captain

Mason and me. I felt something was wrong. The OC motioned me over. I got to him and crouched down.

'Corporal B, Ginge McCarthy was killed and so was Phillip West. The shell was meant for your gun team.'

A flashback of what had happened filled my mind: the smock pulled from my back, the spinning head, the deafness.

'It must have missed you by inches, Corporal B. You OK?' said the CSM.

'Yeah, I'm OK. I'll go and find Hedicker then.'

Captain Mason came over. 'Sir,' he said to the OC, 'Pete Hedicker was killed also. The bearers have now found his body.'

I stood up and walked back to my spot. I was gutted beyond belief. Pete had always been my mate. We had spent many times together drinking in the 'Shot. I'd met his family, too. Now he was dead. Only a short while earlier, I'd been sitting beside him. He'd said what a good spot he had. Now he was dead, killed by a shell meant for me. I will never forget that I survived, while he was killed.

As I sat in a trance, Tommo came to sit beside me. 'Vince, you OK?'

'Yeah.'

'Look,' he said, 'someone had to take that position you were in last night. You and Bob took a lot on. I felt bad when they had to put you in there. You can't blame anyone, OK?'

Tommo was right, but it didn't ease the guilt of survival there, and it never has.

Johnny broke in again about water. Now, this is where you either go mad or get a grip of yourself. If you don't play, joke, laugh in times of war, you'll go nuts. This is the only way that I can explain my next action.

'Johnny, me and Rick will get some water, OK?'

I grinned at Rick and he growled at me. I back-tracked the route we'd taken in the early-morning mist. As I rounded a corner, I came across about eight Argies laid out, being searched and beaten up by the lads. I stopped, took some photos and had a chat with Taff Hedge. He passed me a tin of peaches from an Argie ration pack, then someone shouted, 'Grenade,' and everyone threw themselves to the ground. There was a small 'crack' and we looked up to see white phosphorus falling a few metres from us. A lad was rolling and crawling towards us in frantic haste. He had turned over the body of an Argie and released a lethal booby-trap. He escaped by a hair's breadth. The white phos' landed at his feet, pushing him clear. Deadly stuff, it eats through anything and breathes on oxygen.

We all scattered from the area. Rick and I ran up towards the first clearing, still back-tracking my earlier route. The hand-to-hand fighting was virtually stopped. It was a case of clearing bunkers and dealing with a few stubborn Argies.

I was fully alert now: the sights and actions of the last hour and a half of daylight had dramatically changed me. Today, I am still very much alert to fate. Fate and luck are life's lot. We all had narrow escapes. When you are so close to being killed, you have to switch off from the sights. The initial impact of killing someone, or just missing death, will send you either one way or the other: nuts or numb. Only in rare cases is it nuts. It is human nature to kill. We've been doing it for thousands of years and will carry on doing it. The main source of relief in this sort of situation is laughing and joking. Everyone becomes guilty of thinking, I'll be OK, but I reckon Joe Bloggs will get killed.

Ricky and I ran up to the small gap that Sergeant P had led us through. I squeezed through, followed closely by Ricky. Drained now of colour, the Argie lay as we had left him an hour and a half earlier. His face showed only shock. The blood on his chin and mouth was dark and dry. I stopped and knelt down by him, lifting his arm. He was already beginning to stiffen. I went through his pockets for ID, finding only a small picture of Mary and Jesus and a rosary. But inside his jacket there were two letters that looked as if they had been written by a child. His child? I'll never know. I pocketed the letters and picked up his weapon, which lay at my feet. On close inspection, I discovered that he had been wounded fighting, for his weapon had a stoppage. The half-fed round in the chamber had led to his death. What would have happened if he had cleared the stoppage? Perhaps one of our lads would have been lying there in his place. I might have felt sorry for him. I did in a way, when I thought of his last struggle to help himself, but he had died trying to kill one of us. He had lost his fight; tomorrow it could be me.

We left his body and came to the spot where we had spent most of the previous night, firing our GPMGs. Ricky asked why I had brought him this far back. I knelt by the bodies of Ginge and Westy. I couldn't bring myself to look at them. I simply went to their webbing and removed their water bottles and what food there was.

Ricky looked at me and said, 'You can't do that, they're our blokes.'

'Why fucking not?' I snapped at him. 'We're going to need everything we can get till they get supplies to us.'

Ricky looked at me. He was a big lad but he reluctantly agreed with me.

Once the water and food were in our pockets, we quickly turned away and ran back to our team. There was something eerie about my action and the spot where Ginge and Westy had died. I had just wanted to get out of there quickly. I sat beside Johnny and Tommo.

'Where the fuck did you get this, four water bottles and two chocolate porridges?'

'Ginge's,' I replied.

Johnny gave me a knowing look. 'Well, you're right. Let's have a brew.'

The OC called me over. 'Corporal B, go with Westry and find what you can of intelligence, OK?'

'Yes, sir.'

'Mind the bunkers – they are still hiding and rigging traps, OK?'

'Yes, sir.'

I called Ricky over and we went over the hill into the clearing where the bunkers lay, beneath intercrossing arcs of fire. Burning to one side of us as we came into the clearing was the body of an Argentine soldier. Phos' had reduced him to a blackened state. He was lying face down with his arms tucked under his face, his right leg flickering with dying flames. Beside him lay some cooking pots and ladles. Was he their cook? The body was off limits to us: the phos' was too deadly to touch even after two hours of burning and smouldering.

Looking to one side of what had been a bunker, I saw an arm and a head sticking out. The bunker had collapsed on top of a young soldier. Black and dark-red blood lay thick on his mouth. He looked about sixteen or seventeen.

Rick and I walked fully into the clearing. No other troops were about. The place looked as if a bomb had landed in the middle and killed everyone. I looked about me. It was more than obvious that this was where some of the hardest hand-to-hand fighting had taken place. Twisted bodies lay everywhere. Rick and I looked at each other open-mouthed. It was the most disgusting sight so far.

Two bodies lay on top of a ledge. They were our blokes. DS lay on his back with his SLR on top of him. Both arms were bent at the elbow and pointing up, the fingers half - clenched. We knelt beside him, removed his weapon and took his map case. I didn't want to look at his face but curiosity got the better of me. The face didn't look like his. It was drained of all colour. His eyes were closed but his mouth was half-open. Looking at your own guys dead is harder than you'd think. It moved me. I pulled his beret from his smock pocket and placed it over his face. Rick and I tied his face veil over and around his head. We both felt that no one should see Scotty like this.

Beside DS lay TG, 'Fester'. He was flat on his back but his legs were raised up on a rock. He looked like he was asleep. We moved his legs, placing them gently on the ground as if he was still alive. Then we walked away.

As we stood looking over the clearing, we couldn't help but smell the area. The smell of the whole mountain was disgusting. It was like cheesy socks mixed with mustard, or like a shithouse or a blocked drain. The smell not only got into our clothes but also into our skin. It was many months before it left me and it's another thing I'll never forget.

All around us was a looter's paradise. Weapons lay everywhere, in all shapes and sizes. Clothing spilled out from enemy kitbags. Food lay discarded as if a shop had just been raided. Medical supplies of morphine lay in a heap, and bloody bandages had been left in a sodden pile. And everywhere lay Argie bodies. Soon we were not walking, but stepping over corpses. About ten lay in a small clearing of about ten by ten metres. The smell of rot and decay came into my every breath. I've seen many films and read many books describing war and its spoils but it is not what it seems. Others might feel differently but I thought it was a con. There is no glory in killing.

Ricky went off to one side and shouted into a bunker to see if it was empty, as he hoped. The area had been silent, but, as we looked at each other across the clearing, 'boom, boom' came to our ears again. We looked at each other as if to say, Not again.

All over the mountain guys shouted, 'Incoming!'

I dived into a crater left by an earlier shell. Ricky dived into the opening of a bunker. The shells came in, landing all over the place – not the usual rolling barrage, but pot-shots all over. The whole battalion was under bombardment at the same time. A shell came in with a deadly scream and I buried my face in the freshly turned dirt of my hole as the air was sucked from around me. The shell came crashing down about fifteen metres away, in the clearing. Shrapnel whacked and twanged into the ground, rocks fell all about, and earth rained over me. Showers like this kept landing on us for about half an hour or so. All this time, no one moved. The sound of shelling from Stanley told us it hadn't finished.

They eventually died out, with just the odd shell landing here or there. I stood up and stretched myself. My whole body ached. I felt damp and broken.

Ricky came out grinning. 'Thought you'd got it when the

last one came in. Fucking bastards, aren't they? You'd think they'd come and counter-attack.'

'Yeah,' I replied, 'they certainly know how to put HE on yer.'

As I walked towards a bunker, I suddenly heard voices coming from it, speaking in Spanish. I pulled out my grenades and stepped to one side of the entrance. Bending over, I peeped inside. In each hand, I held a grenade, my forefingers on the pins. I knelt in the entrance, then crawled in a little way. To my surprise, I had found the communications bunker. This was enough for me to decide it wasn't for me, but a heavy discovery for Intelligence. On one side of the bunker lay three or four stack radios about half a metre square, their red lights blinking on and off. Handsets lay on the ground, frantic Spanish voices coming from them. From a mountain of paperwork I picked up a few sheets. They were covered with figures and codes.

As I crawled back into the open I looked to my right, to where I had last seen Ricky. I was about to call him over but came face to face with an enemy soldier peeping out of a bunker that I had not noticed. His eyes opened wide with fright, and so did mine. For a few vital seconds, we stared at each other. If he had had a pistol and had wanted to kill me, he could have, for he must have seen me first. I felt vulnerable. I jumped up with my rifle and ran at him screaming. My bayonet struck the entrance of his bunker as he quickly retreated inside. I pulled out a grenade, removed the pin and was about to throw it in when a pistol and rifle fell at my feet. I looked down at the weapons: surrender or ploy?

Ricky and Sergeant Chris Howard came over the crest

when they heard me scream. Seeing my grenade primed and ready, they immediately grasped my intentions. My rifle now lay against the side of the bunker. Ricky took up a position behind a rock, to cover me, and Chris pulled out his own grenade and removed the pin.

As we stood on either side of the entrance ready to blow them out, a hand waving a bloody bandage appeared. Ricky shouted to us that the Argie was coming out. It was now too late to throw in our grenades. The young soldier looked up at us standing over him. Chris quickly replaced the pin and grabbed him by the collar. Pulling him out and throwing him to the ground, he screamed at him to stay where he lay and backed it up by booting him in the face. I replaced my pin and lowered my head, looking into the bunker. The Argentinean pointed at the bunker and screamed, 'My friend, my friend.'

I leaned into the entrance and shouted, 'Out, out.'

Common sense overcame the language problem. I heard a small scuffle inside and picked up the Argie's discarded pistol to fire a shot into the bunker. He started yelling and this time a pair of legs appeared as a second soldier made his way out. Chris and I grabbed a leg each and ripped him from the bunker. He lay on his back looking and blinking wildly at the daylight. I kicked him in the ribs, motioning him to turn on to his front. He did this quickly. I put his arms and hands behind his head. Ricky joined us. He came up close to the first Argie's head and the soldier covered it with his arms. Chris said that the prisoners were mine to deal with and that he would search the remaining bunkers.

Ricky stood covering me while I pulled the first soldier to his feet. Now and again, we looked into each other's face.

Thankfully, I was the victor. I motioned to him to empty his pockets and he promptly obeyed. We were standing very close to each other. I stopped him and said, 'Do you speak English?'

He looked at me with uncertain eyes.

'English?' I repeated.

He shook his head and then placed his thumb and forefinger together, miming 'a little'.

'Regiment, name?' I asked.

'Seven, I'm Costa.'

'Well, I'm Vince.' I pointed to myself.

'Wince?'

'Forget it,' I said.

I picked up his papers and ID. In a wallet, I found a picture of his family and two letters. I glanced at them. My wallet contained shots of my family too. Some Spanish money fell to the ground. He picked it up and handed it to me. I put it back in his wallet but he handed me his watch and pointed at the money, motioning for me to take it. I looked at him closely. His eyes were watering and he began to cry. 'You take please; you take please,' he insisted.

I pushed his watch and wallet back into his top pocket. His rosary was hanging around his left hand; he had been praying. He looked about seventeen or eighteen. He was crying hard now and shaking. Did he think I still might kill him, or was he crying with relief that his war was now over?

His friend turned to look up at us. Ricky stamped on his head. The first soldier was sniffling but trying hard to control himself. I wanted to tell him that it was OK but I couldn't, for it would have shown weakness on my part. I

187

felt for him, but my exterior had to remain controlled. I looked down at his leg. There was a wound where a single bullet had gone straight through. It was roughly bandaged up. I pointed to the ground and he became subdued. Just then, Lieutenant Oliver came over to us from a ledge. The Argentinean looked up at him and, as soon as he saw his officer's pips, began to shake and come towards me as if I was going to protect him.

'What's the matter with him?' asked the PC.

'Don't know, sir. He's been shaking and crying ever since we got him from his bunker.'

The prisoner looked at us. His face showed curiosity. Ricky stepped forward and started to chat with the PC about the capture. The young Argentinean suddenly stepped back from me, pointed to his leg wound and then pointed at Lieutenant Oliver and his pips, then back to his leg.

'Jesus Christ, I reckon his own officer shot him,' said Ricky.

Lieutenant Oliver regarded us seriously. 'No, couldn't be, could it?'

The youngster began to tremble and cry again. I got annoyed and shouted at him to shut up, which he did. I pushed him towards Ricky and we swapped soldiers. The second prisoner was solid, older in his eyes and looked less frightened. I dominated him throughout the search. His only belongings were letters from home.

Chris Howard reappeared with some guys from his platoon.

'Have you searched them?' he asked.

'Yeah, nothing of value,' I replied.

He turned to tell a guy to take the two prisoners to

battalion HQ, then walked away. The two Argentineans got up and were frog-marched below.

The PC gave me a mixed look.

'Don't worry, sir. I know you wouldn't shoot me,' I said with a grin.

'Bloody disgusting, if he was shot like that,' he said.

'Sir,' I said, 'I've found something. Perhaps Intelligence should come up and see this little beauty.'

I showed him the radio bunker.

'Fucking hell, the full works in there,' he said. 'Stay here. I'll go and get Sig and Int [Signals and Intelligence].'

He went off down and around the corner. I leaned against the side of the bunker with my rifle cradled in my arms, looking around me. I became aware now of more troops walking about and chatting as if on a Sunday stroll. At my feet lay a pile of letters. Flicking through them, I came across two photos of Argentinean troops posing by trucks in their own country. The letters and photos went into my pocket.

I felt a sweat coming over me. I took off my helmet to let my scalp breathe. My hair was greasy and wet with sweat. I looked down at my uniform. It was nearly black with dirt. I felt knackered but my head was buzzing with the excitement of the night and morning.

I glanced across the clearing at the twisted and mangled bodies. Flat on his back, by the bunker from which I had pulled the two Argentineans, lay the body of a third soldier. His head was completely missing. Bits of flesh and bone lay around him. Ricky stood looking down at the corpse. He covered the neck with a rag. I would have done the same, for it was a disgusting sight. Blood had soaked the soldier's whole uniform. What had removed his head, God alone knows.

Ricky came and sat down at my feet, leaning his head on his rifle. Neither of us spoke. We rested for a few brief moments, thinking our own thoughts. Then the OC and the CSM came back with the PC to examine the radio bunker. The OC peeked inside. Behind him was a signaller. The OC took a handset from him and spoke briefly on the net, asking for Intelligence to come up. He looked at me, grinned and said, 'Have you nicked anything from this bunker yet?'

'No, sir.'

'Good. Intelligence will have a field day in there.'

Ten minutes later, they arrived. The young officer smiled as he came up to us. He had a quick chat with the OC, then crawled into the bunker. We all tried at once to see what he was doing. The Spanish-made radio was still working, buzzing away with all sorts of messages. The young officer laughed as he listened. He popped his head out and said, 'They still think that this station is being held. They must think that perhaps the A Company position is still fighting. Anyway, leave this with me. We've already established that they had special forces up here last night. We reckon the snipers played in on that.'

I left them chatting and joined up with Ricky.

By now, the chain of command seemed disorganised. The CO had ordered the remains of B Company to battalion HQ at the base of the mountain. B Company had been so badly battered you could no longer call it a company. Its wounded accounted for 60 per cent of the total so far.

Our support teams filtered into the centre of a hill and took up defensive positions. The counter-attack still hadn't materialised, so we all now walked about looting bunkers and pulling out any Argie corpses that lay hidden. Wreckage covered the whole area: materials, weapons, military kit, spilled all over the hill. You couldn't walk two feet without finding something of interest. I now had my own pistol and time-lapse grenade and an FN automatic rifle over my shoulder to act as a back-up to my own.

I made my way to where we had run through the central bunker layout earlier that morning. The battle had ended some three hours before, but rifle fire could still be heard and prisoners were still being taken. Some Argies were still feebly fighting. No one could relax.

I bumped into TP and Tommo. They grabbed me by the smock and started to run with me. I guessed that they had found something. We ran up a small slope and there, right in the middle of a clump of rocks, was a point-fifty-calibre machine-gun. It was still facing our route of entry on to the mountain. Beside it lay a mountain of ammo, while behind it, lying on his side, was a dead Argentinean. I turned him over. His stiff body flopped on its back, revealing a single bullet hole in the forehead. I pulled the body to the side of the slope and pushed. It rolled two or three times, then stopped.

Tommo had loaded the machine-gun and TP had locked it on to Mount Tumbledown. The valley between us and Tumbledown, which was still held by the Argentineans, stretched for about two thousand metres.

'Hang on,' shouted TP, 'let me see the buggers first.' He scanned with his binos and started to giggle. 'Oh, yes, lovely. Take a peek.'

I looked through the binos, across the valley, and saw a bees' nest of enemy soldiers walking about the hill. A mass of bunkers lay in our sights. After Tommo had had a giggle too, TP took up the firing position. Tommo and I continued to look at the position. TP fired the machine-gun, which burst into a good thumping beat. The tracer rounds flew towards the enemy bunkers. Through our binos, we watched little figures scattering everywhere.

'Jesus, look at them go down,' Tommo screamed.

'Let me have a go,' I shouted.

We swapped places and I fired about one hundred rounds at their positions.

Down the line of Mount Longdon, from A Company's positions, another point-fifty calibre opened up at our targets. When we stopped firing, it was as if no one had ever been walking about the target area.

'That's given them something to talk about,' grinned Tommo. The machine-gun at A Company's position stopped minutes later. I stood up and walked away to find Ricky, so that he could see it all. A booming sound from Stanley erupted in the distance. From my position, I could now see the capital. We all jumped into a crag as the first shells began to fall in a rolling barrage.

I decided to have a snack and got out some compo biscuits. The shells rolled past us and fell up at A Company's position for about ten minutes before the shelling abruptly ended.

'Looks like they're saying "lay off",' shouted TP.

He was right. We decided to leave the machine-gun for now. I carried on eating. Funny how, concerned with eating, I didn't feel anything on that particular barrage. It was as if I didn't have a care in the world. I had got to the stage just then where I felt that if one had got me, so what?

I walked back to the clearing, where some of the lads

were still sitting. I had been gone about an hour. The OC sat relaxing in the sun.

Captain Mason called me over. 'Found anything yet?' he asked.

I grinned and dropped a bayonet covered in blood at his side. 'Well, sir, that's what it's like all over this fucking hill.'

I can remember him picking up the bayonet and wiping it, then he stuck it into the ground next to him. 'Well, thanks anyway,' he said.

I sat down by our GPMG, still guarded by Bob. 'Why don't you have a scan, Bob?' I said.

'Not really interested, Vince. I'm OK here dodging the shells.' He grinned.

The lads had returned in small groups and were resting. A few shells came over now and then but only one or two at a time – a comparatively light shelling, 'just to keep us on our toes', to quote our OC.

17

PERSONAL LOSSES

We had made a brew and Denzil Connick joined us. This Welsh nutter was one of the battalion characters who would laugh at anything, even the weather, which was the last thing on our minds.

Below the cliff line, a party of our lads were burying the 'battle-dead' Argies who had been centralised for this purpose. I tried to see more but Captain Mason shouted for Johnny and me to come over.

'Go to where you were last night: the ACC, Sergeant Pete Morrison [Mentioned in Dispatches], needs a hand with some body bags. Sorry, but you're the first to cross my sight line.'

Johnny and I made our way to where Ginge and Westy lay. I still hadn't looked at either of them; I had refused to make myself the last time I came here. Now I stood and looked down at Westy. His small five-feet-three frame lay as if he was asleep on his back. I couldn't see any marks to show how he died. Lying on his chest, just out of reach of his fingers, was a small greyish teddy bear with a little ribbon round its neck. Westy's face was turned to one side. His left leg was bent slightly at the knee. Jimmy looked down at him with more seriousness in his face than I'd ever seen.

'Oh, Jesus,' I said, 'who put that there?' I felt so utterly helpless, so sad.

'Not sure,' said Steve, 'but I think he had a sister or something who gave it to him before all this shit started.'

Had Westy pulled the mascot from his smock before the fatal shell, or after?

Jimmy tucked it back in his smock again. 'What a fucking game this is,' he said.

Pete Morrison joined us. This guy was excellent. He had been up and down the objective throughout, collecting dead and wounded alike. 'Thank God I've help with these three. I'm fucked, you know.' He held three grey poly bags. He threw them down and went over to a body. 'Right, come on, help me,' Pete said.

We all stood still. No one moved a muscle.

He looked up at us. 'Someone has to do it, lads. Let's get them down the bottom a.s.a.p., yeah?'

I knelt on one side of the body. 'Look, Peter, we're not wanting this, not our guys,' I said.

'Yeah,' said Jim, 'we'll help but, Jesus, this is a fucking bastard.'

Johnny, Jimmy Morham, Steve Wake and I laid out the grey bag and unzipped it ready. A green Argie blanket lay over the body. Steve slowly pulled the blanket off him from the bottom, revealing the wound that had killed him. I grabbed the blanket in frantic haste.

'What's up?' asked Jim.

'Nothing. Let's just put him in with the blanket, OK?'

Everyone got the hint. Johnny and I pulled the body towards us while the bag was slid under him. When it was tucked under him, we gently laid him on to the bag. We then had to push him the other way. As we did this, my hand slipped into the wound. I felt sick at the feeling. I wanted to get up quickly and walk way, to hide somewhere, but I couldn't. I pulled my hand out and wiped it on the grass quickly, the lads looked at me. No one spoke. No one had to; my embarrassment was shared. The bag was zipped up and we took hold of the corner grips. Pete and another lad went over to Westy, while we carried the body down the hill.

The walk was rough and longer than we thought, a steep descent. We stopped two or three times to change hands. We reached the bottom and saw the padre with some of the wounded who were still awaiting evacuation. They lay in groups with medics going among them.

We put down our bag with the rest. The pile was mounting. Among the bodies were Johnny Crow, Sergeant Ian McKay and Corporal Stewart McLaughlin. I didn't know that McLaughlin had died until that moment. The name tags boldly showed who was dead.

A few guys sat to one side, looking up at us as we laid the body down. My eyes met those of the medic from our field ambulance, Jock. He looked so different. He looked as if he had been weeping; his eyes were wide and staring. We grinned at each other.

'Jock, is that you?'

'Yeah, why?'

'You look fucked.'

'To be honest, Vince, you look bloody awful too. I wasn't sure it was you at first.'

I sat beside him, holding my rifle across my legs. I got out a packet of Rolos. 'Here, have some,' I said. 'What's it been like for you down here then?'

'Let's put it this way: I've done all the training possible for this and it still hasn't been what I thought. It's fucking shitty, Vince.'

'Yeah, it's like that up there too.'

Looking at me again, he said, 'Hope tomorrow never comes.'

Our little chat was abruptly halted, as two or three more wounded were brought down. They were A Company men, Artillery. One lad on a stretcher held his leg, screaming. Jock jumped up and shouted to me, 'Here we go again, Vince.'

I ran with him; there was nothing else I could do. Jock pulled down the wounded guy's trousers and half-stuffed, half-pushed a plasma syringe up his rectum. He injected morphine and mustered bandages to the wound, all within seconds of the lad's arrival. The soldier looked up at us all, his wide, frantic eyes staring with fright and concern.

Jock patted him and said, 'You'll be OK.'

I got up and went away. I wasn't any use to them there: the organisation was brilliant.

I walked up the hill through B Company's rest area. I passed the remains of the company, a small group of worn-out troops lying against rocks on the ground. Everyone I saw had strain in his eyes, almost as if they were on a different planet. Taff Goring stood watching me tramp up the short slope again. His face made a picture I'll never forget. His whole face was sunken and his hollow eyes told a story in themselves. I felt for him and the lads sitting around him.

'Hi, Vince,' he said, 'how's it going?'

'The pits,' I said.

We agreed what a shitty game it was.

With Johnny, I crossed over towards our night position. We climbed through the shitpit. Human excrement lay everywhere. The smell was unbelievable. It seemed to lie in every corner. The smell even drifted with us, as if it was chasing us.

When we reached the previous night's gun position, Johnny and I stood on the spent bullet cases and looked at my target arc. It was huge. This side of the mountain was completely open to my right. Only a small clump of rocks here and there obscured a total view of Mount Tumbledown. Halfway along the smooth side of a hill lay a one-hundred-and-six-millimetre recoilless rifle, similar to a Wombat. Was that the weapon that had nearly killed me? Further on, through A Company's position, lay Stanley. With my binos, I watched Argentinean trucks coming and going through Moody Brook, the old Marine barracks.

To my right, Tumbledown buzzed with activity. Argie troops walked about, going from one bunker to another. It was only a matter of time until that battle would begin. Our troops were in twos and threes, still searching and collecting military souvenirs. Johnny nudged me and I looked in the direction he was facing. Sitting behind a small rock were three or four soldiers, Guardsmen, I think, with high-powered binos and a map, busily noting down Tumbledown's enemy positions.

'Well, Johnny, tonight or tomorrow, what do you reckon?' I said.

'Tonight, Vince.'

We turned around to where Ginge had lain, and walked back from the skyline to find the gap through which Sergeant P had led us. In this way, we avoided being seen from Tumbledown. On the ground, I saw bits of clothing and flesh. Everywhere resembled a slaughteryard. We walked down ten metres or so and there was more and more. Stuck on the side of a rock was what was clearly a large piece. Johnny and I moved closer to it and my stomach churned as I saw the nose and cheek of a face. We looked at each other, our eyes wide. I put my bayonet under the flesh and flicked it into the ground, before burying it quickly. Neither of us spoke. I had no doubts, and Pete M confirmed to me, that this was the remains of a mate. Pete told me later that he had died instantly, for only the waist down remained. I felt gutted beyond belief. I had been told of the direct hit that had also killed two others. To see with my own eyes the body and remains was another story.

Walking over a crest, we bumped into Pat Harley. With him were one or two others, though I no longer remember who they were. As I was talking to Pat, I noticed a helmet on the end of an SLR planted in the rock face. Nodding towards this, Pat mentioned that he had come up and found Geordie Lang dead. We rounded the rock face and at our feet lay Doc and Geordie, both on their backs. They had died in an open space with the infamous Tumbledown looking down on them. Geordie had died trying to save Doc. The bastard sniper had caught him in the open as he reached him.

Geordie lay with his mouth slightly open. Gunshot wounds to his chest and stomach meant he had died quickly. Evidence around him showed that he had tried to reach Doc. Had he been calling for help himself? Pat, looking cut up, took Geordie's fags, saying, 'He'd want one of us to have them rather than the rear echelon.'

We turned our attention to Doc, who was more depressing. DM hadn't died quickly. He must, in fact, have been fully aware of his injuries. The top part of his skull was blown away, the brain visible, smashed by a sniper's bullet. Only the fragmented skull had prevented the complete collapse of the side of his head. How he survived the impact God knows. Lying beside him were items from the first aid kit he had been carrying: a field dressing half-open, safety pins at his right-hand fingers near the ground. His left hand held a morphine syringe. This had been used; the thin needle pointed towards him. It must have been his dying act. His radio mike was still attached to his throat. A close friend told me many months later, 'DM fell on his radio. The sending switch was stuck and he was on permanent "send" to all of us. We could hear him gurgling and moaning as he became aware that he had been shot badly. Vince, it sent the signallers nuts, but we were all helpless. The sniper picked at anyone that moved. Geordie tried and lost his life for it. We eventually had to turn to the emergency frequency to establish communications again.'

DM had remained conscious and eventually died on a part of that mountain alone with a lad who had bravely tried to rescue him. The sniper had coldly killed with the aid of a superb head-mounted night sight. He had killed at the slightest movement.

We stepped back with the others as the medics arrived. Our ACC bearers joined us. We watched them carefully place the bodies of two good friends into grey body bags.

The zipping up of the bags took from our sight two heroes who had died for two different reasons, for the principles that had brought us there in the first place. One died advancing on the enemy, the other died trying to save the life of his friend. As the bodies were carried away, the only evidence of their deaths was their weapons sticking into the ground.

Standing back to regain cover, I turned for the last time to look at their rifles crowned by their helmets, the traditional way of marking the spot where a soldier had died. In the distance lay Stanley in full view. The sun was above me. As I looked, I couldn't help but think, They died so near yet so far.

Back at the base clearing, the OC came around encouraging everyone sitting there. The strain showed on everyone's face. The dead lay about us and the smell reminded us all that this was hell itself. Quietly, the OC gave orders for all to spread out and take up defensive positions for the night. Burial parties were busy dragging Argie corpses, either by their legs or by their jackets, through the clearing to a patch being dug by some A Company lads. The bodies went into a makeshift grave; the enemy piled up in full view for everyone to see. A group of Argentinean prisoners helped with the digging and burial, alongside our guys. The Argies wept openly at the sight of their comrades' bodies. One cradled the head of what must have been his friend. A lad from A Company gently tapped his shoulder to remind him that the body had to be buried. He cried out loudly, 'Mama, Mama.' Was that corpse his brother?

We sat watching without pity, without feeling at all. We

were all old men, hard old men with no feelings. Two lads pulled the weeping Argies away while the bodies were dropped and flopped into the shallow grave. Dirt buried the corpses and hid away their deaths for good. The prisoners were led past us back to battalion HQ.

As I write now, feelings do come into it but during war you have to stop registering what you see. You have to laugh about it or play with it, because if you take it seriously you can come up against a barrier that is enough to send you nuts. Do I feel for the enemy now? Only as a soldier at arms, wrapped up in a conflict in which I had to fight. I feel for the Argies who lost their friends. I lost mates. We became united in loss. What a sad pity that politics failed in this case, otherwise we might only have fought verbally across a football pitch. Perhaps men will always want to kill each other.

The OC broke up our background activity – 'Come on, lads, move about now. Get shifted – the shells are still about you; plus we have only one or two hours of light left.'

We shifted our kit and made for some empty bunkers on the side of the hill. Intelligence had it that the attack from the Argies would be coming from the open left side, not the Tumbledown side.

Walking up a small slope with all my kit and hundreds of pounds of linked Argie ammo, I couldn't help but think to myself, Here we go again. Orders for a counter-attack now. Jesus Christ, not again.

The counter-attack was imminent. Johnny and I found a small alcove. It was only big enough for one to squeeze into and Johnny grabbed it. Five metres further down was a well-hidden bunker. Steve Wake and Mal sat over it, guarding it as if it was their castle. After gentle persuasion, I was allowed to join them for tea, so to speak. Johnny and I had two mess tins of chocolate porridge and a big brew to follow.

The temperature seemed to have dropped further that day. The wind bit through us. Ricky came up to me moaning that not a single bergen had reached battalion HQ. I shouted to Johnny that we would collect as many blankets or sleeping bags as we wanted before nightfall. Ricky and I walked over the cliff line again. I thought that the empty bunkers would supply us with our needs.

As we crossed the clearing, a bullet smashed into the rock beside me, less than a metre away. I dropped to the ground, and so did Ricky.

'Where the fuck did that come from, Rick?' I screamed.

'Christ knows.'

We were lying in a small clearing with no view at all. I crawled to a rock and stood up, pointing my rifle in the direction the bullet had come from. Nothing. Rick joined me. Gingerly, I poked my head around the rock face into the clearing. Still nothing. There was a gap of not much more than a metre before it met another rock face. In between the rocks, in the gap, rifles and ammo boxes lay abandoned.

'What do you reckon, Rick? Shall we dash across and see if the bastard fires again?'

'Why not, huh? You first; and I'll scan the area.'

I looked at him thinking, You bastard, but the guy who was shooting had the area well in his sights. 'Right, here goes.'

I ran across the small gap. As a bullet twanged against the rocks above my head, I fell against the rock face.

'See him?' I screamed.

'No, all I see is Tumbledown.'

'Well, it's your turn now.'

He looked at me, grinning, obviously thinking the same as I had. He ran across the clearing but this time the bullet seemed later than the one before as it hit the rocks.

'It's got to be a sniper on Tumbledown, Rick,' I said, 'you're right. Look, go back to Johnny's position and get my GPMG and Bob Geddis's up here.'

He went off. I looked across the valley. Someone over there was watching and waiting for me. The deadly game began.

Johnny came up with Rick. After a quick brief with Johnny, we decided to move to a better position. We ran across the gap together with our heads tucked down. Whack – another bullet hit the rocks. I placed the GPMG between two rocks on the ground. I raised the sights to the max and fired in one long indiscriminate spray at the area where we thought the sniper might be. About one hundred rounds were through the gun before I stopped. Nothing was returned.

Behind us lay three or four bunkers. We grabbed blankets and sleeping bags and found our positions for the night. I sat on my own thinking, Was it really necessary to play with the sniper? Was it really worth it?

I hadn't felt anything at all when firing at the sniper. I certainly hadn't hit him, because I didn't know his exact position. The whole episode wasn't worth it, but many things seem different when you do them rather than think about them.

The Two Sisters had had a shelling from us the previous night. We had a brew and waited, linked enemy ammo lying by our gun, to see if the Argies would counter-attack tonight. We sorted out the stag list with Sas, Steve Ratchford and Clive (the company clerk with our bunker). We had the first seven hours of the night: two hours twenty minutes each.

As I stood or sat by the gun during the night, my only view was of utter darkness, as clouds had completely enveloped us. I was going nuts listening to every noise, every movement. All I could hear clearly was Steve Wake's snoring from the bunker; twice I had to push him to break his breathing pattern. I didn't think of home, victory or anything; my mind was totally wide open to survival, and falling asleep now could kill me.

No one moved that night. The battalion stayed put in their little corners, sleeping or guarding, waiting for the counter-attack. On my shift, I spent more time looking behind me than facing the vast empty space across my arc. Behind me was the very edge of where the battalion had surprised an attack the night before. Surely the enemy had more opportunity to attack from Tumbledown than from the open area in front of me? It didn't make sense to me to guard a suicidal route but I could only follow orders and the Intelligence reports.

Even after changing positions and crawling into my sleeping bag, I couldn't sleep. The Argentinean blankets smelled, and the bag stank like shit. The whole night was a blank, waiting for daylight. The only noises to keep us awake were those of war. The odd shell would crash on to the hill in the night and the ground would shake suddenly with the explosion. Then silence would abruptly return.

The morning of 13 June was cold and wet. The snow had fallen. I crawled from my cramped bunker and stretched my sore limbs. The view across the valley revealed nothing but white snow with blades of grass sticking out of it. As the sun rose, the snow began to melt, but the cold wind remained. It was an ordeal to wake up, move about and motivate myself. I looked up at Johnny sitting on his stinking bag. We sat together and made a brew with the last of the water. Within an hour of daylight, the snow had gone but not the shelling.

'The booming from Stanley was our alarm clock,' Johnny said later.

Shells came in thick and fast, with a vengeance. We crawled into our bunkers again. We listened to dirt, shrapnel and bits of rock thumping into the overhead protection of our bunker. We sat in silence, grinning at the shells as they landed near us, as if to reassure ourselves that if one went we all did. Everyone had gone to ground; no one moved out into the open.

The shelling had become part of our routine – not in the sense that we could get used to it, but in that very important lessons had been learned within the first few hours of the previous day's shelling. The artillery opening up in Stanley had a distinct tone to it. Obviously, the booming from Stanley told us that shelling would arrive, but where? Enemy shells could certainly reach us or other objectives now in our hands. The shell's flight was the telltale sign. Within seconds of the boom, the air space over the mountain would feel as if it was evaporating, and air would start to rush around the hill, telling us unmistakably that Mount Longdon was about to be hit. The scream announcing the shell's imminent arrival was produced by suction. This would grow louder in the last two or three seconds of the shell's deadly flight and that was all the time we had to get down. That loud screaming meant that the shell would land within six to ten metres of us. Some say that the shell you don't hear is the shell that will get you. This may well be true, for I never heard the three shells that nearly claimed my life.

The shelling stopped after about an hour. I lost count of the numbers. What did it matter anyway? One shell or a hundred, they still came.

I crawled from the bunker and the smell of freshly disturbed earth and cordite hit my nose. I sat on my webbing looking at the view across the valley. A shell screamed in over my head so fast and unexpected that I didn't have time to hit the ground; the shell and I landed together as it exploded. I jumped up as the dirt settled, looking down the small slope to see where Steve Ratchford, Sas and Clive were gathered. I saw smoke drifting from where the shell had landed; it looked as though a fire had just gone out there. It wasn't fifteen metres from the others' position and I screamed out, 'Steve, Steve.'

Nothing. I turned to Johnny, who stood by my shoulder. His eyes met mine, and we both feared the worst. My mind was frantic.

'Steve, Steve,' I screamed again.

Nothing. I ran down the small slope and around the little bank that had obscured my view. There, in a tight bundle, sat the three lads, staring straight ahead as if they were in a trance. Their faces told me of shock and anguish. They all slowly turned their heads as if my presence had disturbed their trance.

'Why didn't you answer me, you bastards, why?'

Sas smiled at me. Clive looked at me as if he were the village idiot who didn't understand. Steve put his hand to his ear and shouted as if I were a million miles away, 'What'd you say, Vince?'

I let my rifle butt hit the ground. They were all deaf, all in shock. There were clumps of fresh dirt around their feet. Johnny joined me. I was visibly mad with frustration, but it was mixed with relief that they were alive. I grinned and walked back up to the small bunker. I sat down and turned to Steve Wake. I hadn't spoken my first word when a shell screamed over our heads, in exactly the same route pattern as the one that had just landed. I had been about to ask Steve if he thought the shells were one-hundred-and-twenty mortars, because they seemed different in their flight signal. We all hit the ground again as the shell landed. No sooner had I started to pick myself up than a high-pitched scream rushed into my ears, a deadly sound. I can still hear it today. I looked down to where the shell had hit, in the same area as before. The ground was smouldering, smoke lifting and evaporating.

Five metres from the smouldering hole lay two bodies. The sight of one of them will stay with me till I die. His Para smock was riddled with smoke escaping from every corner, the arms, bottom, the collar. The lad turned on to his back, screaming, 'Oh, God, help me, help me, please.'

I ran down the hill in fright and concern. I dropped to my knees by the screaming soldier. His eyes met mine. Did he register me? I only saw Denzil, Denzil the character we all loved. I wrenched my eyes over to his legs: one was hanging off, ripped to shreds, the bone clearly visible. His screaming churned my stomach – it was like nothing I'd ever heard. He tried to look down at his leg.

'Don't fucking look this way,' I barked. 'Lie back now, hear me?'

He dropped on to his back, still holding his thigh.

Jonah Jones, a 9 Squadron lad, came to my side. 'Vince, I'll deal with him. You see to him,' he said, pointing to Craig.

Craig lay very close to Denzil. Clive rushed to help me. Craig hadn't any visible wounds. He lay quietly as Clive tried to talk to him. I tried to pull his smock open and pull his trousers down to check for a wound.

Denzil screamed and moaned behind me, 'Help me, help me.' Jonah was busy seeing to his leg.

I pulled out my knife and started to cut through Craig's denims and quilted Arctic clothing. My frantic cutting was too slow and I knew it. The doctor skidded in beside me, pulled out his scissors and started to cut through Craig's leggings. I pulled the ripped material to one side; we had reached the skin. His legs had massive lacerations in all directions, spilling muscle and bone, but there was hardly any blood. The doctor shouted at me to tie his muscles together. I pulled out my field dressing and tied the lacerations together. The doctor was joined by a medic who went to Denzil.

I was half-conscious of cries of 'Medic, medic, stretcher-bearer' all down the hill. Craig was lying still. I slid up beside him and looked into his face. It was pale, with no colour at all; his eyes stared into my face.

'You'll be OK, Craig, just hang on, mate, hang on.'

Clive held his head, stroking his forehead, repeating my words.

'Craig, can you hear me?' I shouted.

The doctor pulled and tugged frantically at Craig's clothing, trying to reach more obvious wounds.

'Craig, you'll be OK, hang on.'

He looked at me and a slight smile came across his face, his eyes laughed at me, bright and wild. His grin spread, then all expression faded. He faded away.

'Craig, Craig, don't, keep in there.'

His eyes closed. He died then and there. He was a young soldier, twenty years of age. The records will say, Private CJ. The doctor motioned a bearer to get him on and away. Denzil was also lifted and carried away. I fell on to my bottom. Jonah and Clive patted me on the shoulder. I tried to get up but fell to my knees again. I hadn't realised until then that I was crying, crying without knowing it. I cried with all the pain and sadness. It didn't seem fair.

Johnny came to my side and picked me up. He picked up my weapon and started to guide me to our bunker again. I glanced at Steve and Sas. Sas was crying as well, and Steve had buried his face in his hands. I stumbled up to our bunker, weeping. When I sat down, Steve Wake put his arm around me and whispered, 'You done a brave thing, Vince. I couldn't have gone down there after two shells landed in the same spot. You done all right, mate.'

His gesture didn't register. I cried with exhaustion, hatred and pity. Craig and Denzil remain with me today, Craig who died and Denzil who lost a leg, and so nearly his life.

When people write or tell of experiences of this kind, I know now that they can never really tell the facts for anyone to totally understand, for often the reader is wrapped in his own make-believe game of war. For me personally, this five-minute experience changed my whole life and attitude towards war. Wars will always be fought and I would go again for my beliefs, but I hope never ever again to see a face fade from me. It took nearly a year after

this war for Craig's face to go before I slept, nearly a year
to wipe out Denzil's smock on fire and his scream. Until I
die, it will remain a part of me.

18

'DON'T GET BITTER'

Johnny made a brew and passed me a fag. I looked at it and I giggled. Why not? I thought. Life's short as it is.

That cigarette helped to take my mind from the incidents of the morning.

'You know, Johnny, I'm finished. I'd kill the fucking lot of them now when we reach Stanley.'

'Don't get bitter, Vince, people never accept that, you know.'

I looked up at him and grinned. He was right, perfectly right. Those simple words have remained with me till today, but the frustration remains as well. After all, bitterness is a sign of defeat, whether you win or lose.

Tommo arrived to tell us that Johnny and I, with him, had to go up to A Company's positions for a rocce. 'Looks like the big push tonight, so rumour has it,' grinned Tommo. 'We'll be moving in thirty minutes. Meet by the OC's position. SLRs and mags only, he says – no need for webbing, OK?'

A small group congregated by the OC's position. Standing with weapons and spare mags in abundance, we awaited his instructions. The group was about ten-strong and consisted mainly of detached commanders. Captain Mason was to lead.

The OC called us together for a quick brief. 'I'm not going to keep you long. These artillery shells are active again. You are to recce Wireless Ridge for 2 Para's attack tonight. We will be supporting them with SF, Milan and mortar throughout. You will all keep to this side of Longdon as the Argies are watching every move, from Tumbledown. That is also going to get a shock tonight, from the Guards. You are to note every bunker and position on Wireless Ridge, so you can lock on to them with ease tonight. See you all later.' Captain Mason added that we were to keep evened out because of the enemy artillery.

Johnny, Tommo and the PC were in front of me as we set off climbing through the sharp crags on the north side of Longdon. We passed the wreckage of battle along the whole of the mountain. The Argentinean bodies that still hadn't been visited by our burial parties lay stinking and rotting. Weapons and military equipment lay discarded, evidence of the enemy's flight. Climbing through a small crack one after the other, we gradually made our way into A Company's position. I was surprised that they were so far away from us, about two or three hundred metres. Being near the end of the small party, I was only concerned with watching where I stepped. The muddy slopes made progress awkward. I passed the body of an Argentinean. He lay on his side, rigid as cardboard. The whole side of him that I could see was burned nearly to the bone, his fingers half-clenched in a fist. I looked at his face. His ear was missing, and blood had congealed into a thick, dark mass.

We broke into a small open patch where we gathered for a short rest. A few A Company lads were leaning against the rock, grinning. They just nodded at our party; eye-talk was the only expression needed.

Captain M set off in the lead again. We all kept a little closer now that we were nearing our objective. Stirred by excitement, I only hoped that we would get a closer look at Wireless Ridge and the enemy. We were now well into A Company's position. Their lads gave catcalls and shouted after their mates in B Company, 'Has anyone seen Taffy or Smudge?' and the like.

Brief messages were passed. Our party was spread across some twenty metres when the booming came from Stanley. The boys from A Company disappeared like ferrets into bunkers or small holes.

'Incoming, incoming,' shouted a sergeant as he vanished into his hole.

A rush of air told us we were about to be hit. The party ran for cover wherever they could find it, but we had been caught well out in the open and this was A Company's home, not ours. The scream of the shells deafened me. I spotted a small crater to my right, definitely a shell hole. The air around me had disappeared and the impact was one or two seconds away as I dived in. Two shells landed behind me, about twenty metres away.

Two more shells rolled past us in the direction of our own position. Tommo shouted something. I stood up, only to see everyone diving to the ground again. I hadn't heard the scream of the second salvo. I threw myself into my hole

215

again, curling up like a hedgehog. All I remember next is an earthquake around me. The explosion was so loud I thought my eardrums must have burst. Shrapnel peppered the rocks above me and sprayed the edge of my hole, sizzling on the ground as the lethal, red-hot pieces of metal burned out. I was beyond help. I froze in complete fright, too scared to move in that split second of the shell's impact. Earth showered all over me with such force that I thought I would be buried alive. My ears popped as it landed on my head, face and neck.

'Vince, Vince,' came a whisper.

I wanted to jump up and answer but I had frozen.

'Vince, Vince,' it got louder.

I raised my head and looked over the edge of the small hole that had saved my life. I saw Tommo and Johnny running towards me. As my head popped up, their running slowed to a happy trot. I was on all fours, still holding my rifle. I pushed myself up, the dirt falling from me as if a shovelful had been thrown over me.

'Fucking hell,' Tommo ranted, 'you scared the fucking life out of me. Don't do this to me.'

'What? I haven't done anything.'

I was still in a daze, as Tommo pointed to a smoking hole next to mine five or six metres away, the freshly upturned earth making a crater about the size of a double bed.

'That's what I call a lucky bastard,' grinned Johnny.

Captain Mason and the rest stood at the rear looking on. Once Mason was satisfied that all was OK, we continued on the last thirty metres of our journey. My head was buzzing and spinning. There was dirt in my ears. I recovered quickly but my mind couldn't register the thought of how near I'd been to death.

A second salvo screamed over us as we reached the observation post. Captain Mason turned to us as we grouped up for our recce.

'You'd think they'd seen us arriving, with all these shells lately, wouldn't you?' Sergeant 'Spunky' agreed.

We split into groups, by machine-guns, and started noting the views in front of us. To my right, just over a small group of rocks, lay Tumbledown. I nodded to Tommo that I was going to look at Moody Brook and Tumbledown. As I crawled up beside Spunky, who was also scanning the view, a shout from behind alerted us all to more shells. Three or four screamed over us and landed smack in the middle of A Company. We pushed ourselves up into our positions again.

'Sergeant, Sergeant, I can see them. Over here, quickly.'

We all turned our heads to see an A Company sergeant running up to a young private from A Company, who pointed to a batch of rocks about five hundred metres in front of us. We saw clearly five or six heads bobbing up and down behind the rocks.

Captain Mason crawled in beside us. 'What's up?'

'Don't know, sir. I couldn't say.'

The sergeant shouted for a GPMG to be brought to him. A young gunner ran across the open patch of A Company's position to join them. Lieutenant Oliver shouted for information.

'It's their fucking FOO position. We've been after these bastards all morning.'

Apparently, this was the position that spotted and radioed to Stanley to bring the shells on to us. How long they had been there, no one knew. It could have been since the fall of Longdon or they could have moved into that position during the night.

Spunky and I brought our SLR rifles into aim. I flicked my sights up and on to max range. A burst from the GPMG saw the tracer rounds bounce and hit the area in question. I waited for a moment and a head appeared almost at once. The rifle jerked into my shoulder as I quickly fired two shots. Spunky fired a single shot. Nothing. The GPMG stopped and we all waited again. The seconds seemed like hours. A helmet appeared on the other side of the rocks and we all opened up together, Spunky, me and the GPMG. Bullets crashed into the rocks at the target, tracer rounds bounced into the air. Still nothing. Had we hit them?

Captain Mason shouted for us to stop. 'Come on, let's do what we came here for. I don't want to get into a full firefight.'

I looked at him, then crawled back to Tommo.

'Personally, Vince, I would leave you there. You would get some of this frustration out of yer,' he said, with a grin.

Spunky remained, after telling the captain that as far as he was concerned as long as they had their heads firmly down then they couldn't see what DF to use on us. However, I'd had my little shoot. I now had to prepare my gun position for that night. The shooting continued while we scanned Wireless Ridge. No more shells landed all the while the FOO position was being shot at. Who had been right?

I lay next to Tommo and Johnny. We scanned and searched the ridge through our binos. I could clearly see Argentineans walking about, bunker to bunker. They stood around in groups of two to five, chatting as if standing in the street. I heard Captain Mason say to an officer with our party, 'What's good for them is good for us, yeah?'

The officer grinned, 'Yeah.' He picked up his handset and said a few words.

'Look in, boys, the show's on.'

Booming came from behind us, artillery and mortars that told us the Argies were in for a bang or two. The shells began to land around them. Watching through my binos, it was like witnessing the start of a hundred-metre race, only the participants ran in different directions. We giggled loudly. The small barrage lasted seconds, but it was enough to completely disperse all the Argies who had been walking about.

We noted down all the bunkers in sight, including a group much further back that we had missed at first. We lay there for well over two hours, noting every move the enemy made, every bunker, gun and depth. All groups finished and packed up on receiving Captain Mason's order to move. The PC grinned at Tommo.

'What's with you two?' I said.

'Isn't it great without the platoon sergeant up there flapping about?' grinned the PC.

The joke was unexpected. I hadn't even thought of him until then.

'Don't spoil my day,' I said. 'I was quite happy being shelled until you mentioned that name.'

The journey back was uneventful. As we passed the gunner who was firing at the Argentinean FOO party, he grinned and said, 'All quiet on the Western Front now, isn't it?' My thoughts exactly.

Having passed through the crags and over the littered battlefield, we were back into our positions after three or four hours. We gave the OC all our information. As we made for our bunkers, I crawled up a bank and bumped into the RSM and CO, who were on their way to meet the OC for information.

'Ha, Corporal B, how are you?' asked the RSM.

'Fine, sir. You?'

'OK. So is your pal Connick, so don't worry.'

They both smiled and walked off. This news of Denzil made us all happy. They had made the gesture for reasons of morale as well.

Water supplies and more rations reached us. In our mess tins Johnny and I cooked the biggest, most disgusting pile of food ever thought of.

'What does it matter what it tastes like? The next shell might have our names on it,' said Johnny.

I grinned at this. As I took a mouthful of food, I noticed four black dots coming towards us from the north. My wooden spoon was half in my mouth as I murmured, 'Johnny, what the fuck is …' My words were cut short as four Argentinean jets screamed right over our heads, faster than sound.

My sighting of them and their passing had taken two or three seconds. The roar and crack as they went by was a shock. 'Jesus, those bastards are still trying it on,' screamed Johnny, as they flew over beyond Mount Longdon towards Tumbledown and further.

'Got to hand it to them: they really don't know when to give in, those pilots. Pity the troops don't behave the same way,' laughed Johnny.

We had seen the underwing colours of Argentina clearly. The pilot in one jet had seemed to be looking straight at us, he was so low. I wondered if he really had seen us. It never ceased to amaze me how their pilots managed to hit and run as they did.

Tommo came running up the slope. 'Quickly, get to your

positions, the Argies are going to counter-attack,' he shouted.

'What?' shouted Johnny.

'OC said Intelligence has seen choppers being loaded with troops and taking off in this direction.'

We left our slopes and our mess tins and grabbed our rifles. I slid in beside the machine-gun. Bob came running up to join me. We quickly loaded an extension on the existing belt of ammo. All over the mountain, the Paras got firmly into the crags, weapons pointing north again. We were expecting them to land in the open ground, Christ knows why; to me, it still seems suicidal, particularly in daylight. We waited and waited. About half an hour passed before the shout came through our positions that the enemy had decided to reinforce an area rather than counter-attack.

Mixed feelings had run through me while waiting. My frustration wanted to fight, but my fear said, 'Not again, please.' The incident passed quickly. The battalion went about its routine defence and the jets went on to attack brigade HQ. It seems they knew exactly where to aim, for they bombed it in a series of runs. It was only luck that no one was killed. The pilots managed to hit the command tent. By a miracle, no one was occupying it at the time of the strike.

As last light faded, I did whatever I could to stop thinking about the coming night's battle. I wasn't involved in the Wireless Ridge operation to the extent that I would be with a big target. I was, with all the others, part of the support teams to be used only if needed.

We gathered round the OC in the last flickers of light. It seemed a far cry from the last gathering we had had, around the model of Longdon, back at Estancia. Cammed up, wrapped up, weapons oiled, hundreds of rounds of ammo wrapped around our bodies, we stood feeling the weight of something we had become used to.

19

PARA SUPPORT

The OC and CSM stood side by side, waiting, as we pushed into a small semicircle.

'Gents,' said the OC, 'I cannot take too long on this, due to the shelling. You know what we're doing tonight from your recces this afternoon. Now all I've got to say is, we will not fire on to the Ridge's flank unless 2 Para ask us. They are also fully aware that we will be in a very, very vulnerable spot. From where we will set up our support lines, we will be in the open in every meaning of the word. I have no doubts about this whatsoever, but, if we do open up, well I'm afraid a lot of us will not be coming back to this position after 2 Para's attack. That is how vulnerable we will be. Two Para has assured me that if they are in need then we will come into use, OK?'

'Sir, I would hope 2 Para do use us if needed – it's only right,' said a sergeant from the Milan team.

'Glad to see we know the score,' grinned the OC.

We all grinned. The OC's words didn't worry me at all. I agreed with the sergeant as well. We all felt 2 Para had done a great deal since arriving. This was their second battle. We all felt jealous that we couldn't mount a joint attack.

The OC went on. 'Now for the biggest crunch.'

We all looked at him, wondering what was in store.

'C Company is at this moment getting orders for the attack on Moody Brook and on the pumphouse, finally ending on the racecourse, where eventually a series of assaults and pushes from both brigades will start the big push into Stanley itself.'

All went quiet. I remember thinking, If we end up in Stanley doing FIBUA then that is the time to worry, not tonight.

'Gents, we will support C Company as a fire-based team tomorrow night if this has to be, but let's see what the enemy does after tonight and worry about tomorrow when it comes. It'll be bloody all the way if they don't give in by tomorrow.'

As night drew in, we watched 2 Para moving across our arc. The long, thin line spread out, loaded down with ammo. Through my binos, I could see the Mortars setting up 2 and 3 Para's Mortar Platoons. The cold set in. It was an incredibly cold night on top of everything else.

At approximately 1700 hours, we formed up and set off for the positions for the Wireless Ridge attack. Moving through the crags in the dark brought me memories of two nights earlier. The dark, sinister mountain reminded me of something from a creepy movie, where the bogeyman could jump out at any moment. The weight of all my ammo and equipment brought me out in a sweat within the first hundred metres of the small trek.

We had gone only thirty metres when the OC tripped and nearly fell over an enemy corpse. The body lay on the grass as if it was a sleeping soldier. We all stepped over it as if stepping over litter in the street. Nobody took any notice, except TP, who murmured, 'I wonder if he's been looted?' This brought a grin to everyone's face. Greed for the spoils of war had begun to creep into all of us.

As our party fought its way through the crags, artillery shells came in and landed in small salvoes. The barrage didn't even bring us to a halt. It seemed normal now.

Bob and Sas struggled behind me with the tripod and the GPMG. We each carried approximately three thousand rounds. The weight dug into my shoulders. We moved into A Company's position. The sentry challenged us hesitantly. His sergeant stood beside him, pointing a direction for us to follow through his position.

'Keep moving, lads, we know you're coming through.'

In the shadows, the lads from A Company stood or leaned against rocks, watching us pass through. No one spoke. Heads nodded at friends occasionally. A barrage of illumination lights went up from the Argentinean gun. They exploded with a burst, like fireworks, then descended to earth, floating harmlessly down on their parachutes to the ground. We were near our position now, in danger of skylining ourselves. Hitting the ground, I watched the flares falling with one eye. The area lit up as if it was daylight, yet everything was still. The enemy artillery fired at the mountain, now in our hands, and again a few shells fell on Longdon.

Darkness and stillness enveloped us again. In whispers, we passed the word back along our party to move out. I reached my feet again and saw the heads and shoulders of the others as we moved off Longdon and beyond the 'full back' of Longdon, 'full back' being a term in the CO's orders, as if the mountain was a rugby formation. We left A Company behind and their dark figures watched us go. Our party of twenty-plus men moved on a further twenty-five metres, where we left the Milan team and one gun team as our reserve and defence, only to be used to cover us if we had to do a quick fighting withdrawal.

We stopped and dropped to our knees. The OC crawled forward and returned some fifteen minutes later. The whispered message was passed back along the lines, 'Close up and get ready to crawl the last fifty to seventy metres.'

We closed up and started to half-crawl, half-drag ourselves and our weapons and equipment through the grass, down the slope leading towards Wireless Ridge.

A few flares went up from the Ridge. We lay flat, hugging the ground. No one moved, or dared speak. The enemy positions lay in front of us about five hundred metres away, but the night air always carries noises much further than daylight air. When the lights had faded we crawled the remaining few metres, but caught sight of the OC and PC pushing their hands out in a signal to us to spread out and line up. We formed up into our gun groups. It was now 2400 hours UK time. It had taken us some three hours to reach this point. The dark, the flares, the crags and many other small problems had made the thousand-metre journey long and arduous.

Very quietly and slowly, Bob, Sas and I mounted the GPMG on the tripod. The ammo was placed in one long belt of approximately three thousand rounds. The machine-gun was loaded and cocked slowly. I felt as if the whole world must be listening to it clunk and click into place. All down our fire-based team line, the thumbs-up came back to the OC. All was set, all was in place: twenty guys were ready and waiting with a deadly fire support. Five SMGs and five Milan rockets lined on to the target and the Ridge. All that was needed was the finger pressure to let off this firepower. We waited and waited. Flares exploded, flickered and drifted to the ground.

With minutes to go to 2115 hours local time, time seemed to freeze. I looked to my right and left at times to see the gun crew's heads looking at the Ridge. Every mind was feeling and thinking the same: Come on, let's do it.

I felt for 2 Para. I had so many friends in our sister battalion that it was as if we were one.

The cold crept into our bodies from the ground. Breathing produced a mist from our mouths and noses. The frost crept in with a vengeance. In the last minutes before the battle started, the area was totally calm and so quiet you could have heard a pin drop. Dark clouds drifted harmlessly across the sky. The cold bit into us and the ground.

At 2115 hours, the whole open space in front of us erupted into a massive fireworks display. Two Para's machine-gunners fired from their positions, a steady stream of tracer rounds burst in front of us. The red flare bullets whacked into the bunkers and the ground around them, the ricochets from direct hits spinning in different directions. The artillery shells booming from behind us now showed the strength of our own firepower. The shells crashed into the peat ground, exploding with fury; the killer shrapnel splitting into a million pieces flew in all directions. Both 2 and 3 Para's Mortar Platoons fired on the registered targets, their fire missions striving for the

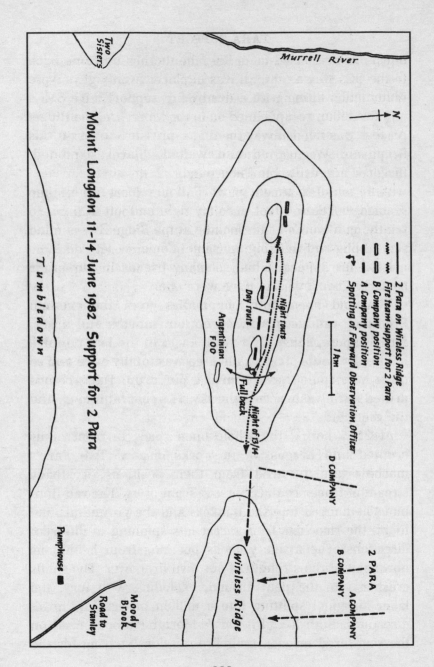

Mount Longdon 11–14 June 1982 Support for 2 Para

———	2 Para on Wireless Ridge
∿∿∿ ∿∿∿	Fire team support for 2 Para
▭ ▭	B Company position
▭ ▭	A Company position
‒ ‒ ‒	Sporting of Forward Observation Officer

1 km

Murrell River

Two Sisters

N

Tumbledown

Night routs

Day routs

Argentinian FOO

Full back

Night of 13/4

D COMPANY

2 PARA

B COMPANY

A COMPANY

Wireless Ridge

Moody Brook

Pumphouse ■

Road to Stanley

effects that took place immediately. The whole area in front of us was a massive display of bullets, shrapnel and illumination lighting, all raining down on the Ridge.

After about twenty minutes during which fire of all types poured down on the Argentineans, the Scorpions and Scimitars belonging to the Blues and the Royals came in to fire their heavy cannon. Their support at this time coincided with 2 Para's D Company moving off their start line into the first stage of their attack. Small arms were soon to be heard faintly, up to our left, as A and B Companies moved into the second phase. The shouting could be heard only when the massive fire support ceased. Shelling and machine-gunning continued until the last moment it was needed. Then the shelling and support fire from machine-guns, Scorpions and Scimitars was elevated above 2 Para's heads, to targets further up the Ridge.

This spectacular display had been going on some two or three hours when we were faced with a different survival task: a battle against the increasingly unbearable cold. The weather had turned so cold now that the lads in our support line were trying not to move any more than they had to. Two Para still weren't in need of us, but hadn't moved into a firm enough position to dispense with us altogether, so another good reason to keep still was that movement might have caused the Argentineans to mistake us for the main attack. We were all conscious that the enemy was still watching our direction. It might have appeared to them at this time that 2 Para's attack was only a diversionary one and that Mount Longdon was the real front stage.

Lying on our stomachs, we took to raising our feet and banging them together behind us in an attempt to restore circulation. I looked down the line at a familiar pattern. Bob looked at me through a small slit in a scarf wrapped around his face. Eye-talk had become a second language to us all. We wanted to help 2 Para, with fire or rockets – anything rather than sit and watch with frustration building up intolerably within us.

The CSM leaned against a rock, watching through the NOD again. He would whisper down to us a report on what was happening and the message would then be passed quickly down the line.

'The Argentines are running to rear positions, firing a few rounds and withdrawing again. Each bunker is getting more and more Argies in every fall-back.'

I rolled over on to my back, quickly slipping on my waterproof clothing, not because it was raining but simply to get an extra layer of clothing on. Bob and Sas followed suit.

'Get that fucking idiot down,' shouted the CSM as low as he could.

I turned to see Sas, standing, trying to get into his waterproof trousers. Bob kicked his legs from under him and the idiot landed on his back. I rolled over to him and trapped him before he could move again.

'Listen, you dickhead, not tonight, you hear me? Be still, be quiet and don't even think about farting.'

I rolled off him and moved back to my position. I had moved too far already as far as I was concerned, but nobody wanted to be six feet under because of him. I felt embarrassed by him. Twice he had acted like a week-one recruit. Things were never to be the same between us.

Moments later, a shell whistled over our heads from the left, followed shortly by another. These were the first of some twenty-six rocket shells that flew over us. The whistle after whistle seemed so close together that it was as if the shells were chasing each other. In fact, what was happening was that the artillery was still far behind us and we were witnessing the naval gun-support ships firing well out to sea, several kilometres away. They were firing in support of the attack on Tumbledown. That battle was well on its way but we hadn't even noticed it, so involved were we in watching our fronts.

The shells came over in steady waves, all capable of landing in a small area of about fifty by fifty metres. We turned our heads and watched them crash into the side of Tumbledown, explosion after explosion hitting the rocks and enemy positions. I recall thinking, Brilliant, if the Guards are getting that type of support they surely must win.

Tumbledown was a tough nut for the Guards to crack, and like us they encountered not just conscripts but also regular and special forces. Their battle, like ours, was to last till daylight.

The cold was now so bad that I and many others were in agony. The frost had set into the ground, our weapons and our equipment, and a thin layer covered the bodies of the lads lying around me, so that their backs looked like part of the terrain itself. The battle raged in front of us, supportive fire bursting out across the open ground. Both battles had been going for four or five hours now. Still we lay waiting. I was desperate to help, irrespective of the danger. It seemed the only way out of the agony of the cold and the frustration of watching.

'Keep quiet, lads, shush,' whispered the CSM.

The changed tone of his voice told us that a different phase was beginning. My ears strained to a new pitch, to feel the air for information. In the distance, Bob and I heard English voices shouting orders, making decisions. Stage Three of the attack on Wireless Ridge was taking place.

D Company, 2 Para, was moving through its objectives up on to the higher part of the Ridge. From the sound of their voices, they couldn't have been more than two hundred or even a hundred metres away. This may seem quite a distance, but at night and in the open it was very close. A blue-on-blue contact could take place very easily.

We kept still. Disturbing D Company might not only destroy their flow and control of the battle but might also be much worse if their commander wasn't aware of our position. We kept perfectly still for about half an hour, while they moved into formation to attack. Once they moved off, a slight wave of relief went through us. The CSM nodded to us with a slight smile: the all-clear. He turned his head back to the NOD to watch the battle.

'The Argies are doing a quick fighting withdrawal. They are moving from bunker to bunker. Get in there.' His voice rose a bit. 'Go on.'

What he was witnessing and whispering to us about was the hand-to-hand fighting with the fleeing enemy. He continued to read us the Argentinean withdrawal as if we were listening to a story from a book. How I wanted to see for myself.

'What the fuck?' he whispered.

We turned to see a shell exploding in the area of D Company. 'That must be the Argies bringing down fire on a DF.'

The shell had been our own and had fallen short. Luckily, mistakes like that were rare.

The Argentineans withdrew, fighting all the way. They were very efficient at DF-ing their own positions every time they fell back, because they had good radio communications. Every time 2 Para secured a bunker position, the shells fell around it. The sheer determination of 2 Para was beating the enemy, with light casualties to themselves. The lesson of massive support fire that they had learned at Goose Green was being put to good effect.

At about 0500 hours, we received a radio message that our support was not needed. We began to pack up and move after some nine hours lying on the frozen ground. My body ached like it had died. I was totally numb all over. My fingers didn't exist. My feet hurt as I stood up.

The battle had slowed to the odd burst of fire. Three Para's support teams moved off, back into our own lines, without even firing a shot. Flares, green, yellow and white, exploded and fizzled down to earth to signal the capture of different areas. Odd shelling crashed into the areas secured. On our left now, as we headed back, was Tumbledown, from which bursts of fire could still be heard. The route back was slow and tiresome. My only thoughts now were of sleep. I was so physically tired that I knew if we stopped I would collapse into a lump.

We reached our positions and fanned out to man our individual bunkers. We set up our guns. I pulled a single Argie sleeping bag up around me and lay on top of the bunker while the rest crashed out all around. I drifted into sleep with one last thought: C Company attacks later today.

Daylight rose over the landscape. The frozen ground sparkled in the early-morning light. The cold began to fade from the air. Now, by contrast with what had happened only hours before, very few artillery shells landed on targets around the mountain ranges. The air around Mount Longdon was calm.

Standing around the OC, we received our last instructions for the attack on Moody Brook and the racecourse. We were to move to Wireless Ridge, now captured completely, and into an area which we would make ready for our thrust down the Ridge into a supporting position for C Company. I clearly remember that I had no nerves left to shred. I felt completely calm and resigned to the fact that we were about to embark on the worst fighting. My attitude had changed. I felt so at ease it was as if I was on an exercise or a day out. The shock of the past three days had given a new dimension to my thinking. Never again will I think, It can't happen to me.

The OC smiled as he finished his brief orders. Many things were still unclear to us; not least, when the attack would take place. Cammed up, ammo wrapped around and across my shoulders, the GPMG on my shoulder as well, I followed the line of troops off the north side of Longdon and headed around the rocky crags leading up to the far side.

After we had tabbed about one thousand metres, with Wireless Ridge clearly visible above us, the absence of troops and the silence of guns in Stanley began to produce some puzzled looks along the line of Support Company. The OC shouted for a halt. We collapsed on the frosty ground to await further orders.

I looked up at the sky, thinking, What now? Who's fucked up this time? Let's just get this part started.

A few shouts came down the line. I leaned forward and

saw the line breaking up and the men laughing. Sergeant Mick Matthews was sitting beside me.

'What's going on, Mick?' I asked.

'Fuck knows, Vince.'

The shouting continued, as messages passed down towards us. A guy three or four positions down from us suddenly turned round and shouted, 'The wankers have surrendered. A white flag is flying over Stanley. Put on your berets. Endex, endex.'

The last part of the message had an ironic ring, because for some of the task force the whole thing had seemed like an exercise.

Mick and I looked at each other.

'Bollocks,' I said.

We stood up to see the remains of 3 Para coming off Longdon in their red berets. Joy washed through my body. Mick and I hugged each other. Nothing more was said. The message had reached everyone.

I slipped off my helmet and put on my beret, which had stayed close to hand throughout. The line moved off with sudden urgency, not to move into position to kill, but to beat the Marines to Stanley. We deserved that right. We now had a different fight on our hands: entry into Stanley.

As I stood looking down at Moody Brook, the red berets stuck out like sore thumbs against the grass. I felt proud. The beret on my head meant more than any task the Army had thrown at me. It meant victory. The feeling is indescribable.

I found myself, for the first time since Estancia, thinking of home. 'Jesus, I have a family thinking of me,' I thought.

As we stepped off the Ridge and descended into Stanley, home was in my mind but I turned to take a quick last glance at a place that had changed my life completely. Many friends had died there, many friends had been severely wounded there, many future friends would never realise it existed. That place has a name I shall remember until I die: Longdon.

20
FIRST INTO STANLEY

As we were coming off Wireless Ridge and heading down towards Moody Brook someone shouted back to us that we had walked straight into a minefield. A sergeant in front stopped dead, as we all did. None of us would take another step. It seemed stupid, now that victory lay in our hands, to be killed by a mine. The sergeant shouted back, 'Right, we're in a bit of a shitty mess here. What I suggest is we take turns leading and tread in each other's footsteps, OK?'

A member of his platoon shouted from behind me. 'Bollocks, *you* fucking lead. You're being paid for that, so let's see it.'

We all started laughing out loud, but the sergeant got really niggled, and started ranting and raving. We all stood our ground. After about five minutes, he set off again, sulking. We followed in his footsteps until we reached safe ground.

At the last peak of the Ridge lay a crumpled body, marked with his SLR and helmet on top. Two Para had lost three more to add to their list from Goose Green. I felt the loss of this lone soldier lying there, as we marched to Stanley.

We passed enemy corpses all the way down to Moody Brook, and a litter of discarded military equipment. As we stepped on to the muddy, trampled road that led to Stanley, it seemed clean compared with earlier scenes. We looked around to see troops spilling off the Ridge, and some off Tumbledown, all heading for the capital.

A BV (a tracked over-snow vehicle) was parked just off the road. There, standing on top posing like Rommel, was our own platoon sergeant, whom we hadn't seen since Estancia.

'Come on, come on,' he screamed. 'Load your heavier kit on to here. We are well in front of those wankers, the Marines, as usual.'

Seeing him standing there like that nearly made me boil over. He was giving orders and acting like he won the fucking war. I looked at him, more with pity than anything else. The platoon passed him the tripods, sights and IWSs. Then we turned on our heels to march into Stanley. Johnny and Tommo were with Tony Jones ('Bones') and Bob Geddis. I ran up to meet them for this famous walk. Bones expressed out loud the same view I held. I added my support. Tommo turned and said, 'We all disagree with him and his attitude, but at the end of the day he's the one with the rank, so let's enjoy this last day without him, yeah?'

We agreed not to talk about the platoon sergeant until after our expected leave period. This was to be short-lived.

We had marched about two kilometres with members of

D Company tabbing with us. We stopped and an officer shouted, 'It looks like they have a few die-hards, lads. Sappers' Hill to our right has enemy still holding. Order has it to take cover.'

Immediately, about fifty of us scrambled into the ditch by the road. Bob came running up beside me and we set up the gun, facing Sappers' Hill, which was some eight hundred metres away. Everyone lay there waiting. The minutes passed slowly. The backlog of troops still trying to reach Stanley were all following us into the ditches, wondering what was up. A radio message informed us that the Guards and Marines were arriving on the other side of the hill and told us not to bother, but to carry on marching. We all climbed out of the ditch and carried on marching. This seemed to niggle a lot of the lads. They cursed the brass for 'shit info'.

The road was littered with weapons, helmets, clothing, bullets and grenades. We all just walked past the pickings, interested only in reaching Stanley.

The road was full of red berets. A few Craphats had joined the Paras' entry. We were content to be in front of the Marines. They had been a constant pain to us throughout. Johnny giggled and remarked on what had happened on the trek across East Falkland when we were some twenty-four hours ahead of the Marines.

'Looking at all the red berets here, I can't see the brigade commander stopping us now, can you?'

We all laughed because, when we had been tabbing to Estancia from Teal Inlet, the brass had got on to the radio net and told our CO, 'For Christ's sake, stop and take a rest, you're making my boys look like week-one recruits.'

The slagging had only just begun.

Lying in the gutter were two dead Argentineans, their faces showing agony, their hands clenched into fists. One had blood covering the front of his combat jacket. The other was peppered with holes. I just glanced at them – it seemed normal now. A bit further on, a helmet lay on its top. Some of the lads passed it back for inspection. Come my turn, I glanced inside to see the top of a head left there. It looked as if the bit from the forehead to the back of the skull remained, with a near-complete brain lying inside. I passed it to the next bloke. I wasn't shocked or even really amused by it. Again, it seemed the normal thing to do, to look at it.

The guy next to me laughed out loud. 'Oh, yes, this is the ultimate souvenir. My missus will love this, pickled as an ornament.' He carried it another kilometre or two before discarding it for some other thing.

While we are on the subject of macabre spoils of war, it needs to be said that the essentials of hand-to-hand fighting have not changed much over the centuries. From the earliest battles, it was the foot soldiers who faced each other, and who did the dirty work. What happens after the battle is not so different, either. Throughout history, fighting forces have had their different ways of despoiling the defeated enemy.

In South America and the Pacific islands, the victors shrank heads as trophies. The Romans often crucified their prisoners of war. In more recent times, the Japanese beheaded and the Germans gassed, hanged and shot POWs, while the Russians took no prisoners. In Vietnam, American soldiers eager for proof of their personal tally of kills severed enemy ears.

Within the British and Commonwealth armies, similar

acts are by no means unknown. In both World Wars, the Gurkhas drew prisoners' blood with their kukris and cut off heads or ears. It is accepted by the government that the Gurkhas do such things, but in the Falklands it was not only the Gurkhas. On two occasions, I saw corpses with their ears missing, and I heard that this occurred throughout the campaign.

The reactions of those without frontline military experience will range from disgust to disbelief. Nevertheless, in the bedlam of battle, the normal standards of behaviour are left far behind, and acts occur that are plainly out of character. It is true that victory is in some cases celebrated by the taking of ghoulish souvenirs. I have no doubt that I will not be the last soldier to make these observations.

We passed the first of the buildings with interest. It was burned to the ground and smouldering. Only its chimneystack remained. We passed some big hangars with huge red crosses on them. Some of the lads went inside and came out waving amputated limbs. One lad waved the arm of an Argentinean as if he was waving goodbye to everyone. This caused laughter along the line of troops, until a concerned officer ordered him to put it back.

Two Para had been in front of us, mixed in with our C Company. Both battalions reached the capital before orders from above halted our advance on the airport where we knew the whole Argentinean Army had gathered. Orders came along the line to rest up until something could be done about lines of organisation of defence.

Our platoon gathered around the back of a house near the racecourse. All the houses seemed to be secured in one way or another. The CO came up to us as we were taking a brew, sheltered from the wind that whipped around us with a light drizzle. He looked tired but was concerned for us all. He asked why we were still in the open and nodded towards some houses that were to be forced open to make ready for the coming night. It seemed to me that I should ask how he was, because he was asking how we were. He was a bit taken aback by my asking. I liked the man and still do. He was perhaps the best CO I have ever served under.

As we prepared to smash our way into the houses, the familiar noise of a helicopter grew louder and louder above the small alleyway between them. The wind from the chopper whipped up more strongly, blowing out the hexie burner. Johnny got up cursing and shouting, 'Why can't those fuckers land elsewhere?'

We walked to a garden to watch the incoming chopper. We looked at each other in amazement when we saw, hovering about ten metres from the ground, an Argentinean helicopter trying to land. A large white bed sheet hung underneath it, flapping in the wind. About fifteen of 3 Para's lads stood looking at it. Some were laughing at the pilot, whose face we could see very clearly. He was obviously worried that we were about to shoot him out of the sky. Some lads pointed their rifles at the chopper, motioning it to land. It swayed from side to side as it hit the ground. The engine's hum quickly died as the pilot and crewman were hauled from the craft. They were dragged to the side of a shed and stripped of all their papers and weapons. Johnny and I were in fits of laughter because the Argies must have thought they were being searched. They were, but just for souvenirs. Even their airborne jackets disappeared into a hidden corner. After some minutes, they were marched off into captivity. We then saw our lads crawl all over the chopper, stripping it for souvenirs. One lad sat in the pilot seat pretending to fly it, as if at a fairground. He hummed and buzzed his own sound effects. We all curled up laughing. Eventually, a sentry was placed on the helicopter to stop it being stripped beyond use.

We made our way back to our kit. Tommo had smashed into a house and was pulling all our kit into the kitchen. Myself, Johnny, Bones and the PC made for the master bedroom. Mark Hammel and Gaz Easter joined us. We closed the door to avoid being 'spammed' for dirty jobs. I thought to myself how funny it was that we should hide with our own boss in there with us. He didn't want the brass chasing him either. We all bounced on the bed like big kids. Mark decided a double bed was too small for six guys, so a grass-drawing contest was held to choose the two to have the bed. Mark and Gaz won. Under the bed, Johnny found a huge tin of beans and tins of peaches and luncheon meat. I elected myself cook. I slipped into the kitchen and brought back the biggest pot. Sweeping my arm across the dressing table, I removed all the make-up and ornaments. I placed two bricks on the table, lit the hexie and emptied the tins into the pot for cooking in five minutes flat. We all produced our dirty, sticky mess tins from our webbing and ate the stew like pigs. Bones complimented my cooking, but became concerned when I told him the peaches had also gone in.

Later, we received orders to move up to the end of the racecourse and collect all our belongings, which were being flown down from Estancia and Longdon. The last flickers of daylight were creeping over Stanley when we reached the main shed. Fifty to sixty guys had congregated in the area, all members of 2 and 3 Para. Seeing those happy and familiar faces was a morale-booster. A Marine officer was shouting for some help from everyone. When one Tom turned on him and shouted, 'Fuck off, Cabbagehead, it's your turn to work now,' the officer went potty, screaming for his name et cetera. Everyone cheered and shouted abuse at the officer, who eventually stormed off, much to our pleasure.

The choppers came in to rest quickly. Kit fell from them at all angles and we ran to collect it. A central collection point was established. Two hours passed before our platoon's kit arrived. I collected my bergen and my souvenir bag from Longdon and we all slipped away from what was obviously going to be an all-night rubber-dick task.

As we entered the house, our morale fell flat when we saw the sergeant was there. There was hardly any mud or dirt on him and his smiling face made me want to vomit. I retreated to the bedroom with the others. It was now about 2100 hours, but the excitement at the thought of home and victory was buzzing like mad in my head. Sleep? No way.

The platoon sergeant entered the bedroom and addressed the PC, to whom we had not only taken a liking but who also supported our views on the sergeant.

'Sir, a curfew is being placed on all troops until daylight. A sentry must man the kitchen only. Apart from that, everyone is to stand down and get some sleep.'

The PC grinned and acknowledged the sergeant. A stag list was set up for one hour per man. Each had to sit and stoke the peat stove – some task!

That night, I lay twisting and turning for hours. The

confined space of the bedroom made nearly all of us feel claustrophobic. Come morning, the windows were fully open, and the wind was blowing violently into the room. The previous three to four weeks of living in the open had adapted us to the open air. It was about a month before I regained the normal tolerance to an indoor atmosphere.

After a night of little more than dozing, relief came with the daylight. Standing outside with just my SLR in my hands, I looked across the rows of back gardens towards the mountain ranges. Thoughts of the previous days were still very fresh in my mind. Bones joined me with Rob Jeffries. There and then, we decided to go on the loot. We quickly moved up on to the lower slopes of Sappers' Hill and among the racecourse bunkers.

The Argentineans had laid out their bunker system in a very neat and careful manner. Row upon row of deep bunkers ran all along the racecourse and well into Stanley itself. They had obviously meant to fight all the way. What had caused them to surrender so quickly? It was said later that Mendez had not wanted a FIBUA battle, because casualty figures were running very high. If this was so, surely the Argentineans should have kept to their bunkers. Had his army run completely out of control, forcing surrender?

In the bunkers were rows of one-hundred-and-five-millimetre artillery guns, point-fifty-calibre machine-guns and one-hundred-and-six-millimetre rifles. They were all set up facing in the direction of what would have been C Company's line of advance. The whole area was littered with military equipment. The spoils proved the best thing about the war.

We each picked up an Argie kitbag from the bunkers, then the three of us ran from bunker to bunker looking for anything that might take our fancy, from bayonets to discarded letters. Slowly, my kitbag filled up. Occasionally, I would see something I liked better and have to throw an item away. Bones and I picked up some shell cases and squeezed them into our kitbags. Beside us, a big one-hundred-and-five-millimetre gun stood, silent now, as we rooted around it.

'Bones,' I said, 'this gun is still facing Longdon. Look.'

He did. The gun barrel facing our previous position was sinister, eerie. I stood on a box at the end of the barrel and looked down it.

'Fuck me, Bones, the bastard's still loaded.'

Swapping places, he said, 'Obviously in a hurry to retreat, yeah?'

The small lanyard which was attached to the firing mechanism moved slightly in the wind. I placed my hand on it and said to Bones, 'If I pull this cord it'll be the biggest ND of the war, yeah?'

Laughing, we walked off. With our kitbags loaded on our shoulders, we made our way back to the bungalow. Rob joined us, with his share of pistols and grenades and an SMG, hanging from different parts of his body.

'Why don't you pack them away like us?' I asked.

'Don't matter if I'm caught anyway, 'cause I'll just get some more,' he said, laughing.

We bumped into Tommo, Johnny and TP, who had all been doing the same as us. It seemed weird that we had all finished looting at the same time. Johnny made a brew and we sat around chatting. The platoon sergeant walked in on our conversation.

'Right, no more fucking off. You can all stay here and area-clean the outside of this building, OK?'

We all looked at this very professional barrack-room soldier. I burst out laughing, which sent him off into a right tantrum.

'Bramley, you have no discipline. You do as you're told, hear me?'

'Hear you? Hear you, yes. But see you? No.'

We glared steadily at each other.

Tommo broke in. 'Look, Vince, you go and find food and we'll stay here. Fair?'

The tension snapped, with the sergeant merely shouting and screaming his orders and then walking off. We all looked at each other like schoolboys revelling in their naughtiness.

Sergeant or not, I had no respect for that man and I wasn't going to be a yes-man for his bullshit in the middle of an empty battlefield.

TP, Rob and I slipped off, leaving Tommo to have a chat with the platoon sergeant. The PC was very much on our side, letting us do our own thing.

As we stood on the road outside, Johnny mentioned that we would be getting Argie prisoners to area-clean that afternoon.

'So, fuck off now and do your own thing before it's decided we also need haircuts!'

We all walked back down towards Moody Brook. An Argie lorry came up behind us, driven by some 2 Para lads. We waved them down.

'Here, we're off to Moody Brook for some looting. Coming?' shouted the company driver.

'You're on,' laughed TP.

We jumped on the back of the lorry and sped off along the three or four kilometres of the only road. Along the

247

way, we passed scatterings of troops making their way into Stanley for the first time.

'Anything left for us?' shouted one group.

'No, we're charging five pounds as a taxi service though.'

As we passed them, the 'fuck off' fingers went up as they turned to finish their last slog of the war.

21

SPÓILS OF WAR

We entered the pumphouse at Moody Brook that had been the Marines' barracks at the time of the enemy invasion. The smell of damp hit our noses straight away. All the walls were pocked with bullet holes and shrapnel marks. A few Marines were kicking and searching through the items on the floor. I found a decent pair of Argie boots in my size and slung them over my shoulder.

The Marines came up to us and started chatting. The bad atmosphere between us was only slight now.

'This used to be my old sleeping spot,' said one.

'Were you here on their invasion, mate?' I asked.

'Yeah, and look at it all now. They told the world they captured us all without killing any of us. You know something? When we were guarding that idiot Governor, they stormed this building with everything they had. We wanted to fight them without surrendering, but that's history now.'

A 2 Para lad said, 'Yeah, I know how you feel. It'll be years before the joke of "hands up, here come the Marines" goes.'

We all laughed: the damage was done.

Our lorry back to Stanley picked up a few lads struggling with their kit. The three Marines with us motioned the driver to stop at a large shed off the road. We backed the lorry up and parked, then we entered the biggest 'free' military supply shop there ever was. Even the troops we had picked up joined in. Inside, there were about fifteen guys already looting. The shelves were packed roof-high with anything you could want: sock, boots, combat jackets, webbing, food, medicine. Most of it was USA stamped and made. I filled every space on my body with kit. TP and I ended up throwing items into a groundsheet and tying all the corners up. When we left the shed, the lorry had gone, but we found a wheelbarrow lying on its side in the ditch. In the kilometre or so back to the bungalow, we picked up anything we fancied.

The morning passed in pleasure. It was the best day's 'shopping' I can ever remember. Once in our new home, we loaded all our kit into one area, as did the rest of the platoon. Tommo had found whisky and beer hidden somewhere he wished to keep secret, but we shared out all the other goodies evenly. My only worry was how on earth I was going to carry it all home: bayonets, helmets, boots, clothing of all sorts.

The PC entered our Aladdin's cave and pissed himself laughing. 'I haven't got a disciplined group of professional soldiers here. I've got football hooligans in disguise,' he said. 'Where's my share?' That was his last word on the matter.

At midday, we all received six prisoners each to guard while they cleaned the area our own platoon sergeant had wanted us to clean. In my group, they were all typically Latin types, young and scared-looking. I marched them round to the front of our bungalow to join TP's group. All the prisoners started to dismantle a bunker in the front garden.

TP leaned against the wall of the building shouting to groups of Marines now entering Stanley. 'What took you, wankers?'

Two Marines stopped and looked him up and down. One shouted, 'We're fucking pissed off with you bastards, too, you know. Why don't you guard those little cunts instead of slagging us?'

'We are,' I said. 'Trouble is we've been here so long waiting for relief that they're our mates now.'

'Fuck off, Para shit.'

'Now, now, lads. Let's not get too upset,' laughed TP.

It was easy to see that a fight was brewing. The prisoners had stopped work and were all watching the display with open mouths. The PC arrived to cool the situation by ordering the Marines on.

After the incident, TP got all the prisoners together and taught them a routine that they had to perform to the signal of a clap of hands. The next group of Marines passing was greeted by myself and TP clapping, followed by twelve Argies shaking their fists in a wanking gesture. The Marines looked at each other with open mouths, then started to laugh with us. One shouted, 'Cool, cool, I like it!'

'At least that lot had some sense of humour,' laughed the PC as he watched us from the bedroom.

This reminded us of the time when one of the radio ops

used a prisoner to carry his radio around the battlefield. The unfortunate Argie was tethered to the op by a power cable and whenever the officer wanted to use the radio the prisoner was hauled over like a dog on a lead.

The clearing up took days. Each day the prisoners came down the road to us regularly at 0900 hours. We had the same prisoners for four days and they slowly ground to a halt. At one stage, we all ended up standing round a small radio in the kitchen, listening to the World Cup taking place in Spain. One of my prisoners could speak a little English, and translated the score for the others.

One afternoon, the platoon sergeant came in screaming, 'What the fuck are these little shits doing in here?'

The atmosphere always changed when he was around. Tommo told him it was Naafi break.

'Bullshit, get them out.'

The prisoners were marched back outside and I went with them.

Tommo said, 'Where're you going?'

'Simple,' I said, 'I'm going with my prisoners to the nearest hut to listen to the football.' This we did, for the remainder of the day.

On the second day, Mark and Gaz moved out to another house. Each house or bungalow was home to a platoon now. The second day also saw the start of the shits for most of the battalion. The mild form of dysentery spread like wildfire. At the bottom of one garden, we built a hasty shitpit, using oil drums with planks for a seat. It became a regular event to see guys running for this area, and in some cases not making it. The water supply was next to nothing, because the enemy had blown up the pumphouse before surrendering. The troops got very thirsty. A can of

Coke was like gold dust. Even precious souvenirs were swapped for a drink of some sort.

Late that second day, after the prisoners had marched off to their central spot, Clive, Bones and I went off on another loot. This time we found a hut with a padlock securing the door. We drew straws to see who would smash it off. Clive lost. Bones and I hid in a ditch in case the door was booby-trapped. How lax and carefree we had become, gambling for this task with a draw of the grass. Looting became a gamble with life.

Clive removed the padlock with ease. On entering the hut, which was the size of a large room, we stood in complete silence as we scanned the shelves. The left side, by the door, was filled with rifle magazines, loaded ready for dispersal. Primed grenades stood on one end of the far side. In front of us lay row upon row of medical equipment. On the right were brand new rucksacks, boots and socks. A desk stood in the centre of the shed with paperwork still in its 'in' and 'out' trays.

The left side didn't interest us. Weapons were now last on our list. After all, Stanley was full of weapons. However, standing in one corner was a portable toilet. We all rushed at it together. I won the race and there I sat for the first time in four weeks – on the throne – while the other two rooted around. Luxury.

I picked up new equipment to swap with the old I already had back in my kitbags. I opened drawers, searching for anything of value. Combing through the items in the shed and picking what we wanted took about half an hour. As we pulled the door to behind us, Clive mentioned the live grenades and wondered if we should nick a few.

'What's the point?' I said. 'We've enough already.' He agreed. That night I tossed and turned in my sleep, causing Johnny to wake me up.

'What's the fucking matter with you, Vince? Talk about moaning and talking in your sleep.'

This was the start of the nearly seven months of nightmares I would have to endure. Always it was the same dream: Denzil rolling about on the ground with smoke coming from his smock. I lost sweat by the bucket and spent many hours lying awake. My wife Karon could not, or would not, understand the problem, much to my frustration.

Next morning, as I stood outside the back door sipping one of Johnny's brilliant brews, Clive came running up from the side of the bungalow.

'Vince, that hut we were in yesterday – come quickly, have a look.'

Clive, Bones and I went down the road to where it stood at the back of some larger sheds. We couldn't get near it, as it was surrounded by white mining tape protecting an area of at least fifty by fifty metres. A 9 Squadron lad stood guarding the entrance to the sealed area.

'What's going on, mate?' asked Bones.

'Well, some lucky bastards broke into a portable bomb, apparently. As you go inside, the shelves on the left are full of mags and grenades. They didn't touch any of it. Whoever went in only looted the clothing side.'

'So, what's wrong with that?' I asked.

'Oh yeah, sorry,' he said. 'My boss went in there late last night to see if it was rigged. Well, you guessed it,' he said, laughing. 'He found a bomb reckoned to be about seventy pounds placed under all the weapons. A pressure bomb, lads. If the lads who had looted it had lifted one or two items from the shelf – bang! No more drinking in Aldershot.'

My hair stood up on end, and I must have turned white. Only Bones remained at ease.

'Cheers, mate,' he said.

We all walked away and stopped around the corner.

'Fuck me,' I said, 'I feel sick.'

Clive was leaning against a wall almost in convulsions.

'Shitting hell – if Clive had picked up those grenades, Vince,' said Bones, 'we'd all be gone.'

'Look, I reckon it's best that firstly we don't talk about it and, secondly, we keep it to ourselves, yeah?' said Clive.

'Deal.'

Of all the events of the previous few weeks, this must have been the silliest act of them all. My looting days ended there and then. We had become so careless with our own lives that greed had dominated everything. My personal feelings had been numb about a lot of things during the fighting, but that was because I felt I had to adapt to the circumstances of war. Greed had overtaken my personal feelings only after the surrender. War was a dirty business. The Argentineans played dirty even though, or perhaps because, they knew they would have to surrender. Booby-traps were a part of their defence. My greed had led me to overlook this fact.

Back at the house, I made a cuppa and sat on the doorstep with Johnny, telling him about the stupid loot. He, as always, curled up laughing, turning it into a joke. The guy had style.

My prisoners halted by the front gate and broke off and joined me. The six guys looked ill and tired of it all. I expect we all looked the same. I shared my brew with them, making two more cups with my rations, and they stopped cleaning to sip the tea. The water was heavily purified, so it tasted tangy.

At dinnertime, TP's prisoners and mine all sat chatting together at the back of the bungalow. The Argie who spoke a little English helped us all exchange names. Not one Argentinean could say 'Vince'. I was always 'Wince'.

Some who read this may say that familiarity breeds contempt. I agree with being careful about this – in the right place and at the right time. But, for the time those prisoners were with TP and me, 'Wince' became my name and we told each other about our different home backgrounds. Most of them I found excitable and eager only to return home, like all of us. Also, they believed their actions to be right in attacking the Falklands. They couldn't believe that they had been beaten. Their attitude towards us as soldiers expressed nothing but praise. Should we admit that we had just about run out of ammo when they surrendered? Should we be thankful that they were using the same calibre ammo in their rifles as we did in ours?

Most of the Argie prisoners with me were naive conscripts. Many people will say that the whole Argentinean Army we fought consisted of young conscripts, but this is wrong. Many of the units on the mountains had elite back-up forces, trained in sniping and holding their ground in a deadly manner. Let me illustrate this with the following story.

Back in Aldershot, after leave, I was standing in the pay office with a guy from B Company, who wishes to remain anonymous. After we left, we walked back to the Naafi together. He was leaving the regiment having been wounded so badly that his army career was over.

'Vince,' he said, 'X and I were pinned behind a small rock. A sniper had us in his sights and was shooting at anything that moved. X moved to the side and saw a group of Argies whispering together not three metres away. X beckoned me to look at them. Both of us saw them suddenly crawl towards us. They actually crawled right into our laps. I just pointed my SLR at the head of one of them as he came past. I blew his brains out there and then. The three others screamed for "no shooting". X and I dragged them into our position, then some of the company did an assault through our position that left us in a more secure position. X wanted to waste the men, now prisoners, and move on. They just looked at us in complete silence. A platoon sergeant came, half-crawling, up to us. We explained the situation. He looked at the prisoners. One spoke perfect English, with an American accent. We were really surprised, Vince, I can tell you. We questioned them for some minutes. All spoke perfect English, praising our soldiering. The sergeant fucked off and came back after ten minutes or so. He took X aside, while I guarded the prisoners. X came back to me and said, "Get them over this ridge quickly." We pushed them the fifteen metres, out of view, then suddenly X let rip, shooting them all dead. I helped to make sure they were completely dead, if you know what I mean.'

I said to him, 'So what, why the big scene?'

'Vince, look, mate, they were Yanks. Orders came from above to waste them, mate.'

'How did you know they were Yanks. Speaking with that accent may only mean they were schooled there?'

'They told us, Vince. That was their mistake. After all, let's look at it this way, politically both Maggie and Ronnie were meant to be helping each other in this war. The existence of Yank mercenaries can't be in the best interests of the higher ranks, can it?'

In my view, he was right. Whose corpses did we bury on that mountain? We will never know.

Four and a half years later, in 1987, I spoke to X in a London pub. X is now also out of the Army. He confirmed the story in every detail. The existence of US mercenaries was common knowledge among the Paras. X was told to keep his mouth shut or something bad might happen. The government didn't like the story. So why do I tell this story, which some might think shameful? Simply because those mercenaries were trying to kill us too. Certainly, I believe both the lads who told this story. I particularly trust X, for he was one of my closest friends in 3 Para.

22

REMEMBERING THE DEAD

Working with the prisoners was at times boring and frustrating. This was because going home was in sight. They almost certainly felt the same. Rumours from the brass had us twisting and turning for the ten or twelve days we remained there. The priority was to get the Argies home. Even I could see that, since there were some ten thousand enemy soldiers on East Falkland. The last thing we needed was a riot.

On the fourth or fifth day after the surrender, orders came from the high and mighty that the prisoners were to be moved to the quayside and shipped off home on the *Canberra* and *Norland*. We gathered our small parties together on the road in front of our bungalow and formed them up to march off. As it wasn't their normal time for finishing work, some of them became fidgety and nervous. Tommo was busy swapping items of military kit with some Argies lucky enough to be driven away on a lorry: his cap, badge and so on.

TP managed to find an Argie who could speak English and explained through him to the group of thirty prisoners that the reason they were going home so quickly was because their neighbours in Chile had invaded and they were now needed for another war. Many of the prisoners bit on the joke and got very worked up. It was only after three or four minutes of seeing us curled up laughing that they realised and shared the joke with us.

The one prisoner I had taken a liking to was looking really down. I passed some compo biscuits and an orange into his pocket and patted him on the shoulder. I never did find out his name or address. I really wish I had done now; it would have been interesting to see if both our societies would have accepted contact between us. I know that many of the lads on the ships guarding the prisoners did exchange addresses with them.

A young Argentinean officer, still equipped with his side-arm for self-protection (against his own troops, I must add), drew the prisoners to attention. Their drill was reluctant and carefree; losing the war had shaken their morale and discipline. As they marched away, the young Argie who I had befriended turned and looked at me. He smiled and waved. 'Goodbye, Wince. Goodbye, Wince.'

I smiled and waved back, with a thumbs-up for him. He continued to wave for at least a hundred metres. He wasn't the only one waving: the majority of the group did the same. I turned to see most of our lads saying goodbye as I had. We were all wrapped up in our own thoughts. Many fellow soldiers from that war will think differently about it, but for me the simple wave from that lone Argie brought home the crazy reality of war. A few days before, he and I could easily have been trying to kill each other in the bedlam of battle. Now, as he disappeared, friendship could have been possible between us.

The platoon moved back into the bungalow for a brew-up. Sitting around in the living room, we chatted generally about the rumours from above. When would we be going home? How much leave would there be? The PC sat at the table by the window, sipping his brew. He looked out and warned us that the platoon sergeant was coming in. As one man, we waited to gauge his mood.

He entered the room with a smile. 'Home by mid-July, lads, OK?'

We all felt happy to have some positive news. He then dished out blank telegrams that allowed us each twelve words. I wrote a brief message telling my wife that all was OK and to get a carry-out in. Tommo produced a bottle of whisky again and we gathered around to toast the end of what Johnny called 'an exercise and a half'. To our amazement, the platoon sergeant, GD, took the bottle and poured the drinks, before treating us to a 'didn't we do well' speech.

Later that day, the bullshit continued. Some of it was obviously necessary, as there were too many men just sitting around. But we at the lower end of the hierarchy felt that, after all the hard work of tabbing across the bloody island, and then the battle, we deserved peace and quiet and to be left to do our own thing, within reason. Area-cleaning with inspections was the last thing we needed. However, our sergeant felt differently from most platoon sergeants in the battalion.

What made me mad was that I still had bad feet, so bad that I was still hobbling a little. I had found a pair of wellington boots, to allow the air to get to my feet. Slowly, my feet began to feel better, then in came the sergeant moaning about 'mixed dress' and ordered me to remove the wellies. It was impossible to explain to him anything that was common sense. As I was about to take off the wellies, in walked the CO, RSM and OC on a walkabout. The CO stood there in the living room and chatted to all of us. He turned to me and asked, 'How're the feet, Bramley?'

'Still a bit sore, but healing,' I said.

'Well, those wellies should help anyway, yes?'

I looked at the sergeant, who was wide-eyed. I turned back to the CO and said, 'Yes, sir. They are a great help.'

After the CO had left, with the whole platoon near to screaming with laughter, I still had to remove the wellies.

Next morning, all ammo of all types was collected by the CSM and stored away. We spent the day scrubbing and cleaning all our kit and weapons. We performed this lazily when alone. Bullshit orders were causing more moans than anything.

I think it was on the sixth or seventh day that our battalion marched down the main road through Stanley to the large red church for a memorial service for both 2 and 3 Paras. We filed in quietly. Both battalions squeezed in to listen to the sermons for the dead and wounded. I sat among the row upon row of troops listening to the roll call. It wasn't the best of feelings. As the names passed of those I knew personally, the list seemed endless – and I was gutted by how young many of them were. I had to think how lucky we had been. In comparison with previous wars, our casualty figures were small. But in another way I felt that the figures were high, because these had been our friends. No battle is easy. Skills were exploited to good effect, to keep the figures of dead and wounded as low as possible. Tactics were used to best advantage, to take all enemy positions quickly.

On leaving the church, we formed up and marched back to our bungalows. The *Canberra* and *Norland* returned empty of those who had been the enemy. We spent the remainder of that day cleaning up the houses for the owners' eventual return.

As I stood in the kitchen, I heard a knock at the door. I opened the door, and standing in the rain were two civilians. They came inside, smiling. They were friends of the house owners, who had been shipped back to England by the Argentineans. They looked over the house while we chatted. Seventeen of us were sitting in various parts of the house, all watching them as they came among us. They eventually stopped to stand by the fire in the living room. The lady warmed her rump, looking across the room to the view of the sea and the bay.

'Move yourself, Jeffries. Let the man sit there,' said the sergeant.

Smiling, the man sat down and started talking about how the war had started at this end. We sat and listened to his views on the Falkland Islands Company. He explained that he and his wife had been heavily involved in trading.

'Well, then, it's partly your greedy faults for all this then, isn't it?' announced Tommo.

'Yeah,' Johnny joined in.

'What have you lads been told?' asked our shocked guest.

'Only that if you hadn't been so bloody eager and ready in your dealings with the Argies they perhaps wouldn't have got the wrong idea, thinking the Islanders would welcome their rule,' answered the PC.

'Rubbish. Absolute rubbish.'

'That's the biggest load of balls I've heard yet,' his wife agreed, nodding with her husband.

'Well then, explain why you dealt so heavily with them,' I said.

'Because of convenience.'

'Well, convenience has killed a lot of people. What with some big fat Intelligence wanker in London and you lot, we now have a completely new era developing here, because I personally can't see the situation changing for years, can you?' said Tommo.

The couple stood up. Feeling very much out of place now, they moved to the back door to leave. The platoon could be heard giggling in the living room.

'Irrespective of the causes, lads, we are grateful you came. Never forget that, OK?' said the lady.

'That's OK. Life is a bitch at times,' I said.

'By the way, why did you come round today?' asked the PC.

'Two reasons. Firstly, to say thanks for keeping the house clean.' (If they had come in two hours before they did they'd have had a fit.) 'Secondly, to say goodbye and thanks.'

'Goodbye,' said Tommo.

'Yes, you're leaving tomorrow, I believe?' murmured the bloke.

'Yeah, that's right,' answered the PC.

'Well, we'll be off now. Thanks again.'

The door closed. The lads in the other room had piled to the doorway of the kitchen. All eyes were now focused on the PC. He looked at us all with a slight grin. 'OK, OK. I was going to tell you, but this couple arrived as I was about to announce it. Sorry, OK?'

'By God, sir, you're lucky you don't look like a Argie, because you're heavily outnumbered here now,' laughed Johnny.

That night, the platoon packed every little piece of kit into its kitbags ready for the early move. I crammed my souvenirs into any spare corners I could find. After briefing, we discarded the weapons because of the threats of jail and cancellation of leave. My only concern was to get leave and forget this dump. What a mistake. As it turned out, customs back in England never even looked at us. I could have brought anything through. Perhaps some of the lads did.

I don't remember much about the last night in that room, only that Johnny and I lay there chatting for some hours. I slipped into a light sleep, thinking about how I would get a shower the next day.

We piled out of the house leaving Bones to mop the last of the muddy footprints from the kitchen floor. We formed up on the road. In a bergen with two kitbags plonked on top and my 'confiscated' weapons in my hands, I must have looked like an overloaded mule as I staggered up the road. The rest didn't look any better. After we had staggered three hundred metres, an Argie lorry pulled up empty. It was soon filled with our platoon and kit, arms and legs sticking out at all angles. We moved off, bound for the pier.

We unloaded and joined a huge queue, where we waited for our turn to shuffle the length of the pier to the landing-craft. Standing at the end of the queue, grinning like a cat, was Divvy Richards from 2 Para. We chatted until departure time. I discovered that Tam had died at Goose Green and that Russell, another close friend, had been wounded. Many other 2 Para lads were on the list. As I climbed on to the landing-craft, I found myself thinking that it was funny that none of us felt anything for the island itself. I personally was glad to see it fade from view as the landing-craft moved off towards our ship, the *Norland*.

The familiar bobbing of the craft in the waves reminded me of the start of this adventure. The fact that we were clambering on board this time was the biggest difference. Our sergeant stood on the lower deck shouting orders again.

Johnny laughed out loud. 'I don't believe him, I really don't!'

We left our kit in one corner of what was the car deck of the ferry. Along with the rest of the platoon, I fought and pushed myself up the countless flights of stairs to find my cabin.

Once we had found our cabins, we returned twice to bring up our kit. Two hours passed before we were all secured in the allocated areas. Waiting on board were our personal kitbags containing fresh uniforms. Johnny and I filled our two-man cabin with kitbags. Johnny stood outside while I sorted and stacked mine in one small corner, then vice versa. With our fresh kit and towels, we set off to find the showers. After going up and down stairs, we eventually found them. Luckily, there were only four or five guys waiting.

We pissed ourselves laughing when we entered the shower room to see one lad bent over with his mate busily cutting off what we call 'clinkers' – pieces of shit stuck to the anal hairs. 'Clinkers' were something we all had. But I preferred to cut mine off myself. 'I'd never trust anyone with scissors,' I said to Johnny, laughing.

REMEMBERING THE DEAD

It was the longest and best shower I have ever had. Black water was still running from my hair after three washes. The dirt and grime on my hands had almost become part of my skin. My body odour, especially under my arms, was reminiscent of a pig farm. We had all noticed the ship's crew keeping well back from us. They had screwed up their noses and told us that we stank. Because we had been living together so closely, we hadn't even noticed it.

In my clean uniform, shaven and with fresh socks, I was a new man. I packed my dirty kit in a poly bag and placed it at the bottom of one of my kitbags. When I finally arrived home and emptied this bag for washing, green mould had grown over everything.

I joined a queue for tea, then, back in my cabin, I lay thinking, day-dreaming really. Suddenly, my stomach turned over. I fell from my top bunk and headed for the toilet. I spent the next twenty-four hours flat out on my bunk with the worst bout of sickness and diarrhoea I'd ever had. I was starved of food and water and given plenty of pills and an injection by the medics, who were busy looking after about a hundred similar cases. As a result, I soon returned to the land of the living.

23

A FRIENDLY RIOT

A scale 'A' parade was called in the main bar. Both 2 and 3 Paras and all our attachments stood squeezed together to listen to the brigadier give a 'rousing' speech on how well we had all performed. Most of us yawned at yet another boring Rodney thanking us.

'Gentlemen,' he said, 'it gives me great pleasure to thank you all for your tremendous courage throughout this campaign. It was also great to see the rift between the red and green berets buried forever more ...'

'Fuck off, hat,' came one shout from the back of the red berets standing bunched together.

The abrupt insult only stalled the commander for a few seconds, then he shrugged it off with a broad grin. 'As I was saying, the red and green have always hated each other and it is nice ...'

'We still fucking hate the wankers, too!' came the next shout.

All the officers were looking into the huge crowd of Paras, trying to find the culprits. All the Paras were laughing loudly.

'Well, it seems you still have the humour you're famous for. It's great to see that you will be home first and ...'

'Yeah, flying home through the back fucking door,' came the last shout.

A few of the lads started booing the commander and his hangers-on. This died down after stern looks from our own officers.

'Gents, it's been nice seeing you and working with you. I salute you.'

He saluted us and walked away from the sweaty room.

We had all, as junior ranks, felt that the separation of Paras and Marines on our return home was fully necessary, and perhaps one of the most sensible things to be done in this war by the administration side. But many of us thought that for the *Canberra* to sail into Southampton docks with only the Marines on board was yet another insult to our work. The glamour of their homecoming, the blaze of publicity, seemed to say, 'We won the war, look at us.'

In fact, they had done their jobs as well as any others there, but the Paras fought the worst of the battles, 2 Para having two battles under its belt, the only unit to do so in the campaign. And what of the Artillery, whose help was a godsend to us? The reader may say I sound bitter that the Paras did not sail home to a heroes' welcome. But I am not bitter about this. I felt at the time, and still feel, that any publicity was the last thing we needed. What I believe is encapsulated in the words of Major General Thompson: 'There is no such thing as a returning hero, only a returning soldier.'

A FRIENDLY RIOT

The *Norland* set sail and we slowly steamed our way out of the harbour away from East Falkland, some of us forever. Rawley and I stood, with many others, watching it grow smaller by the minute. Jutting out around the edge of this view were the mountain ranges around Stanley. Mount Longdon stood among them, cold-looking and, to my eyes, ugly. Our battalion had lost twenty-three men there, with more than sixty wounded. There were nearly a hundred of our lads missing from the ship as we sailed. As the island disappeared altogether, I felt no loss. I felt only for myself now. Gone were the days when I had thought of war as a game.

The ship sailed through the cold waters of the South Atlantic and on into the warmer waters, heading for Ascension Island again, from which we would fly home. It was now the first weekend of July 1982: Airborne Forces Day. After the evening meal, the battalion all headed for the junior ranks' bar to celebrate this annual event. Much to our disgust, the senior ranks had restricted each man to four cans of beer for the whole evening. The troops made it well known that they considered this well out of order. We all knew that the officers were drinking themselves silly in their bar, as were the senior ranks. Yet again, it was the Toms who had to suffer. The sergeants even opened all four cans of each man's beer when he bought them. Whoever gave the order for us to have only four cans each made a big mistake, for within an hour the queues had got longer and louder with shouts of 'Fuck off to your own bar' directed at the few sergeants there.

The duty orderly sergeant stood by the door, agreeing with the complaints but helpless to do anything about them. Beer was smuggled from the hull by many of the

271

ship's crew, who were also sympathetic. The barmen eventually gave up rationing and a party soon followed. 'Wendy', a 100-per-cent homosexual, played the piano and sang songs on request. Everyone was eventually pissed, either with beer or simply the atmosphere.

The Paras sang all their favourite songs, among them 'The Zulu Warrior' and 'Old MacDonald Had a Farm'. The latter is performed naked on a table with a partner, simulating animal acts to the song. For example, we would sing, 'And the rams were doing it there, and the rams were doing it here,' while one of the partners played the ram. People might think we behaved like homosexuals, but while the way the lads acted and fooled about together would seem offensive to civilian eyes, it was purely an expression of camaraderie.

The 'Dance of the Flaming Arseholes' was the finale of most piss-ups. A volunteer, who is either very brave or very drunk, stands naked on a table with a toilet roll or newspaper rammed between the cheeks of his arse. To the chant of 'Alla, zoomby, alla zoomby', the paper is lit by the nearest guy with a lighter. As the paper catches and the flames get closer to his rear end, the lad dances quicker and quicker. Normally, the volunteer's pubic hair is non-existent after this little routine. It might leave him sore, but it raises a roaring cheer around the hall or bar if the lad has braved it long enough to satisfy the crowd.

We had a couple of new songs that night. One of them began with a chanting rhythm, singing about 3 Para being the first to be called up for the war. Then came a bit about 2 Para quickly leaving Aldershot to join us. The last part was a collection of insults about 1 Para, who didn't get to join us at all. That was just in jest, because deep down we knew that, if 1 Para had joined us, the war would have been better for having the Paras there in full strength.

The second song was about a very sad incident, but very appealing to the army sense of humour. It was an adaptation of the old First World War song 'Pack Up Your Troubles In Your Old Kitbag'. We sang, 'Pack up your brother in your old kitbag.' This stemmed from the story of a young Argie, captured in Stanley, who, when trying to board the *Canberra* for his homeward journey, had been discovered with the remains of his dead brother in his personal kitbag. He had kept the body with him for the long march in retreat from us because he didn't want to leave it behind. A lot of the lads felt for the Argie, but it was impossible to let him take home a rotting body. It was taken from him for decent burial.

At around ten o'clock, a few sergeants gatecrashed our bar and tried to lead the entertainment. Within minutes of their arrival, a fight had started on one side of the lounge. I was standing with Kev Connery, Paul Reid, Johnny, Big Jacko and Quincey of the 2 Para Mortars. Fighting by the piano caused Wendy to jump up and down and scream at the lads to stop, in a female voice. This helped, and caused laughter all round, but within minutes a few more fights had started. Everyone has seen the typical saloon-bar fight in the Westerns. Well, that's exactly what happened on Airborne Forces Day, 1982, on board the *Norland*.

The fighting spread like wildfire across the whole room, everyone scrapping with anyone they chose. Tables, chairs, beer cans, even bodies, flew through the air in every direction. Big Jacko and I backed our way to the wall, watching and screaming with laughter at the whole scene. Two lads crashed and rolled together off a table in front of us, punching hell out of each other. Four to six others attempted to pull them apart, but ended up fighting each other. I couldn't stop laughing. Suddenly, Quincey shouted at me, 'Stop laughing,' then smacked me in the side of the head. I retaliated and Jacko tried to separate us. We rolled on the floor, punching and kicking like the other four or five hundred lads in the bar.

After what seemed hours but was in fact minutes, Johnny and Jacko succeeded in separating us. I stood up, still laughing. The place looked more and more like a cowboy saloon. We all decided to take a break from the mess and go up to Quincey and Jacko's bunk for a quieter beer. Ducking the flying chairs and beer cans, we wove our way from the lounge.

As we ran down a corridor towards the bunk, we saw two lads walking ahead of us. Suddenly, a lump of wood came from a doorway, hitting one of them on the head and a snatch party flew out and mugged them of their beer. We stopped and retreated to a different corridor, but the fighting had now spread out of the lounge and into most of the corridors. It was no less than a shipboard riot. Even Bones and Ratch were scrapping in one corridor as we tried to pass.

The fights lasted until the early hours. Abandoning Jacko's drinking session, Johnny and I made our way back to our own cabin and supped a few cans there.

Next morning, as we sat in the galley eating breakfast, everyone had black eyes, swollen lips and cut faces. The amazing thing was that only a handful of lads bore grudges against their fighting partners of the night before. Everyone chatted happily about the way they got caught and hit, or how they hit back. They merrily swapped stories of their new battle experiences.

A FRIENDLY RIOT

Why did the riot start? We all agreed overwhelmingly that the brass's small issue of beer on Airborne Forces Day infuriated most of us because it added to our frustration. We also agreed that the riot had resulted from a massive release of the tension caused by our personal experiences during the war. Our punishment was no drinking for about two days. However, by this time, we all had our secret supplies anyway, so the evenings were spent sitting in the corridors outside our cabins, drinking and swapping stories.

We arrived at Ascension Island soon after Airborne Forces Day. The warm weather brought the lads out on deck to feel the hot sun for the first time since our departure. The island looked different from when we had last seen it. Now, it was Paradise, the start of a homeward journey. Before, it had been the start of a nightmare.

We anchored just offshore and a flight plan was posted to the battalions. The flights would take a number of days to get both battalions home. The first flight received a massive welcome home from the public, family and friends, with Prince Charles and Sir Anthony Farrar-Hockley, who was one of the fathers of the Parachute Regiment, attending.

Johnny and I, Skip and a few more of our platoon ended up on flight ten, near the last. We weren't worried; this suited us to a tee. We watched the *Norland* slowly empty of our comrades. Johnny and I spent the last few days and nights bumming around the bar, drinking. We felt very much the same: that we wanted a quiet welcome, please. Neither of us even felt that we wanted our families to meet us. We wanted just to get on the plane, land and jump on the military transport that would take us to Tidworth.

The *Norland* started to fill up with the relief troops for the Falklands. They were a Scottish battalion, but I no longer remember which. They were posted with us at Tidworth. The ship's corridors were suddenly filled with fresh-looking, clean troops, all eager to listen to the war stories. Johnny and I reflected on how innocent they looked. Some lads that had moved into the cabin opposite ours sat with us on our last night on board, with a massive carry-out of beer. They had noticed the opposite about us. One said, 'Have you looked in the mirror lately?'

'Why?' asked Johnny.

'Because your faces, particularly your eyes, look, or make you look, so old.'

Next morning, I looked into the mirror after my shave. I stared at myself. I looked into my eyes closely. The lad was right. In some way, they did look different. They have never changed since, either.

24

A DIFFERENT KIND OF WAR

'Flight ten to the upper deck now, please,' came the signal we all wanted to hear.

With all our kit, we started to fight our way along the corridors to the deck.

'Hey,' came a shout from behind us, and we turned to see two Jocks leaning in a doorway.

'Have a nice flight home, lads, but sorry to spoil your day: we've been shagging your wives while you all got wasted!'

Johnny looked at me to boogie (fight). I stared at them, but the childish remark didn't arouse the anger they wanted. I simply smiled and said, 'That's OK, we're going home to shag yours now, and you'll be down south much longer than us.'

Johnny pissed himself laughing while they started screaming and swearing. We walked off into the heat of the sun for our flight home. Within two or three months, the

Sun did a front-page story that bore out my prediction. The Jocks' battalion suffered a large percentage of divorces.

A chopper ride to the airfield brought us home to dry land again. We quickly bought duty-frees and climbed aboard the DC10. Within two hours of leaving the *Norland*, we were up and looking down at the ship anchored in the bay. A pretty air-hostess came along with grub and drinks, while we all clambered over each other to look into the aisles, to see her arse and legs as she walked up and down. Skip pushed me and Johnny off him. He was sitting next to the aisle.

'Talk about dogs on heat!'

'Come on, Skip, don't be an old fart. She's lovely, and after looking at your boat race for three months I think I'm in love. Ha, ha.'

After the meal, we fell into a relaxed sleep only to be awoken as we landed at Dakar for refuelling.

We all clambered out on to the tarmac to see the locals filling up the plane and staring at us as if we were Martians. Once the plane was refilled, the pilot could not achieve a connection with his engines. We sat watching the mechanics fiddling with their tools and banging about in the engine. I turned to Johnny and said, 'This is something fucking different, mate. If you think I'm getting on that plane after witnessing the world's best mechanic in action there, then you're in for a shock.'

The pilot eventually came and stood in the doorway of the plane, by the wing, and shouted for attention. The Paras all looked at him with interest.

'Gents, we have a small problem. Please be patient. We are going to bump-start the engine that's giving the trouble, quickly release the starter motor and then get the other engine going. If this fails, I will take off and bump-start it in the air, then come and pick you up, OK?'

'Fuck off, you maniac,' shouted a lad from Signals.

'What did you say, young man?'

'I said, "Fuck off", pal. If you think I'm going to watch something from a sketch by Monty Python and fly home in that, then you're mistaken. You're not taking me.'

We all cheered and backed him up, with comments like, 'Next, you'll be asking us to push the fucking thing down the runway to gather speed for take-off!'

An officer stood up and calmed us down, laughing. He was in agreement with us and had a chat with the pilot. Two hours passed, with the mechanic working flat out while a large group of Paras stood below him with their hands on their hips, watching his every move as if they were aircraft technicians.

Once the engine was finished, we all stood back as it turned over for the first time. However, we were all still adamant that we would rather wait for the promised back-up flight and refused to board.

Again, the captain came to the doorway, his plane humming quietly. 'Right, come on, lads, let's be fair and get home.'

'Fuck off,' came our reply.

We'd been shot at, bombed and fucking bossed around like garden gnomes down south, but we were not going to step on to a dodgy plane.

The captain walked off. Minutes later, the young air-hostess was standing in the doorway. All went quiet.

'Come on, lads, if I'm willing, so must you be.'

Everyone laughed out loud, one lad shouting our thoughts: 'If you're willing, so am I. Your place or mine?'

She turned red at the joke, but pleaded with us in a sexy voice like a naughty schoolgirl. The plane was filled with troops and ready for take-off in seconds. The wonder of females!

We spent the last part of the long-drawn-out journey looking at the fuselage of the plane. An expected failure of the engine was very much in our minds.

'Vince,' said Johnny. 'Do you think the families have been warned of our homecoming?'

'I don't know, but personally I'd rather they wait at home for me. It's a bit heavy all these reports of crazy families and friends going mad over us.'

'Yeah, you're right. Still, we'll see.'

This was perhaps the last important conversation of the campaign that Johnny and I held.

When we stepped off the plane at RAF Brize Norton the next morning, we were hit by an English summer in full blaze. As we entered the airport lounge, the doors were slung open to a screaming crowd of relatives, who charged towards us. My mother climbed over chairs to hug me, with all the rest of my family in close pursuit. My wife came up to me. I was tense and made unsure by all the noise and shouting. It made me scared in a peculiar way. Karon looked hard and almost angry. 'Hello, Vince,' was all I got from her.

After a little research of my own, I haven't met anyone else from the task force who didn't get a kiss from his wife. It seems silly to write this because, given the choice of whether to have my family there or not, I would have said no. But not to get even a kiss from my wife confirmed to me that trouble at home was my new war. My parents were obviously overwhelmed to have me home and this was touching, for I, like many others, didn't feel we had done anything out of the ordinary. After all, war is what we were trained for.

Customs proved to be a simple walk-through. How I cursed and kicked myself for not bringing home more spoils of war. I quickly parted from my family and Karon, because my quarters were in Tidworth, and climbed aboard the army coach.

All was very quiet on the journey. The English countryside made me feel like an alien. Johnny tapped my shoulder from behind. 'Vince, the trees, man. Look at them.'

I looked at the trees. They were part of what was making me feel an alien. They were all in full bloom, bright-green leaves in the wind. There was traffic on the roads, shops, people walking about doing their own thing. It all seemed unreal. After only three months away, it was a shock to see civilisation again. The odd thing was, I felt anger. Anger at everyone for doing their own thing. It was as if something in my head was urging me to shout at them as they walked along the streets, 'Hey, you lot, licking your fucking ice-creams, there's a fucking lot of injured guys over there. Friends have been killed, but all you're interested in is yourselves.'

Just frustration, I know. The general public was concerned, but it didn't seem like it just then. I wasn't expecting a medal, or even a pat on the back. I really didn't know what to expect. Even so, I found it hard to be calm.

Back in my quarters, I started to fight a completely different war, against boredom. The first thing I did was to throw open all the windows, because the claustrophobia I felt almost made me ill. The wind came rushing in, much to my relief, but not Karon's. Within an hour, I had to go out and walk about. Karon and I walked around Salisbury shopping, but still the people annoyed me as they crowded together, pushing and shoving.

That night, I was restless, sweating and walking about the house. I sat for two or three hours by the open windows in the lounge. I couldn't stop thinking of how the lads who had been hit by shrapnel or bullets were coping.

Next day, we went home to Aldershot. A banner hanging from the front top window of our house saying 'Welcome Home' was touching, but somehow embarrassing. I didn't want anyone to know where I had been. I started to grow a beard on this six-week leave, to hide my identity as a soldier.

What hit me most was that I really hated the leave at first. It was so fucking boring. There was no way I could relax. If I had been asked to go and do a tour of duty in Ireland, I would have gone. More than anything, I felt the pinch of no longer having my friends around me. We had been together so tightly over the last few months that it was as if now I had severed an arm. The buddy-buddy system that we had needed to literally survive wasn't there any more and the sheltered life now seemed to me far too boring to endure.

I made a point of not talking about my experiences to any member of my family, including my wife. But I do remember sitting up in bed one evening, turning to my wife and giving her a very mild insight into what had really happened. I was sick to death of the press's views and of the publicity of a country still high on the war. I told Karon what had happened to Denzil and CJ. The blank look she gave me, with a half-smile, told me she wasn't interested and couldn't understand me at all. I never said anything again. I tried to look at it from her point of view instead. She was sick of the war, of the Army and of me going away. Whenever I bumped into one of the lads, I seemed more at home and relaxed talking our private language with him than I did with civvies and my own family. If I had had my own way, I would have gone on the biggest bender ever, but I knew that was the easy way out. I remember buying the LP *The Friends of Mr Cairo* by Vangelis. That record had been played daily to us over the intercom on the *Canberra* on the journey down. The track 'I'll Find My Way Home' had been an instant hit with the troops.

The days at home turned into weeks. I finally returned to camp with many other Paras who had chosen to help unload the *Elk* in Plymouth of all the remaining 3 Para equipment. Next day came notice of a further six weeks' leave. It was sending me nuts.

Karon and I moved into new quarters in Aldershot. Setting up the new home gave me something to do for a while. As I walked into town on the first morning after our arrival, the sun was out and kids were playing in the small swing park. It was a typical summer's day, quiet and nice. All of a sudden, a jet fighter flew over us with a scream and I ducked and was halfway into a doorway before I realised it was peacetime now. Karon looked at me, half-giggling. I smiled to cover the embarrassment that engulfed me.

There is no doubt that I was slowly unwinding over the long leave, but the boredom also gave me more time to think about my experiences. Worst of all were my nightmares about the war. At first, they came nightly; later they faded and returned intermittently. I always had the same dream, of Denzil's smock and CJ's face passing before me. I would wake up in a bed so wet that a bucket of water might have been thrown over me. Sometimes Karon would be sitting there waiting for me to come round, but only because I had lashed out.

The nightmares lasted about six months or so. Today, I can see and understand everything that happened to me. I now know that I wasn't alone. The most comforting words I ever had to help me did not come from any of my family. My family were concerned, but could never really understand what I was going through. Those words came from my friends in the pub as we drank during the leave. Johnny turned to me and said, 'Vince, I've had a few turns in the night, you know.'

That made me sit up and see clearly that I wasn't alone, and when you're not alone you're stronger.

I sit here today, 24 years later, and feel so different from how I felt then. My whole outlook has changed about the Army and my aims in life. I still think back occasionally to the wind-swept hills of the Falklands. Many things still niggle me: for example, the QM stopping the balancing of our SF guns at Estancia or the men at the rear keeping back the overboots for themselves. The list is endless, and, even though they are trivial points, it's the little things that niggle the Tom.

I fully believe that we, as a nation, performed the most excellent of tasks. I am fully behind the decision to send the task force and I wouldn't hesitate to fight again for our country and its beliefs. People who whinge about the decisions taken in a war they weren't involved in are to me the most misguided of all. Take the sinking of the *Belgrano*.

Nobody at home has the right to say it was wrong, when thousands of British lives could have been at stake. I believe the sinking saved more lives than it claimed. Nobody, but nobody, will change my view on that. Also, we should remember that the Argentinean regime of that time had shown scant regard for human life. What if the boot had been on the other foot? No, we British had been kicked once too often.

Summing up, the most striking events to affect me throughout the war were obviously the deaths of my friends. In 1982, I regarded these friends as those in 2 and 3 Paras only. Now, after learning about others' experiences and after watching and reading others' accounts, I see that the whole task force was my friend. I watched a Marine sergeant in a TV documentary, his eyes showing the emotion of his story, and the sight told me we were all the same.

I still feel a bit angry that the wounded went unnoticed. A propaganda film on the task force's arrival home showed only the Paras and the Marines and a Navy homecoming. Can you remember seeing the badly wounded coming through the gates? I think not. Nobody wants to see the effects of carnage.

I am a full supporter of Maggie and her decision to invade the Falklands, but I am very concerned at the massive censorship of all the material that has come through since the battles. One reporter said to me in Stanley, 'I've got a one-hundred-page report here. What's the bet the Home Office and the shits behind their desks let no more than ten pages through?'

The whole campaign was handled with more of a 'Big Brother' approach than any before. You mustn't say this or say that. I feel the government dug a tiny piece of their own grave with this policy, for all the truths will come out in the end.

My personal attitude to life changed also. Never again will I think that war is just a game, like on TV. It is very different from how it is portrayed in books and films. We con ourselves into the killing game, don't we? I remember very clearly watching from the window of my quarters five or six kids playing a war game. Some were even dressed in combat gear and carrying small toy machine-guns. I watched with interest their tactics in attacking a cardboard box that was meant to be an enemy-held position. The two kids defending rolled over and pretended to die when overrun by the goodies. After being 'tigged' by their friends, they got up to resume the game. From knee-high, we start to practise what is human nature, to defend and kill. The one big difference between their game and the real one is that you don't get up after really being shot. War is the legal killing of people and can be very scary. War is kill or be killed.

We must also remember that a lot of the command structure at junior rank level can be almost too difficult to maintain in the heat of battle. Then, what becomes a winning factor is the determination of the private soldier, his lone 'get up and go and do' attitude. We must take our hats off to the junior ranks of all services, for they are the backbone of the war machine in that they have to kill at close range. We are lucky to have what is perhaps one of the best fighting forces in the world, thanks to our system of training and to our discipline.

Even today, I feel frustration about the war. I was so psyched up to carry on with the fight into Stanley that the

Argentineans' surrender made me disappointed as well as happy. I try very hard to keep out of fistfights now, as I wouldn't like to lose my self-control. Am I alone in this feeling, or are there hundreds or thousands of other time bombs out there?

Other experienced veterans may be sympathetic to all I've said. We can only wait for the next war now, to practise the art of killing again. I hope I'm there to help. Finally, I must quote a First World War veteran who told me, so many years before I joined up, 'You'll like the Army, Vince, but not the war, it's 'orrible, boy.' He was right. I didn't like it. Then again I did.

POSTSCRIPT

Corporal Stewart McLaughlin (B Company, 3 Para) The imposing black bulk of Mount Longdon confronted the lads of B Company, 3 Para, as we prepared to advance. Were they true, the Intelligence reports of enemy reinforcements on our objective that very night? Were our tactics right – a silent night attack?

Nervous fingers twitched on the trigger, stomachs were in turmoil. The battalion was now in position; H hour had arrived. The cold, frosty but clear night of 11 June 1982 was to change many lives, and to take lives too.

One man among the ranks was more concerned about the lives of his section of men than the coming advance, for he was to control their actions. Corporal Stewart McLaughlin, twenty-seven and married with two young sons, was a true Paratrooper. He was stocky and of medium height, a tough leader, SAS-trained, highly professional and very experienced. A brilliant career lay ahead of him.

Throughout the campaign, McLaughlin had pushed his men hard across East Falkland, the reality of war constantly in the forefront of his mind. He was helped in this by enjoying the hard-won respect of those men.

The battle started when Corporal Brian Milne stepped on an anti-personnel mine. Bullets and bedlam swiftly followed, our commanders asserting control of the extended line of troops. Corporal McLaughlin's section hit the ground within seconds of the enemy opening fire on them. Having checked that his lads were unwounded, he began to seek out a route along the slopes of the next position.

Just as Corporal McLaughlin was about to give the command to move, a scream from Private Pete Hindmarsh told everyone that he had been hit. Each man froze, and young soldiers completely new to battle didn't know what to expect. Pete cried out for help, which prompted the Argentineans to increase their fire.

Corporal McLaughlin took control by firing a sixty-six-millimetre rocket at the enemy. Then, leaving good cover, he dashed to help the private, thirty or forty metres away. On reaching him, he shouted for covering fire, picked him up in full kit and still under fire carried him back to safety, where a medic attended to the wounded soldier.

Private Grant Grinham, Corporal McLaughlin's rifleman, pressed forward with his 2 Section more confident and relaxed after witnessing his leader's actions. With renewed determination, they advanced up the mountain under a hail of bullets.

B Company as a whole started to sustain more casualties, and slowed down. They advanced up the slope by darting from bunker to bunker until they reached a new static position. Their advance had caused the company and platoon to split up, so that Corporal McLaughlin found that he had new men attached to his section. He at once took command of them and gave them tasks, one of the first of which was to suppress an enemy point-fifty-calibre machine-gun. This they did rapidly.

Lieutenant Mark Cox, the platoon commander, was one of a number of young officers who were under huge pressure. Corporal McLaughlin took the PC aside and tried to reason with him. Now, in effect, part of 5 Platoon was under the corporal's command. Constantly in touch with his men, Corporal McLaughlin took the platoon to the top of Mount Longdon. All the while, 4 Platoon were fighting ferociously on their flank, advancing from bunker to bunker.

B Company reached the enemy's main line of defence, on the very summit. There the mountain dipped away into a crater, where bunker after bunker of defences confronted them. Immediately, the enemy opened fire, killing four or five men. Among them was Lance-Corporal Murdoch, who fell horribly wounded and died leaving his radio on permanent send.

The lads had been fighting their way for three or four hours up the dark, craggy mountain, the Argies remaining hidden in their bunkers on every strategic crag and corner.

Having seen many members of his platoon killed or wounded, Lieutenant Cox was distraught. Corporal McLaughlin reassured his men but could not calm the PC, and in desperation CSM Weeks punched the PC in the head.

Quickly, 4 and 5 Platoons now worked their way into the crater, grenading, bayoneting and firing into bunkers as they went. Corporal McLaughlin, leading, shot any enemy in sight. No prisoners were to be taken. In any case, B Company, with many dead and wounded by now, lacked the manpower to deal with prisoners.

The OC, Major Mike Argue, controlling from the rear from behind a rock, irritated his men by ordering them to go further and faster. But how could they, with the enemy snipers, equipped with efficient night goggles, shooting everything that moved? Corporal McLaughlin relayed messages requesting support through his sergeant, John Ross. In response, naval gunfire and artillery were brought in to soften up the enemy. Soon Argentineans were wandering about, dazed by the huge explosions all around them. They were shot on the spot.

B Company surged forward. Corporal McLaughlin, standing up in the face of enemy fire while his men were static on the ground, shouted and cursed at them to keep up the momentum. They responded by killing efficiently and without emotion. Under fire, they followed McLaughlin, destroying the enemy. Their training had been of the highest standard in the Army. Many NCOs were letting their men control themselves, realising that they were better off in pairs or small groups. The private soldier needed little encouragement, despite seeing his friends wounded and killed. It was the Toms and JNCOs who won the battle.

The enemy withdrew again. Corporal McLaughlin, still in full control and not having lost a single one of his men, was now reorganising them. Short of ammo but their morale high, they relaxed a little. McLaughlin was emptying his bowels in a bunker when an Argentinean who had been hiding inside sprang up at him. Still squatting, the corporal shot him between the eyes. When he emerged and told the others, they at once saw the funny side of it. The imperative to kill or be killed was ever present.

The CO ordered B Company's OC to make a further push along the summit. The company was by now reduced to half its original strength and the remaining men were worn out. Yet they drove themselves on, engaging in hand-to-hand fighting among the crags. The reality of the frontline seemed not to matter to the higher-ranking officers, who were in the middle or at the rear.

Enemy artillery fire rained on the summit, pinning down Paras and Argentineans alike. Amid this onslaught, Lieutenant Cox, now more in control of himself, with Private Kevin Connery, charged and destroyed three enemy soldiers in their bunker. Both men were later Mentioned in Dispatches.

Suddenly, during another lull in the fighting, Corporal McLaughlin leaped up and charged forward under fire, hurling grenades and firing sixty-six-millimetre rockets at the enemy positions. His section joined him, and reached a new line of cover without casualties.

Throughout the night, Corporal McLaughlin controlled A Platoon, whose men had come to respect greatly his leadership and courage. Every move he had his men make was carefully thought out, so that full momentum was maintained.

As day broke, B Company had been reduced to about thirty men, a third of its strength only twenty-four hours earlier. Undaunted, CSM Weeks set about organising a new formation.

Corporal McLaughlin rested with the other survivors, who took over an abandoned enemy bunker for a smoke. The next task was to secure their defences. As they rested, they listened to Argentinean shells landing all around the mountain, and rifle fire as A Company stormed along the summit, mopping up the last of the enemy resistance. Corporal McLaughlin came out from the bunker to see men from Support Company following up A Company's advance and helping to secure their objective against any counter-attack.

It had been a very long night and a bloody battle. Daylight revealed bodies lying everywhere, but also brought some relief for the survivors. The calm was abruptly shattered when there was a flash near the ground, followed by a terrific bang. A rocket fired from Mount Tumbledown across the valley had exploded almost among the B Company lads.

Private Grinham, who at the time had been crawling backwards from the bunker, had a leg blown off. He screamed in shock and agony, only to be told to shut up by Corporal McLaughlin, who himself had received a wound to his back and lung from a large piece of shrapnel, and was still half-joking about what had happened.

Nearby Paras rushed to their aid, and were told by Corporal McLaughlin to attend to Private Grinham first. The private was rushed to the field hospital and from there to the hospital ship *Uganda.* A little later, Corporal McLaughlin was being helped down to the first aid post by Private Hicks of D Company when a mortar hit them. Both men were killed instantly.

Before long, the men of the battalion were to hear each other's stories of individual heroism among their ranks. That of Corporal Stewart McLaughlin received particular recognition. Every private who fought alongside him knew of his daring actions throughout that night. His courage and initiative had helped save lives in both his section and his platoon.

Medals and citations are customarily awarded to those who have deserved them. The 'brass' alone decide whose contribution should be rewarded in this way. It is not for the rest of us to say who should get a medal. Even so, the news that Corporal McLaughlin was to receive no posthumous award was greeted with dismay and anger by all the privates, the JNCOs and many SNCOs and officers. Let it be clear that, while no one expected a medal, not even the South Atlantic Medal, official recognition was held in high esteem. The many soldiers who received medals or were Mentioned in Dispatches, in some cases for an action lasting only thirty seconds, were proud, and rightly so.

Among the men of 3 Para, there remains strong agreement. If a corporal can control for most of the night the major part of a platoon in addition to his own section, and do duty beyond his rank throughout a brutal, bloody fourteen-hour battle, that soldier deserves the highest decoration. Such a soldier was Corporal Stewart McLaughlin.

AFTERWORD: NIGHTMARES

It's been a good few years since this book was first published. A lot has been said and done. Some people have said, 'What a great book'; others have pronounced it, 'Too raw for the public to understand.' You will have your own opinion now that you have nearly finished these pages.

One big sorry saga that erupted from these pages came when a police inquiry was launched into the conduct of troops in the Falklands. Today, the findings of this inquiry are sitting on some shelf, collecting dust and rightly so. I was as horrified as the next man when it was launched back in 1992. However, as always, there are two sides to every story. Ironically, during the whole saga, I never named names.

Following assassination in the media by people who have never been on the frontline and after being hounded, pestered, followed and bugged, it all ended as quickly as it started. With nothing further to write, the media just filed the story away as if nothing had ever happened. The only newspaper that kept out of the inquiry was the *Sun*, always the troops' favourite and supporter. Why couldn't other newspapers follow its example?

If anyone thinks fifteen minutes of fame is fun, I'm here to tell you it is not. Forget money, don't go anywhere near it – I never did. For eighteen months, I had a procession of hacks in my face as the inquiry kept popping up on the news. When the inquiry first began, one newspaper offered me a lump sum that would have paid my mortgage off, for an exclusive with all the dirty details. Tempting, wasn't it?

But I do have morals, and strong ones at that. Today, I can look in the mirror and honestly say, 'I never sold out.' I never betrayed the Regiment, or my colleagues who fought on that mountain. I do think about the three ex-Paras from my old battalion, whose names I could mention, who tried to sell their stories and now stand alongside comrades at reunions and smile. I wonder what they see every time they look in the mirror.

At the end of the day, selling your story may be a money-spinning adventure but I found it was a nasty backstabbing, cut-throat business. I'm not here now to name names (except one or two) because I ended up taking the blame for something that was not what I wanted to say in my book. In certain media circles, I got treated worse than a serial killer.

For years, I have been the man who 'wrote that book'. Yes, it's true I wrote a book, but did I name names or sell out? No. That still pisses me off today, and to date no one has ever returned to say 'sorry'. But I'm not bitter about it. I just sat down and wrote a second book, had it published and carried on my simple life as just another Joe Bloggs living out his days. I'm happy with that. But I will tell you, although I still have enough material to write another book on this subject, I never will. All the material is collecting dust, just like the government files are.

Back in the early summer of 1992, a political journalist asked me for a coffee at Westminster. Was he wanting a story or just sounding me out? The chat was friendly enough: a copy of my book sat next to him; it had been out for over a year.

I had no problems with this; everyone I knew enjoyed the book. He informed me that certain politicians were pushing for questions to be asked about the conduct of some troops during the war. I was surprised. He told me of the existence of letters of complaint from an ex-Para, who wanted the matter dealt with at a higher level.

'What letters? Which ex-Para?' I asked.

He said, 'Be wary, Vince. You could be a possible scapegoat.'

I hadn't a clue what he was on about; I was certainly confused about his meaning. Weeks passed, I thought no more about this meeting. I went on holiday. It was while I was on holiday that, smack, bang, wallop, I saw the headline news: the government had launched an inquiry under Malcolm Rifkind to investigate allegations (featured in this book) into the conduct of 3 Para on Mount Longdon. My face was there on TV for all to see. Scotland Yard were to do the dirty work. Suddenly, I found myself screaming, 'What the hell do the suits think they're doing?' The race was on in the media to find out more; the hyenas were let loose in search of a scoop. On my arrival home, I found my answer-machine was overwhelmed with messages. The press, TV and everyone else kept knocking at my door.

'No comment, no comment,' I replied. Cheques were waved: No! No! No!, I replied. One paper started ringing at two o'clock in the morning, until I unplugged the phone. Eventually, it died down. I was in an utter state. Plus I was getting paranoid. I had to climb over my back fence every day on the way to work. I was picked up by my work partner Martyn Benson, who throughout this ordeal remained as solid as a rock. He was, and remains, a diamond to me.

I received a call from Denzil Connick, who put me under the wing of an old hack, who being loyal to the Paras wanted the same outcome as me: the Regiment's name intact. Alistair McQueen, Irish and solid, this guy saved my sanity. Thank you. He guided me through the media snakepit, protecting me and advising me. He made sure the truth of what I said was printed. Every interview I did was always aimed at stopping the inquiry and in praise of 3 Para.

I cocked up once when one particular paper just wouldn't let go. They sent the same journalist to my door time and time again. So I whacked him. Big mistake: next day, I was assassinated on the front page. As Alistair said, 'You cannot hit hacks, Vince, they will be judge and jury in their columns.'

At one point, after clearance by the Argentine government through my solicitor Julie Nixon, I found myself with Denzil, Dom Gray, Alistair and the legendary photography Ken Lennox (famous for his photo of Maggie leaving Downing Street in tears). We were on a plane to Argentina to do a joint story about ex-foes meeting each other to discuss the war. Two armed security guys went with us everywhere, even to a Latin tango bar run by exiled Cubans. What a night out! The whole thing was a success, but, before we travelled back, the synopsis for my second book was already in place. But that is another story.

It was around this time that the *World in Action* team approached me. They had collected a fair bit of information, enough to warrant a programme. I agreed to be interviewed once they had captured on film the letter-writer who was the source of the inquiry, which I wanted turned on its head.

It was once said to me by an MP in a bar after a TV show that the government needs to wash its dirty linen now and then, just to show the world that it can. Today, our troops are being hounded in Iraq for spitting. And aggressive fighting men on the frontline are now expected to act like policemen.

Before I can go any further, I must explain how this book came to be published. It was never meant to be like this: the manuscript was a rough bundle of papers so my father could read about my experiences. Nothing more, nothing less. However, the text found its way to a publisher.

Next thing I know, there I am sitting with publishers thinking, Wow. Before I signed a contract, the manuscript was passed to my old regimental HQ for approval. I received a reply, saying it was a good book, and it would be nice to have the exploits of 3 Para on the record. The book hit the shelves and ticked along with good reviews.

All I had wanted was recognition for 3 Para and to explain how troops suffer to achieve government aims. In my opinion, this war was the most heavily censored war of all time and I wanted to put across the experiences of the ordinary soldier.

Well, my turn did come. Throughout the Scotland Yard inquiry, the police travelled up and down the country searching for witnesses and piecing together events. Many lads called in to tell me the score. At least these lads could see the bigger picture. I received a call from Julie Nixon, my solicitor, informing me that I had to attend an interview at Aldershot Police Station. My fear and anxiety was indescribable.

Although Julie was calm, collected and supportive, I knew I was going to be grilled. The two detectives were smart and intelligent, as well as being overpowering in their seriousness and professionalism. We shook hands. I respected them immediately, and I felt sorry for all the lads who had to endure the raking up of old ghosts, memories and mental scars. I know I couldn't assist them. The bravery of all 3 Paras was more important. 'No comment, no comment,' I kept saying.

After about two hours, I was informed that they might require me at a future date, and that it would be advisable not to get involved with the media, as charges of looting or murder could be raised against me or others.

I wanted to scream, 'Tell the suits to bury it, stop this now!' How could they (the suits that is) even think about a trial?

I walked from the station into fresh air and freedom. I feel angry towards the Tory government, whom this war helped re-elect who were now stabbing the troops in the back. Time passed, weeks, months, and then every now and then the story would pop up and disappear as it turned into the next day's fish and chips wrapping paper. But, to me and everyone involved, it was a long nightmare.

World in Action did screen its programme, putting

forward their view and mine. I had known for many months the source of the letters and had had many verbal confirmations as to who really kicked this off. Ex-Captain Mason, Support Company 3 Para, had written to an MP who had always moaned about the legalities of this war. The letters were written over a period of time and were filed even before this book was first published. They became a kind of eventual launching pad for the inquiry.

The bigger picture is that lots of men were dragged through this inquiry because of a misinterpretation of orders. That is also how this inquiry ended after eighteen months of nightmares, with a thirty-second slot on the TV news and half a column in the papers. The line was 'It's not in the public's interest to pursue this any further' – to me that was the right conclusion and what I had been fighting for.

Who ended the inquiry? Well, most probably it was the same suit who started it all in the first place.

You may sense my anger at the word 'suit' throughout this small chapter, but it was a big chapter and nightmare for me, my family and all those 3 Paras who were grilled. To me, suits are faceless bureaucrats who can abuse their power and ruin lives without losing sleep. Sadly, they run this country. But we don't learn by history, do we? The same things are happening today in Iraq. Just as in the Falklands, the suits will be wined and dined, while the troops will always have to suffer.

As for me, well, I've said my piece now; it's put to bed. I'm not a first-class author or military critic, but I will always speak out in defence of the troops. I do some lectures and have fallen in with the rank of 'Joe Public'. I have lost a few friends, and some have returned to say

'Sorry'. That's fine. I know the crap we all went through. I'm happy with my work and my colleagues. Hopefully, I will retire peacefully and gracefully.

Acknowledgements are normally carried at the front of a book, however, I wish to do this now. John Blake and Lucian Randall, who have reprinted this book, are thanked wholeheartedly. There are many friends who have stuck by me throughout: Paul Reid, Jez Hemming, Mark Rawlings, Jon Cook, Dom Gray, Martyn Benson, Mark Eyles Thomas, who as a 17-year-old boy has already made a success of his life. Alistair McQueen and Julie Nixon who assisted me when I was alone against the powers that be. Everybody needs friends and family to get them through life. My family closed ranks and supported me throughout. They are all heroes to me.

But one person remains my main strength, my wife Karon. She may not have given me a welcome-home kiss, and we did get divorced soon after the war, but we quickly remarried and brought into the world our daughters, Beth and Meg. It is she and she alone to whom I owe so much, a quiet, inoffensive, routine girl who has endured years of nightmares with me.

My nightmares exist to this day, the nightmares of the inquiry and the war. She never moaned once and she is the one who wakes me gently when I moan at night. She has quietly supported me for nearly twenty-four years. She is also a war veteran in my eyes and should wear my medals, and I'm sure there are other wives the same out there. One day the nightmares may end for everyone who suffered but for now, as when all wars end, the casualty list is bigger than you think.